THE
African-American
YELLOW PAGES

THE
African-American
YELLOW PAGES

A COMPREHENSIVE
RESOURCE GUIDE AND
DIRECTORY

Stanton F. Biddle, Ph.D., editor

An Owl Book

HENRY HOLT AND COMPANY   •   NEW YORK

Henry Holt and Company, Inc.
Publishers since 1866
115 West 18th Street
New York, New York 10011

Henry Holt® is a registered trademark
of Henry Holt and Company, Inc.

Published in Canada by Fitzhenry & Whiteside Ltd.,
195 Allstate Parkway, Markham, Ontario L3R 4T8.

Library of Congress Cataloging-in-Publication Data
The African American yellow pages : a comprehesive resource guide and
directory / Stanton F. Biddle, editor.—1st ed.
       p.   cm.
    "An Owl book."
    Includes index.
    1. Afro-Americans—Information services—Directories.   2. Afro-
Americans—Services for—Directories.   3. Afro-American business
enterprises—Directories.   4. Afro-Americans—Societies, etc.—
Directories.   I. Biddle, Stanton F.
E185.A2575   1996
973'.0496073'0025—dc20   96-15092
                                                                    CIP
                 ISBN 0-8050-4070-6
Henry Holt books are available for special promotions and premiums.
          For details contact: Director, Special Markets.
                   First Edition—1996
                 Designed by Victoria Hartman

          Printed in the United States of America
      All first editions are printed on acid-free paper. ∞

             10 9 8 7 6 5 4 3 2 1

❂ CONTENTS ❂

Subject	page	Subject	page

◉ **ACKNOWLEDGMENTS** ◉

This book would not exist without the research skills of Joneil Adriano, the diligence of Christine Chiang, and the guidance of Mitch Rose, the agent.

❂ INTRODUCTION ❂

- What organizations help African-American engineers?
- What are the African-American historic sites in Boston?
- Which organizations offer business advice for young black entrepreneurs?
- Who can help trace a family tree back to Nigeria?
- Is there a store in San Francisco to buy traditional African art?

The African-American Yellow Pages provides the answers to these questions and thousands of others. A national resource of organizations, businesses, historic sites, services, publications, etc., of particular interest to African-Americans, this book covers the broad range of African-American life from the arts to the everyday—museums, career advice, colleges and universities, health care, vacation sites, even the best black-oriented Internet sites.

The African-American Yellow Pages provides a wealth of vital information for the African-American community. The women's organizations listed are for African-American women. The banks are black owned or majority owned and serve the black community. The hair and skin clinics specialize in the concerns and problems of African-American men and women. The fraternities are black fraternities. This easy-to-use directory lends itself to a number of uses, from the completion of everyday tasks to making business partnerships, from personal and career development to navigating the Internet, from voicing concerns to African-American officials to opening a bank account.

The African-American Yellow Pages is the first all-inclusive national directory that documents the wide range of services and organizations that are either owned by African Americans and/or fulfill the needs and concerns of the African-American community. It is designed to be useful for a wide variety of audiences: politicians, professionals, creative artists, performers, small business owners, educators, librarians, students, journalists, community organizers, families, and individuals. With well over 2,000 entries, no other resource offers in a single volume such a broad range of information.

Scope of Publication

This publication is national in scope; however, where appropriate it includes information on international businesses, institutions, and organizations. It also includes information on local and regional businesses, institutions, and organizations that have special significance. Information is given on businesses owned and/or managed by persons of African descent; businesses that have identified the African-American community as their target audience; institutions that have identified the African-American community as their primary constituency; and organizations composed primarily of African Americans or that have been established to provide services to or address the concerns of the African-American community.

A team of researchers has culled information from government agencies, business organizations, African-American associations, national directories, databases, Internet sites, suggestions from individuals, and other sources.

Every effort has been made to be as up to date as possible, but as with any phone book, organizations move after publication. If you know of an organization whose address or telephone number has changed or that should be included, please write to the author in care of the publisher and we will update any reprints.

Organization

Under each category, entries are listed by three criteria: state, city, and name of organization. In this manner, all of the related organizations in a city will be listed together.

Each entry appears under a primary category, and several also appear under an additional category, reflecting the dual focus of the organization. The W. C. Handy Museum, for example, appears under Museums and Music.

Each entry is numbered individually according to the order in which it appears in the book. An index of the names of all organizations that appear in the book with their entry number is included for easy reference. In addition, there is a subject index for people interested in finding particular services, rather than specific organizations. This subject index is organized thematically, according to the ten areas of African-American life covered by this book:

ARTS & HUMANITIES. Companies, institutions, and organizations whose primary focus is the arts (visual, performing, etc.), culture, and writing. Includes arts and crafts organizations, museums, musicians and vocal artists, other performing artists, and related organizations.

BUSINESS & INDUSTRY. Business and other commercial organizations, as well as organizations that provide assistance to African-American businesses. Not-for-profit bodies will be included in area of endeavor. Organizations of businesspeople would also be included in this section.

EDUCATION. Organizations and institutions involved in education and career enhancement. These include schools, colleges, universities, adult education programs, scholarships, and fraternities and sororities.

HEALTH & HEALTH CARE. Institutions and organizations involved in all aspects of medicine and health. Because AIDS and sickle-cell anemia are two diseases that are of particular concern to African Americans, organizations that provide assistance to people with these illnesses have been given their own specific category.

MEDIA. Businesses and organizations involved in all aspects of the communications industry. This includes all aspects of print and broadcast media and Internet services and sites that are of particular interest to African Americans.

POLITICS & GOVERNMENT. Individuals, institutions, and organizations involved with politics, government, and government services. National, international, state, and local government offices are included here, as are civil rights and other public policy groups.

RELIGION. Organizations and institutions that serve the spiritual needs of African Americans. The historical significance of religion in African-American communities is also noted here.

SCIENCE, TECHNOLOGY & THE ENVIRONMENT. Individuals, institutions, and organizations involved in all aspects of the applied sciences or environmental conservation.

SOCIAL SERVICES. Institutions and organizations that provide services designed to help and improve the welfare of individuals and/or the African-American community. Organizations are listed according to the type of service they provide.

SPORTS & ATHLETICS. Individuals, institutions, and organizations that commemorate the involvement of African Americans in athletics or that are designed to increase their participation in specific sports.

THE

African-American

YELLOW PAGES

❂ ADOPTION ❂

1.

**Black Adoption Placement
& Research Center**
1801 Harrison St
Oakland California 94612-3403
510-839-3678

2.

Black Adoption Program & Services
3200 Wayne Ave
Kansas City Missouri 64109-2062
816-921-0654

3.

Black Adoption & Foster Care Center
951 Jeanerette Dr
St. Louis Missouri 63130-2719
314-863-1321

4.

National Adoption Center
1500 Walnut St
Philadelphia Pennsylvania 19102
800-862-3678

5.

Adopt Black Children Committee
P.O. Box 442
Houston Texas 77001
713-670-1118

Odessa Sayles, President

❂ ADVERTISING ❂

6.

Mayo Communications International
250 S San Fernando, Suite #212
Burbank California 91502
818-842-8810
818-841-6296—Fax

Karen Mayo, President/CEO

7.

Black Public Relations Society
Los Angeles California 90000
213-962-8051

8.

African Marketing Corp Limited
1614 Newton St, NE
Washington DC 20018-2318
202-526-2690

9.

Anderson Communications
2245 Godby Rd, SW
Atlanta Georgia 30349
404-766-8000
404-767-5264—Fax

Business-to-business, consumer advertising, creative, direct mail, media, public relations, sales promotion, African-American specialty.

10.

Brainstorm Communications
228 S Wabash Ave, 10th Floor
Chicago Illinois 60604
312-922-9797
312-922-9365—Fax

Vince Sanders, General Manager
Business-to-business, consumer advertising, creative, media, sales promotion, African-American specialty.

11.

Burrell Communications Group Inc.
20 N Michigan Ave
Chicago Illinois 60602
312-443-8600
312-443-0974—Fax

Thomas J. Burrell, Chairman/CEO
Consumer advertising, creative, media, public relations, sales promotion, infomercial, African-American specialty.

12.

E. Morris Ltd.
820 N Orleans, Suite 402
Chicago Illinois 60610-3051
312-943-2900
312-943-5856—Fax

Eugene Morris, President
Consumer advertising, public relations, sales promotion, African-American specialty.

13.

Equinox Advertising Inc.
980 N Michigan Ave, Suite 1180
Chicago Illinois 60611
312-951-5366

Bernie Washington, Partner; Bill Daniel, Partner; Stuart Rankin, Partner
Advertising agency.

14.

Proctor & Gardner
One Illinois Center, Suite 321
Chicago Illinois 60601-4284
312-565-5400
312-565-5450—Fax

Barbara Proctor, President

15.

R. J. Dale Advertising Inc.
500 N Michigan Ave, Suite 2204
Chicago Illinois 60611
312-644-2316
312-644-2688—Fax

Robert J. Dale, President
Business-to-business, consumer advertising,

creative, direct mail, media, public relations, African-American specialty.

16.

Vince Cullers Advertising Inc.
676 N St. Clair, Suite 2222
Chicago Illinois 60611
312-649-7777

Vince T. Cullers, President

17.

RAI MOBE
7724 Oak Ave
Miller Beach Indiana 60602
219-938-1888
219-938-1988—Fax

Yvette Jackson Moyo, President
Conceptualizes the advanced marketing symposium, Marketing Opportunities in Black Entertainment (MOBE). A marketing services company that provides and develops marketing for corporations and organizations.

18.

African American Marketing
1187 Payne Ave
St. Paul Minnesota 55101-3642
612-774-6917

Advertising agency.

19.

Advertising Experts Ltd.
280 N Central Ave, Suite 210
Hartsdale New York 10530
914-948-8144

Al Anderson, President

20.

Caroline Jones Advertising Inc.
1290 Avenue of the Americas, 37th Floor
New York New York 10104
212-262-8181
212-333-4208—Fax

Caroline Jones, President
Advertising agency.

21.

Exhortation Public Relations Inc.
305 Madison Ave, Suite 1740
New York New York 10165
212-557-3697
212-370-5206—Fax

Beverly L. Cook, President

22.

Haricome Advertising Inc.
596 W Broadway, Suite 501
New York New York 10001
212-334-4321
212-334-4393—Fax

Ron D. Harris, President
Business-to-business, consumer advertising, creative, media, public relations, African-American specialty.

23.

Lockhart & Pettus
79 Fifth Ave, 10th Floor
New York New York 10003
212-633-2800
212-661-7729—Fax

Keith Lockhart, President

24.

The Mingo Group Inc.
228 E 45th St
New York New York 10017
212-697-4515
212-697-4515—Fax

Samuel J. Chisholm, President
Direct mail, sales promotion, Hispanic specialty, African-American specialty.

25.

North American Precis Syndicate
201 E 42nd St
New York New York 10017-5704
212-867-9000

National publication and distribution service.

26.

Powell Advertising & Design Inc.
214 E 24th St, Suite 5A
New York New York 10010
212-889-7724
212-889-7682—Fax

Ken Powell, President

27.

Tri-Ad Consultants
101 W 57th St
New York New York 10019
212-246-1138

Charles Richardson, President
Advertising agency.

28.

Uniworld Group Inc.
100 Ave of the Americas
New York New York 10013-1699
212-219-1600
212-274-8565—Fax

Byron E. Lewis, Chairman/CEO
Consumer advertising, creative, direct mail, media, public relations, sales promotion, telemarketing, recruitment, Hispanic specialty, African-American specialty, event marketing, and promotion.

29.

Communiplex Services
2081-B Seymour Ave
Cincinnati Ohio 45237
513-731-6300

Steven Reece, President
Advertising agency.

30.

Focus Communications Inc.
1675 One Dallas Centre
Dallas Texas 75201
214-954-0286

Kenneth W. Carter, President/CEO
Advertising agency.

❂ ADVOCACY GROUPS ❂

31.

Black Americans for Family Values
2554 Lincoln Blvd
Marina Del Rey California 90291-5082
310-823-5871

32.

Black Women Organize for Political Action
518 17th
Oakland California 94601
510-763-9523

This group was formed in 1968 and works on political issues of interest to its members. It holds monthly meetings and uses committees to help develop programs in keeping with its goals.

33.

A. Philip Randolph Institute
1444 I St, NW, Suite 300
Washington DC 20005
202-289-2774

Norman Hill, President
Seeks to eliminate prejudice and discrimination from all areas of life; educate individuals and groups on their rights and responsibilities; assist in the employment and education of the underprivileged; combat community deterioration, delinquency, and crime. Fosters cooperation between the labor force and the black community through voter registration, labor education, and trade union leadership training.
1964

34.

African American Coalition
1100 6th St, SW, Suite 209
Washington DC 20024
202-488-7830

A nonprofit organization that lobbies and works with Congress and the D.C. city council for programs and legislation that are beneficial to African Americans and immigrants from Africa and the Caribbean. Attempting to extend the assistance of the Marshall Plan to African nations.

35.

National Association of Minority Political Women USA
6120 Oregon Ave, NW
Washington DC 20015
202-686-1216

36.

Voter Education Project Inc.
604 Beckwith St, SW
Atlanta Georgia 30314
404-522-7495

Ed C. Brown, Executive Director
VEP provides financial and technical assistance to local voter registration and education drives in the old Confederate states of Alabama, Arkansas, Florida, Georgia, Louisiana, Mississippi, North Carolina, South Carolina, Tennessee, Texas, and Virginia. It also provides policy research and technical assistance to African-American elected officials.
1962

37.

African Leadership Office
494 S Emerson Ave
Greenwood Indiana 46143-1953
317-889-0456
317-882-8854—Fax

Dr. Mike Henderson
Missionary organization for leadership development and training in Africa. Nondenominational Christian persuasion.

38.

African American Voters League
310 S Broad St
New Orleans Louisiana 70119-6416
504-822-2890

Colleen Johnson
Scholarship foundation, community service organization, and political organization. Sponsors a feed-the-needy program.

39.

National Political Congress of Black Women
P.O. Box 411
Rancocas New Jersey 08073
609-871-1500

40.

Black Men & Women Against Crime
1225 E 5th St
Winston Salem North Carolina 27101-4363
910-773-0992

41.

African Americans Informed & Delivering Solutions
North Olmsted Ohio 44070
216-962-3666

42.

African-American Voters Coalition
340 N Holtzclaw Ave
Chattanooga Tennessee 37404-2305
615-622-1727

43.

Black Women United for Action
6551 Loisdale Ct
Springfield Virginia 22150-1808
703-922-5757

☼ AIDS ☼

44.

Minority AIDS Project
5149 W Jefferson Blvd
Los Angeles California 90016-3800
213-936-4949

45.

African American AIDS & Addiction Hotline
Oakland California 94601
510-452-3700

46.

African American AIDS Support Services & Survival
Oakland California 94601
510-273-9996

47.

AMASSI (African-American AIDS Support Services & Survival Institute)
3419 Martin Luther King Jr. Way
Oakland California 94609
510-601-9066

This human and social services center was designed to provide an affirming and safe place of care and support for diverse sexual communities with emphasis on people of color, primarily African American. Not only an AIDS organization, AMASSI focuses on the importance of self-love, empowerment, and affirmation, both in AIDS prevention and healing and in living in a racist/homophobic society in general.

48.

Black Coalition on AIDS
1042 Divisadero St
San Francisco California 94115-4409
415-346-2364

49.

National Minority AIDS Council
300 I St, NE
Washington DC 20002
202-544-1076

50.

African American AIDS Network
711 S Kedzie Ave
Chicago Illinois 60612-3319
312-722-4400

51.

Black Educational AIDS Project Inc.
123 W 24th St
Baltimore Maryland 21218-5001
410-889-8822

52.

Minority Task Force on AIDS
505 8th Ave, 16th Floor
New York New York 10018-6505
212-563-8340

Nonprofit providing support services for people with AIDS or HIV+, programs for housing, food deliveries, Monday-night dinners, support group, case managers and staff for counseling or referrals, help with financial services and prison release, prevention, education and outreach, legal department with legal issues.

53.

Minority AIDS Outreach
2128 11th Ave N
Nashville Tennessee 37208-1105
615-391-3737

❂ ALCOHOL & DRUG ABUSE ❂

54.

Minorities Alcoholic Treatment Alternative
1315 Fruitvale Ave
Oakland California 94601
510-261-7120

55.

Sacramento Black Alcoholism Center
2425 Alhambra Blvd
Sacramento California 95817
916-447-0234

56.

Concerned Citizens on Alcohol & Drug Abuse
3115 Martin Luther King Jr. Ave, SE
Washington DC 20032
202-563-3209

Samuel Foster, Executive Director

57.

Blacks against Dangerous Drugs
460 6th Ave S
St. Petersburg Florida 33701-4633
813-822-8429

58.

National Black Alcoholism Council
53 W Jackson, #828
Chicago Illinois 60604
312-663-5780

Maxine Womble, Chairperson

59.

Black Alcohol & Drug Service Information
1501 Locust St
St. Louis Missouri 63103-1810
314-621-9009

60.

Urban Minority Alcoholism Outreach
2500 E 61st St
Cleveland Ohio 44104
216-881-5533

61.

Black Alcoholism Outreach Program
1323 W 3rd St
Dayton Ohio 45407
513-225-5556

Ronald Long, Consultant

62.

Minority Alcoholism Program Halfway House Inc.
66 Burnett St
Providence Rhode Island 02907-2527
401-785-0050

❂ BANKS, BANKING & SAVINGS & LOAN ❂

63.

Citizen's Federal Savings Bank
1728 Third Ave N
Birmingham Alabama 35203
205-328-2041

Dr. A. G. Gaston, President/Chairman of the Board

64.

Commonwealth National Bank
2214 St. Stephens Rd
Mobile Alabama 36601
205-476-5938

Alpha Johnson, President/CEO

65.

Gulf Federal Bank
901 Springhill Ave
Mobile Alabama 36646-0217
334-433-2671

66.

Tuskegee Federal Savings & Loan Association
301 N Elm St
Tuskegee Alabama 36088
205-727-2560

Richard R. Harvey, Managing Officer

67.

Enterprise Savings & Loan Association
1219 E Rosencrans Ave
Compton California 90282
213-591-5641

Cornell R. Kirkland, President

68.

Broadway Federal Savings
4229 S Broadway
Los Angeles California 90037
213-232-4271

69.

Broadway Federal Savings & Loan
4501 S Broadway
Los Angeles California 90037
213-232-4371

Elbert T. Hudson, Chairman

70.

Family Savings & Loan Association
3683 Crenshaw Blvd
Los Angeles California 90016
213-295-3381

71.

Founders National Bank of Los Angeles
3910 W Martin Luther King Blvd
Los Angeles California 90008
213-295-3161

Carlton J. Jenkins, Managing Editor

72.

Golden Coin Savings & Loan Association
170 Columbus Ave, Room 210
San Francisco California 94133

Winfred Tom, President

73.

Community Federal Savings & Loan Association
4490 Main St
Bridgeport Connecticut 06606

Donald Finch, Managing Officer

74.

African Development Bank
2001 Pennsylvania Ave, NW
Washington DC 20006-1850
202-429-5160

75.

Development Bank of Washington
2000 L St, NW, Suite 702
Washington DC 20036
202-332-9333

Jerry Apodaca, President

76.

Independence Federal Savings & Loan Association
1229 Connecticut Ave, NW
Washington DC 20036
202-626-0470

William Fitzgerald, President

77.

Industrial Bank of Washington
4812 Georgia Ave, NW
Washington DC 20011
202-722-2014

D. Boyle Mitchell, Chairman & President

78.

United National Bank of Washington
3940 Minnesota Ave, NE
Washington DC 20006
202-828-4300

Samuel Foggie Sr., President

79.

Peoples National Bank of Commerce
3275 NW 79th St
Miami Florida 33147
305-686-0700

Frances Tyler Sr., Vice President

80.

Metro Savings Bank
715 Goldwyn Ave
Orlando Florida 32805
407-293-7320

William L. Young, President

81.

Citizens Trust Bank
P.O. Box 4485
Atlanta Georgia 30302
404-659-5959

I. Owen Funderburg, President

82.

Mutual Federal Savings & Loan Association
205 Auburn Ave, NE
Atlanta Georgia 30303
404-659-0701

Hamilton Glover, President

83.

First Southern Bank
P.O. Box 1019
Lithonia Georgia 30058
404-987-3511

Herbert K. Orise, President

84.

Carver State Bank The
701 Martin Luther King Jr. Blvd
Savannah Georgia 31401
912-233-9971

Robert E. James, President

85.

African American Charitable Trust
320 N Michigan Ave
Chicago Illinois 60639
312-237-6600

86.

Community Bank of Lawndale
1111 S Holman Ave
Chicago Illinois 60616
312-533-6900

Joyce Wade, CEO

87.

Drexel National Bank
3401 S King Dr
Chicago Illinois 60616
312-225-9200

James Shirley, President

88.

Evergreen Bank
5235 W 63rd St
Chicago Illinois 60638
312-582-6300

Has several locations in Illinois. Call for more information.

89.

Highland Community Bank
1701 W 87th St
Chicago Illinois 60620
312-881-6800

George H. Brokemond, President

90.

Illinois Service Federal Savings
4619 S Dr. Martin Luther King Jr. Dr
Chicago Illinois 60653
312-624-2000

91.

Independence Bank of Chicago
7936 S Cottage Grove
Chicago Illinois 60619
312-881-6800

Edgrick C. Johnson, President

92.

Seaway National Bank of Chicago
645 E 87th St
Chicago Illinois 60619
312-487-4800

Walter E. Grady, President

93.

First Federal Savings & Loan
7990 Scenic Hwy
Baton Rouge Louisiana 70807
504-775-6133

Henry Stamper, Executive Vice President

94.

Life Savings Bank
7990 Scenic Hwy
Baton Rouge Louisiana 79874

Ernest Johnson, President

95.

Liberty Bank & Trust Company
3939 Tulane Ave
New Orleans Louisiana 70160
504-483-6601

Alden J. McDonald Jr., President

96.

United Bank & Trust
2714 Canal St
New Orleans Louisiana 70119
504-827-0060

Marvin D. Beaulieu, President

97.

Advance Federal Savings & Loan Association
1405 Cold Spring Ln
Baltimore Maryland 21239
301-323-9570

John Hamilton, President

98.

Harbor Bank of Commerce
133 Federal St
Baltimore Maryland 21201
410-528-1800

Ronald A. Homer, Chairman

99.

Ideal Federal Savings Bank
1629 Druid Hill Ave
Baltimore Maryland 21217
301-669-1629

Dr. W. O. Bryson Jr., Chairman

100.

National Association of Urban Bankers
1010 Wayne Ave, Suite 1210
Silver Spring Maryland 20910-5600
301-589-2141

Paul R. Wiggens, President; Lloyd Griffin, Vice President; Richard Holmes, Treasurer; Beverly Brown, Secretary; Adele D. Jackson, Executive Director

101.

First Independence National Bank
44 Michigan Ave
Detroit Michigan 48226
313-256-8250

Don Davis, Chairman

102.

Home Federal Savings Bank
9108 Woodward Ave
Detroit Michigan 48202
313-873-3310

Wilburn R. Phillips, President

103.

OmniBank
10474 W Jefferson Ave
River Rouge Michigan 48218
313-843-8856

104.

First Commerce Savings Bank
P.O. Box 3199
Jackson Mississippi 39201

105.

Douglass Bank The
1314 N 5th St
Kansas City Missouri 66101
913-321-7200

Sarah Swaters, Vice President

106.

Gateway National Bank
3412 Union Blvd N
St. Louis Missouri 63115
314-389-3000

William X. Smith, President

107.

New Age Federal Savings & Loan Association
1401 N Kings Hwy Blvd
St. Louis Missouri 63113
314-361-4100

David Harper, President

108.

City National Bank of New Jersey
900 Broad St
Newark New Jersey 07102
201-624-0895

Louis E. Prezeau, President

109.

Carver Federal Savings Bank
121 Dr. Martin Luther King Jr. Blvd
New York New York 10027
212-666-8139

110.

Carver Federal Savings & Loan Association
75 W 125th St
New York New York 10027
212-876-7573

Richard T. Greene, President

111.

Freedom National Bank
275 W 125th St
New York New York 10027
212-678-8408

George A. Russell, President

112.

Mutual Savings & Loan Association
112 W Parish St
Durham North Carolina 27701
919-688-1308

F. V. Allison Jr., President

113.

United National Bank
P.O. Box 1450
Fayetteville North Carolina 28302
919-483-1131

Leonard Hedgepeth, President/CEO

114.

American Federal Savings & Loan Association
701 E Market St
Greensboro North Carolina 20071
919-273-9753

115.

Greensboro National Bank
P.O. Box 22046
Greensboro North Carolina 27420
919-373-8500

Robert S. Chiles Sr., President

116.

Mechanics & Farmers Bank
P.O. Box 22046
Greensboro North Carolina 27702
919-683-1521

Ms. J. W. Taylor, President/CEO

117.

American State Bank
P.O. Box 6389
Tulsa Oklahoma 74148
918-428-2211

Leon Evans Jr., Executive Vice President

118.

Berean Saving Association
5228 Chestnut St
Philadelphia Pennsylvania 19139
215-472-4545

Ron Green, President

119.

**Dwelling House Savings & Loan
Association**
501 Herron Ave
Pittsburgh Pennsylvania 15219
412-683-5116

Robert R. Lavelle, CEO

120.

Heritage National Bank
205 E Liberty Station
Pittsburgh Pennsylvania 15206

Deidre Sledge, Operations Manager

121.

Victory Savings Bank
1545 Sumter St
Columbia South Carolina 29201
803-733-8100

James A. Bennett, President

122.

Tri-State Bank of Memphis
180 S Main St
Memphis Tennessee 38101
901-525-0384

Jesse Turner, President

123.

Citizen's Bank
401 Charlotte Ave
Nashville Tennessee 37219
615-256-6193

The oldest continuously operated black-owned bank in America.
1904

124.

First Texas Bank
P.O. Box 29775
Dallas Texas 75229
901-525-0384

William E. Stahnke, President

125.

Standard Savings & Loan Association
P.O. Box 8806
Houston Texas 77288
713-529-9133

Gloria R. Hall, Executive Vice President

126.

Unity National Bank
2602 Blodgett
Houston Texas 77004
713-526-3971

Larry Hawkins, President/CEO

127.

First State Bank
P.O. Box 640
Danville Virginia 24543
804-793-4611

Sylvester L. Jennings, President

128.

People's Savings & Loan Association
101 N Armistead Ave
Hampton Virginia 23669
804-722-2575

129.

Imperial Savings & Loan Association
211 Fayette St
Martinsville Virginia 24114
703-638-7545

William B. Muse Jr., President

130.

New Atlantic Bank
415 St. Paul's Blvd
Norfolk Virginia 23510
804-623-6155

Hillary Holloway, Chairman/CEO

131.

Emerald City Bank
2320 E Union
Seattle Washington 98122
206-329-3434

Leon Smith, President

132.

Sound Savings & Loan Association
1006 Second Ave
Seattle Washington 98114

Cathy Boydston, President

133.

Columbia Savings & Loan Association
2000 West Fond du Lac Ave
Milwaukee Wisconsin 52302
414-374-0485

Thalia B. Winfield, President

134.

North Milwaukee State Bank
5630 West Fond du Lac Ave
Milwaukee Wisconsin 53216
414-466-2344

Snow Mitchell Jr., Chairman

❂ BASEBALL ❂

135.

Negro League Baseball Apparel
P.O. Box 25
Brentwood Maryland 20722
800-255-2289

Free catalog.

136.

Negro Leagues Baseball Museum
1601 E 18th St, Suite 260
Kansas City Missouri 64108
816-221-1920

Memorabilia and tributes to some of the
greatest baseball players in history.

137.

**National Baseball Hall of Fame &
Museum**
Main St
Cooperstown New York 13326
607-547-9988

Heroes of the Negro leagues, as well as recent
African-American baseball heroes, are en-
shrined here.

❂ BASKETBALL ❂

138.

**Naismith Memorial Basketball Hall of
Fame**
1150 W Columbus Ave
Springfield Massachusetts 01105
413-781-5759

Tribute to the great players of basketball,
many of whom are African American and have
so dramatically transformed the game.

❂ BOOKSTORES ❂

139.

Beacon Book Club
Alison Alston
AALSTON213@aol.com

Mail-order book service specializing in African-American best-sellers and other books celebrating Afrocentric culture. Book list features over 250 selections including audio books, biographies, calendars, entertainment, fiction, health, children's books, mysteries, and many more, all with the convenience of mail-order delivery.

140.

African Book Mart
2440 Durant Ave
Berkeley California 94704-1611
510-843-3088

141.

Aquarian Bookshop
3995 S Western Ave
Los Angeles California 90062
213-296-1633

Bernice Ligon, Owner

142.

Black & Latino Multicultural Book Center
23 N Mentor Ave
Pasadena California 91106-1709
818-792-0117

143.

Marcus Books
1712 Fillmore St
San Francisco California 94115
415-346-4222

Julian Richardson, President

144.

African Child Bookstore
3415 E Colfax Ave
Denver Colorado 80206-1801
303-399-7206

145.

Hue-man Experience Bookstore
911 23rd St
Denver Colorado 80205
303-293-2665

Clara C. Villarosa, President

146.

JMA Enterprises Inc.
218 46th St, NE
Washington DC 20019-4639
202-398-3787

Aretha S. Frizzell, President/CEO
Reading is exciting when the story is about you. That's the message of JMA Enterprises Inc., a create-a-book dealer. JMA uses a computer and laser printer to make personalized children's storybooks and other items. Let's encourage our children to read.

147.

African-American Bookstore
3600 W Broward Blvd
Fort Lauderdale Florida 33312
954-584-0460

148.

Afro-In Books & Things
5575 NW 7th Ave
Miami Florida 33127-1401
305-756-6107

149.

African-American Heritage Book
515 Northwood Rd
West Palm Beach Florida 33407-5817
407-835-3551

150.

Afro American Awakening Book
1710 45th St
West Palm Beach Florida 33407-2150
407-848-3224

151.

Shrine of the Black Madonna
946 Gordon St, SW
Atlanta Georgia 30310
404-752-6125

Barbara Martin, Director

152.

African American Book Center
7524 S Cottage Grove Ave
Chicago Illinois 60621
312-651-9101

153.

Afrika North Bookstore
4629½ N Broadway
Chicago Illinois 60640
312-907-00005

154.

Afro-centric Bookstore
234 S Wabash Ave
Chicago Illinois 60604-2304
312-939-1956

155.

DuSable Museum Gift Shop/Bookstore
740 E 56th Place
Chicago Illinois 60637
312-947-0600

Useni Eugene Perkins, Executive Director

156.

Black Heritage Books
Evanston Illinois 60204
708-864-0700

157.

Afrikan-American Book Source
3490 Village Ct
Gary Indiana 46408-1426
219-981-2133

158.

Authentic Book Distributors
P.O. Box 52916
Baton Rouge Louisiana 70892
504-356-0076

Kwaku O. Kushindana, Business Manager

159.

Afro-American Book Stop
7166 Crowder Blvd
New Orleans Louisiana 70127-1970
504-246-6288

160.

African American Books Plus
8640 McGilford Rd
Columbia Maryland 21045
410-730-0779

161.

Pyramid Bookstore
3500 East-West Hwy
Hyattsville Maryland 20782
301-559-5200

Hodari Ali, Owner

162.

Afro-American Book Source
P.O. Box 851
Boston Massachusetts 02120
617-445-9209

Charles Pinderhughes, President
"Your Black Bookstore by Mail."

163.

Savanna Books
858 Massachusetts Ave
Cambridge Massachusetts 02139
617-868-3423

Gail Pettiford Willett, Director

164.

African American Books
892 State St
Springfield Massachusetts 01109-3136
413-781-2233

165.

Progressive Books
6265 Delmar Blvd
St. Louis Missouri 63130
314-721-1344

Johnson Lancaster, Manager

166.

African University Book Store
1661 Amsterdam Ave
New York New York 10031-6107
212-281-8650

Specializes in books on ancient African history.

167.

Liberation Bookstore
421 Lenox Ave
New York New York 10037
212-281-4615

Una G. Mulzac, Manager

168.

Positive Images Unlimited Bookstore
137-07 Bedell St
Rochdale Village New York 11434
718-949-2535

Brad McLeod, Manager

169.

Afro-centric Connections Book Dealers
116 E Walnut St
Goldsboro North Carolina 27530-3649
919-731-4404

170.

Afrikids
108 William Howard Taft Rd, Suite 2
Cincinnati Ohio 45219
513-569-8286
513-569-8284—Fax

Keena Mcdowell-Smith, CEO
Afrikids offers educational books, games, toys, and resources for African-American children ranging from preschool through junior high school, as well as parenting books. All materials available by mail order.

171.

African Book Shelf The
13240 Euclid Ave
Cleveland Ohio 44112-4524
216-681-6511

172.

African & Islamic Books Plus
3752 Lee Rd
Cleveland Ohio 44128-1410
216-561-5000

173.

Hakim's Bookstore
210 S 52nd St
Philadelphia Pennsylvania 19139
215-474-9495

Dawud Hakim, Owner

174.

African Appeal Book Store
Chattanooga Tennessee 37400
615-624-2318

175.

Black Images Book Bazaar
142 Wynnewood Village
Dallas Texas 75224
214-943-0142

Emma Rodger, President

176.

Amistad Bookplace
1413 Holman St
Houston Texas 77004

177.

JustUs, Inc.
498 E 630 N
Lindon Utah 84042
800-706-1133, Ext. 2238
http://www.shopsite.com/justus

JustUs is an African-American bookstore that offers uplifting books about the African-American experience. They have the largest selection of African-American books on-line.

178.

African American Books Unlimited
Milwaukee Wisconsin 53200
414-442-3663

❁ BUSINESS ASSISTANCE & DEVELOPMENT ❁

179.

Alabama Minority Supplier Development Council Inc.
3100 Cottage Hill Rd, Suite 218
Mobile Alabama 36606
205-471-6380
205-470-4190—Fax

Darlene M. Moore, Executive Director

180.

African American Business Council
1577 C St
Anchorage Alaska 99501-5138
907-263-9885 or 907-263-9886

181.

Minority Business Development Center
Anchorage Alaska 99501
907-274-5400

182.

African-American Summit
5040 E Shea Blvd, Suite 260
Phoenix Arizona 85254-4610
602-443-1800

The Rev. Leon Sullivan, Summit Chairman and Convener
The African-American Summit was initiated by Rev. Leon H. Sullivan and key African gov-ernment officials to focus on closer coopera-tion and ways in which African Americans and friends of Africa might assist in creating prag-matic strategies and meaningful programs to assist with the development of sub-Saharan African countries.

183.

Arizona Minority Supplier Development Council
5151 N 16th St, Suite F-136
Phoenix Arizona 85016
602-274-4647
602-277-8559—Fax

James E. Salmon, Executive Director

184.

Minority Business Development Center
7777 Alvarado Rd
La Mesa California 91941-3616
619-668-6232

185.

Minority Business Development Center
1000 Wilshire Blvd
Los Angeles California 90017-2457
213-892-1632

186.

Southern California Regional Purchasing Council
3325 Wilshire Blvd, Suite 604
Los Angeles California 90010
213-380-7114
213-380-8026—Fax

Hollis Smith, President

187.

African Enterprise
128 E Palm Ave
Monrovia California 91016-2851
818-357-8811

188.

Minority Enterprise Group of Southern California
Newport Beach California 92660
714-720-1465—Fax

189.

African Business Referral Association The
1212 Broadway
Oakland California 94612-1841
510-238-5170

190.

Northern California Purchasing Council
1970 Broadway, Suite 710
Oakland California 94612
510-763-8162
510-763-8727—Fax

Marilyn Waits, Executive Director

191.

Minority Business Development
451 W 5th St
Oxnard California 93030-7049
805-483-1123

192.

Minority Business Development Center
1779 Tribute Rd
Sacramento California 95815-4406
916-649-2551

193.

Minority Business Development Centre for Monterey County
14 Maple St
Salinas California 93901-3229
408-422-8825

194.

African International Development
988 Market St
San Francisco California 94102-4002
415-771-4506
415-771-5481—Fax [telex ITT 470 271]

Sunday Peters, President/CEO
Consulting, engineering, management consulting, purchasing agents, foreign-resident buyer, agriculture. Africans and African Americans. Export management.

195.

Minority Assistance Service
3004 16th St
San Francisco California 94103
415-552-5466

196.

African Development Resources Group
620 W Santa Anita Ave
San Gabriel California 91776-1024
818-308-3410

197.

Minority Business Entrepreneur
3528 Torrance Blvd
Torrance California 90503-4827
310-540-9398

198.

Minority Business Enterprises
1220 Oakland Blvd
Walnut Creek California 94596-4304
510-935-7494

199.

Rocky Mountain Minority Supplier and Development Council
Minority Enterprises Inc.
940 Speer Blvd
Denver Colorado 80204
303-595-9638
303-595-0027—Fax

James Laurie, Executive Director

200.

Connecticut Minority Purchasing Council
General Electric Company
Bridgeport Connecticut 06607

Clarence T. Williams, Executive Director & CEO

201.

Minority Entrepreneur Network Association
955 Connecticut Ave
Bridgeport Connecticut 06607-1200
203-335-7599

202.

African American Union
3048 Stanton Rd, SE
Washington DC 20020-7881
202-610-0529

Minority business development.

203.

Links Inc. The
1200 Massachusetts Ave, NW
Washington DC 20005
202-842-8686

Marion Schultz Sutherland, President
Founded as a public-service organization; today over 8,000 members in 240 chapters in cities in the United States, Nassau, Bahamas, and Frankfurt, West Germany focus Links' activities around four program areas: the arts, services to youth, national trends and services, and international trends and services.
1946

204.

Minority Business Development Agency
14th & Constitution Ave, NW
Washington DC 20230
202-482-5741

Office of Public Affairs, 202-482-4547
Assists business development centers nation-

wide in starting up and expanding competitive minority-owned firms. This federal government agency does not provide loans, but does provide managerial counseling and marketing and technical assistance. Over 100 minority development centers to provide services for the minority community.

205.

National Association of Investment Companies
1111 14th St, NW, Suite 700
Washington DC 20005
202-289-4336
202-289-4329—Fax

JoAnn H. Price, President
This is an alliance of small business investment companies licensed by the Small Business Administration to provide capital to businesses owned by socially or economically disadvantaged Americans. Total private capital investment in the MESBIC program exceeds $100 million.

206.

National Business League
1511 K St, NW, Suite 432
Washington DC 20005
202-737-4430

Benjamin S. Ruffin, Chairman; Sherman N. Copelin, President; Franklin O'Neal, Senior Vice President
Organizational vehicle for minority businesspeople. Promotes the economic development of minorities, encourages minority ownership and management of small businesses, and supports full minority participation within the free enterprise system. Maintains file of minority vendors and corporate procurement and purchasing agents.

207.

Florida Regional Minority Purchasing Council
7900 NE Second Ave, Suite 2501
Miami Florida 33138
305-757-9690
305-757-8376—Fax

Windell Paige, Executive Director

208.

Black Business Investment Fund— Central Florida
315 E Robinson St
Orlando Florida 32801-1912
407-649-4780

209.

Minority Business Consultants & Contractors
725 S Goldwyn Ave
Orlando Florida 32805-2903
407-521-6330

210.

Minority Business Development Association
2410 N East St
Pensacola Florida 32501-1617
904-432-2375

211.

Black Business Investment Corporation
2001 Broadway
West Palm Beach Florida 33404-5669
407-845-8055

212.

Georgia Minority Supplier Development Council
243 Marietta St
Atlanta Georgia 30303
404-523-7919

Ernie Lee, Executive Director

213.

Minority Business Development Agency Regional
1371 Peachtree St, NE
Atlanta Georgia 30367-2301
404-347-3438

214.

Minority Business Referral Service
4336 Covington Hwy
Decatur Georgia 30035-1211
404-286-4830

215.

Paragon
2527 Park Central Blvd
Decatur Georgia 30035
404-322-9181

Lou Walker
Motion picture production, public relations, management consulting, miscellaneous publishing.

216.

Minority Economic Task Force
P.O. Box 447
Washington Georgia 30673
706-678-4450
404-678-4451—Fax

M. V. Booker, President

217.

Minority Business Development
1132 Bishop St, Suite 1000
Honolulu Hawaii 96813-2830
808-531-6232

218.

Chicago Regional Purchasing Council
36 S Wabash Ave, Suite 725
Chicago Illinois 60603
312-263-0105
312-263-0280—Fax

Maye Foster-Thompson, Executive Director

219.

Minority Economic Resources Corporation
2570 W Devon Ave
Chicago Illinois 60659-1810
312-694-3989

220.

Minority Enterprise Development Information Association
7046 S Crandon Ave
Chicago Illinois 60649-2239
312-324-2927

221.

Minority Business Network
550 S Greenwood Ave
Decatur Illinois 62522-3315
217-422-7222

222.

Minority Business Development
1840 Oak Ave
Evanston Illinois 60201-3670
708-866-1829

223.

Minority Business Development Center
567 Broadway
Gary Indiana 46402-1910
219-883-5802

224.

Indiana Regional Minority Supplier Development Council
300 E Fall Creek Parkway, North Dr,
Suite 403
Indianapolis Indiana 46205
317-923-2110
317-923-2204—Fax

Donald E. Jones, Executive Director

225.

Minority Business Development Center
4755 Kingsway Dr
Indianapolis Indiana 46205-1545
317-257-0327

226.

National Association of African American Entrepreneurs
P.O. Box 1191
Indianapolis Indiana 46206
317-466-9556

Linda Clemons, CEO
To encourage the economic growth and development of minority business enterprise, the organization provides support in the areas of business planning, marketing, and technical and financial assistance. It also provides matchmakers with major corporations, major networking events on the local, state, and national level, discounts on travel, express mail service, retail products, etc. Membership is open to individuals, small businesses, organizations, and supporting corporations.

227.

African/Caribbean Enterprises
1514 W Broadway St
Louisville Kentucky 40203-3516
502-585-1577

228.

Kentuckiana Minority Supplier Development Council
One Riverfront Plaza
Louisville Kentucky 40202
502-625-0000

Betty J. Fox, Executive Director

229.

Gulf South Minority Purchasing Council Inc.
935 Gravier St, Suite 1710
New Orleans Louisiana 70112
504-523-7110
504-592-7232—Fax

Helen S. Stanwood, Executive Director

230.

Maryland/DC Minority Supplier Development Council
9150-B5 Rumsey Rd, P.O. Box 2069
Columbia Maryland 21045
301-596-5560
301-997-2040—Fax

Charles R. Owens, Executive Director

231.

Africa Cultural Center Inc.
13815 Marianna Dr
Rockville Maryland 20853
301-871-1397

Mohamed A. Khadar, Director & General Founder
A duly established, tax-exempt, nonprofit corporation that provides the public and members with cultural, educational and information programs about Africa and the Caribbean. The center serves as a distributor of food and clothing to needy African families and as a contact point for those interested in conducting business in West Africa.

232.

Minority Business Assistance Center
133 Federal St
Boston Massachusetts 02110-1703
617-457-4444

233.

Minority Business Development Agency
10 Causeway St
Boston Massachusetts 02222-1047
617-565-6850

234.

New England Regional Minority Purchasing Council
Four Copley Place, Suite 125, P.O. Box 145
Boston Massachusetts 02116
617-578-8900
617-578-8901—Fax

May Ling Tong, Executive Director

235.

African Technology Forum
Massachusetts Institute of Technology
Cambridge Massachusetts 02139
617-225-7477
http://web.mit.edu/africantech/www

Marion L. Buchanan

ATF publishes a unique magazine on science and technology in Africa and provides consulting services and networking opportunities for technical and business professionals involved in African development. Articles and organization information can be found online.

236.

Minority Business Associates
4B Doamon Mill Sq
Concord Massachusetts 01742
508-371-2997

237.

Minnesota Minority Purchasing Council
2021 E Hennepin Ave, Suite 370
Minneapolis Minnesota 55413
612-378-0361
612-378-9342—Fax

Jane Winston, Executive Director

238.

Mississippi Minority Supplier Development Council
P.O. Box 20092
Jackson Mississippi 39209
601-948-2253

Vern Gavin, Executive Director

239.

Kansas City Minority Supplier Development Council
106 W 14th St, Suite 701
Kansas City Missouri 64105
816-472-6464

Gregory D. Baker, Executive Director

240.

St. Louis Metropolitan Minority Supplier Development Council
4144 Lindell Blvd
St. Louis Missouri 63108
314-534-8916
314-534-7206—Fax

Joseph Bulter, Executive Director

241.

Omaha Regional Minority Purchasing Council
1301 Harney St
Omaha Nebraska 68102
402-345-2212
402-346-7050—Fax

Terrie J. Miller, Executive Director

242.

Minority & Women's Business Enterprise Coordination
Reno Nevada 89509
702-858-1700

243.

African Business to Business Program
55 Washington St
Orange New Jersey 07052-5536
201-672-6666

244.

Rio Grande Minority Purchasing Council
5000 Marble, NE, Suite 108
Albuquerque New Mexico 87110
505-265-7677
505-265-7690—Fax

Richard E. Lavers, Executive Director

245.

New York–New Jersey Minority Purchasing Council
60 John St, 4th Floor
Brooklyn New York 11201
718-243-6000
718-858-9010—Fax

William R. Garner, President

246.

Upstate New York Regional Minority Purchasing Council
4455 Genesee St
Buffalo New York 14225
716-632-8422
716-632-1053—Fax

Mary J. Hayes, Executive Director

247.

African American International Trading Inc.
40-22 College Point Blvd
Flushing New York 11354-5100
718-461-2591

248.

African Business Consultants
107-12 Jamaica Ave
Jamaica New York 11418-2239
718-849-8243

249.

Africa Export
150 W 28 St
New York New York 10001
212-633-0365

250.

African Minerals Resources Exchange
4 Park Ave
New York New York 10016-5339
212-532-5449
212-532-4680—Fax

Frank Weston, President
Provides African businesses with opportunity to reach the vast mineral and material wealth of African diaspora. Economic institution that converts mineral and material wealth into currency.

251.

Interracial Council for Business Opportunity
51 Madison Ave, Suite 2212
New York New York 10010
212-779-4360 or 800-252-4226

William A. Young, President
The Interracial Council for Business Opportunity, founded in 1963, is a full-service business development organization devoted exclusively to minority business development.

252.

Minority and Women's Business Development
1515 Broadway
New York New York 10036-8901
212-827-6170 or 800-STATE-NY

Information and phone numbers to help women and minorities start businesses.

253.

Minority Business Forms Inc.
276 Park Ave S
New York New York 10010-6408
212-529-1266

254.

Minority Operated Management Inc.
1 Beekman St
New York New York 10038-2203
212-791-4240

255.

National Minority Business Council Inc.
235 E 42nd St
New York New York 10017
212-573-2385

John F. Robinson, National President & CEO
Education and training, international trade.

256.

National Minority Supplier Development Council
15 W 39th St, 9th Floor
New York New York 10018
212-944-2430

Harriet R. Michel, President; Arthur C. Martinez, Chairman
Composed of individuals, corporations, associations, foundations, and other organizations who are members of regional purchasing councils. Promotes networking and business opportunities, offers consultative, advisory, and informational services and technical resources to minority businesses and regional and local purchasing councils. Chartered to increase procurement and business opportunities for minority business of all sizes.

257.

Minority Business Development
350 North St
Rochester New York 14605
716-232-6120·

258.

Minority Business Exchange
215 Tremont
Rochester New York 14608
716-436-4377

259.

Carolinas Minority Supplier Development Council
700 E Stonewall St, Suite 340
Charlotte North Carolina 28202
704-372-8731
704-334-5739—Fax

Malcolm R. Graham, Executive Director

260.

Minority Women's Business Enterprises
Charlotte North Carolina 28200
704-336-4138

261.

**Minority/Women's Business Enterprise
Winston-Salem**
City Hall
Winston Salem North Carolina 27100
910-727-8040

262.

**Cincinnati Minority Supplier
Development Council**
300 Carew Tower
441 Vine St
Cincinnati Ohio 45202
513-579-3137
513-579-3102—Fax

Mark F. Green, Executive Director

263.

**Cleveland Regional Minority Purchasing
Council**
200 Tower City Center
50 Public Sq
Cleveland Ohio 44113-2291
216-621-3300
216-621-6013—Fax

Ames W. Wade, Executive Director

264.

**Minority Contractors Assistance
Program**
20475 Farnsleigh Rd
Cleveland Ohio 44122-3850
216-283-4700

265.

**Columbus Regional Minority Purchasing
Council**
37 N High St
Columbus Ohio 43215
614-225-6959
614-469-8250—Fax

Michael D. Gordon, Executive Director

266.

**Greater Dayton Minority Purchasing
Council**
Chamber Plaza
Dayton Ohio 45402
513-226-8265

Robert R. Lowe, Executive Director

267.

Minority Business Assistance Association
1116 W Stewart St
Dayton Ohio 45408-1970
513-443-0316

268.

Minority Business Development Council of N.W. Ohio/MCBAP
303 Morris St
Toledo Ohio 43602
419-244-3111
419-259-8208—Fax

Mark A. Urrutia, Executive Director

269.

Minority Business Development Council of Northern Ohio
303 Morris St
Toledo Ohio 43602-1869
419-249-4800

270.

Minority & Small Business Incubator Building
303 Morris St
Toledo Ohio 43602-1869
419-249-4740

271.

Oklahoma Minority Supplier Development Council
525 Central Park Dr, Suite 106
Oklahoma City Oklahoma 73105
405-528-6732

Debra Ronder-Moore, Executive Director

272.

Regional Minority Purchasing Council of Central Pennsylvania
915 S 13th St
Harrisburg Pennsylvania 17108
717-233-5502

Wanda Pritchett, Chairman

273.

Minority Business Development Agency
Philadelphia Pennsylvania 19092
215-597-9236

274.

Minority Business Network
Philadelphia Pennsylvania 19092
215-748-2191

275.

Minority Contractor's Business Development
1000 Ivy Hill Rd
Philadelphia Pennsylvania 19150-3232
215-242-6606

276.

Minority Venture Partnership
1315 Walnut St
Philadelphia Pennsylvania 19107-4719
215-546-1687

277.

New Jersey–Pennsylvania–Delaware Minority Purchasing Regional Council
One Winding Dr, Suite 210
Philadelphia Pennsylvania 19131
215-578-0964
215-578-2832—Fax

Thornton C. Carroll Jr., Executive Director

278.

Opportunities Industrialization Centers of America
1415 N Broad St
Philadelphia Pennsylvania 19122
215-236-4500

The Rev. Leon Sullivan, Chairman/Founder;
Herman Art Taylor, President/CEO

279.

Philadelphia Commercial Development Corporation
1315 Walnut St, 6th Floor
Philadelphia Pennsylvania 19107
215-790-2200
215-790-2222—Fax

Dr. Romeo A. Horton, President
Since 1977, CDC has provided a comprehensive program of financial managerial and technical assistance to small minority firms. More than $90 million in financing has been secured for more than 900 firms in the fields of manufacturing, retailing, advanced technology, and construction.

280.

Minority Enterprise Corporation of Southwestern Pennsylvania
5907 Penn Ave
Pittsburgh Pennsylvania 15123
412-363-9660

281.

Pittsburgh Regional Minority Purchasing Council
One Oliver Plaza, Suite 3004
Pittsburgh Pennsylvania 15222
412-391-4423
412-391-3132—Fax

John H. Adams, Executive Director

282.

Minority Suppliers
631 S Chester Rd
Swarthmore Pennsylvania 19081-2315
215-387-1600

283.

National Economic Association
Office of Vice Provost
University Park Pennsylvania 16802
814-865-4700

James B. Stewart, President; Alvin E. Headen, Jr., President-Elect; Alfred E. Edwards, Secretary-Treasurer

284.

Puerto Rico Regional Council
P.O. Box 2410
Hato Rey Puerto Rico 00919
809-759-9445
809-756-7670—Fax

Jacqueline Matos, Executive Director

285.

Black Enterprises Inc.
1807 Black Hwy
York South Carolina 29745-8723
803-684-4971

286.

Tennessee Minority Purchasing Council
Building 3, Suite 235, Maryland Farms
Brentwood Tennessee 37027
615-371-8980
615-371-8869—Fax

Cheri K. Henderson, Executive Director

287.

Minority Business Bureau
1828 McCalla Ave
Knoxville Tennessee 37915-1419
615-525-7550

288.

Black Business Referral Network
1177 Madison Ave
Memphis Tennessee 38104-2227
901-272-7272

289.

Mid-South Minority Purchasing Council
4111 S MSU B St
Memphis Tennessee 38111
901-327-6672
901-327-6678—Fax

Carol B. Crawley, Executive Director

290.

Minority Business Development
5 N 3rd St
Memphis Tennessee 38103-2610
901-527-2298

291.

Dallas–Fort Worth Minority Business Development Council
2720 Stemmons Freeway, Suite 1000
Dallas Texas 75207
214-630-0747
214-637-2241—Fax

Yvonne Wooten, Executive Director

292.

San Antonio Minority Supplier and Development Council
301 S Frio, Room 244
San Antonio Texas 78207
512-270-4554
512-270-4501—Fax

Cynthia Travieso, Office Manager

293.

Global Marketing Resources
609 Half Mile Branch Rd
Crozet Virginia 22932
804-980-3425

Ruby Spradford-Boston, President
Marketing consultant firm for African-American businesses. Creates and implements marketing strategies: special projects, fund raising for nonprofits, asset management.
1994

294.

**Tidewater Regional Minority
Purchasing Council**
1216 Granby St, Suite 9
Norfolk Virginia 23510
804-627-8471
804-627-3272—Fax

295.

**Virginia Regional Minority Supplier and
Development Council**
201 E Franklin St
Richmond Virginia 23219
804-780-2322
804-780-3171—Fax

Adele Johnson-Crawley, Executive Director

296.

**Northwest Minority Supplier
Development Council**
660 SW 39th St
Renton Washington 98055
206-657-6225
206-657-6721—Fax

Thor R. Briggs, Executive Director

297.

**Wisconsin Supplier and Development
Council**
4222 Milwaukee St, Suite 26
Madison Wisconsin 53714
608-241-5858
608-241-9100—Fax

Floyd Rose, Executive Director

298.

Minority Business Development
1442 N Farwell Ave
Milwaukee Wisconsin 53202-2913
414-289-3422

299.

Minority Business Joint Certificate
2323 N Martin Luther King Dr
Milwaukee Wisconsin 53212
414-265-7680

❂ CAREER DEVELOPMENT ❂

300.

Black Progress Review Office
3010 Wilshire Blvd
Beverly Hills California 90210
310-285-0112

Publication for minority recruitment at corporations and school districts.

301.

Minority Employment Journal
110 S La Brea Ave
Inglewood California 90301-1768
310-330-3670

302.

Hawkins Co. The
5455 Wilshire Blvd, Suite 1406
Los Angeles California 90036
213-933-3337

Executive search firm.

303.

Sampson Associates
4100 Redwood Rd, #359
Oakland California 94619
510-531-4237

Executive search firm.

304.

Montgomery West
220 Montgomery St
San Francisco California 94104
415-956-6010

Executive search firm.

305.

Minority Placement Services
1229 Albany Ave
Hartford Connecticut 06112-2156
203-278-6611

306.

Black Education & Employment Network
Washington DC 20007

307.

Black Human Resources Network
1900 L St, NW
Washington DC 20036-5002
202-331-7398 or 202-775-1669

308.

Black Employment & Education
2625 Piedmont Rd, NE
Atlanta Georgia 30324-3012
404-469-5891

309.

Executive Source International
550 Pharr Rd, Suite 840
Atlanta Georgia 30305
404-231-3783

Executive search firm.

310.

Mitchell-Street Associates
Merchants Business Centre
Atlanta Georgia 30274
800-636-2477

Executive search firm.

311.

Excel Executive Recruiters
140 Wynchase Lane
Fayetteville Georgia 30214
404-719-9745

Executive search firm.

312.

Robert L. Livingston Recruiting & Staffing
P.O. Box 568
Lilburn Georgia 30226
404-925-8687

Executive search firm.

313.

Corporate Plus
3145 Tucker-Norcross Rd, Suite 206
Tucker Georgia 30084
404-934-5101

Executive search firm.

314.

Carrington & Carrington Ltd.
39 S LaSalle St, Suite 1125
Chicago Illinois 60603
312-606-0015

Executive search firm.

315.

Ellington & Associates
1755 Park St, Suite 200
Naperville Illinois 60563
708-305-0088

Executive search firm.

316.

Juan Menefee & Associates
503 S Oak Park Ave
Oak Park Illinois 60304
708-848-7722

Executive search firm.

317.

Career Communications Group
729 E Pratt St, Suite 504
Baltimore Maryland 21202
410-244-7101
410-752-1837—Fax

Tyrone D. Taborne, President & CEO
The country's largest minority-owned media services company producing information about education and careers for black and Hispanic professionals.

318.

OSA Partners Inc.
2 Park Plaza, Suite 600
Boston Massachusetts 02116
617-357-7333

Executive search firm.

319.

Minority Employment Program
2345 Main St
Springfield Massachusetts 01107-1907
413-736-8470

Job training and educational services.

320.

Joe L. Giles & Associates
18105 Parkside St, Suite 14
Detroit Michigan 48221
313-864-0022

Executive search firm.

321.

Benford & Associates Inc.
300 Town Center, Suite 1333
Southfield Michigan 48034
810-351-0250

Executive search firm.

322.

Wing-Tips & Pumps Inc.
P.O. Box 99580
Troy Michigan 48099
810-641-0980

Temporary agency.

323.

S. E. Heifner & Associates
3954 Portland Ave S, Suite 2
Minneapolis Minnesota 55407
612-827-0267

Executive search firm.

324.

Inroads
1221 Locust St, Suite 410
St. Louis Missouri 63103
314-241-7330

Reginald D. Dickson, CEO & President
A program that encourages corporations to
sponsor internships for minority students and
pledge to develop career opportunities for the
interns. Prepares black, Hispanic, and Native
American high school and college students for
leadership positions within major American
corporations in their own communities.

325.

Howard Clark Associates
231 S White Horse Pike
Audubon New Jersey 08106
609-467-3725

Executive search firm.

326.

Aces Employment Consultants
P.O. Box 1513
Linden New Jersey 07036
908-925-8836

Executive search firm.

327.

Hillman Group Inc. The
1032 South Ave, Suite 232
Plainfield New Jersey 07060
908-561-6255

Executive search firm.

328.

Bruce Robinson Associates
Harmon Cove Towers, Suite 8, A–L Level
Secaucus New Jersey 07094
212-541-4140

Executive search firm.

329.

Your Accountant of New Jersey
255 Route 3 E, Suite 201
Secaucus New Jersey 07094
201-866-5122

Executive search firm.

330.

P. S. P. Agency
188 Montague St
Brooklyn New York 11201
718-596-3786

Executive search firm.

331.

A. D. Fleming Group Inc.
139 Fulton St, Room 818C
New York New York 10038
212-349-6060

Executive search firm.

332.

Interspace Interactive Inc.
521 Fifth Ave
New York New York 10017
212-867-6661

Executive search firm.

333.

Johnson Group Inc. The
1 World Trade Center, Suite 4517
New York New York 10048
212-775-0036

Executive search firm.

334.

Milo Research
60 E 42nd St, Suite 1762
New York New York 10017
212-972-2780

Executive search firm.

335.

Minority Temporary Agency Inc.
41 E 42nd St
New York New York 10017-5301
212-697-7500

Temporary agency.

336.

National Minority Business Council Inc.
235 E 42nd St
New York New York 10017
212-573-2385

John F. Robinson, National President/CEO
Education and training, international trade.

337.

Minority Executive Search
6001 Landerhaven Dr
Cleveland Ohio 44124-4190
216-449-8034

Executive search firm.

338.

Minority Personnel Service
5424 N 5th St
Philadelphia Pennsylvania 19120-2802
215-457-5660

339.

Minority Workforce Cooperative
339 Blvd of the Allies
Pittsburgh Pennsylvania 15222-1917
412-281-6321

340.

**African American Apprenticeship
School The**
1011 S Willett St
Memphis Tennessee 38114-1846
901-725-5494

341.

Minority Employment Recruiting
101 W Pleasant St
Milwaukee Wisconsin 53212-3963
414-271-6376

342.

Minority Training Project
6815 W Capitol Dr
Milwaukee Wisconsin 53216-2056
414-353-7240

❂ CHAMBERS OF COMMERCE ❂

343.

**Birmingham-Jefferson Metro
Chamber of Commerce**
1713 Fourth Ave North
Birmingham Alabama 35203
205-323-1887

Kenneth Owens Jr.

344.

Black Chamber of Commerce
654 Discovery Dr
Huntsville Alabama 35806
205-971-9700
205-971-9090—Fax

Buford Crutcher

345.

Mobile Black Chamber of Commerce
962 Dr. Martin Luther King Ave
Mobile Alabama 36603
205-438-1442
205-438-1439—Fax

346.

Arizona Black Chamber of Commerce
1155A Plaza Maria
Sierra Vista Arizona 85635
602-459-3436
602-459-8682—Fax

347.

Arkansas Black Chamber of Commerce
1411 College St
Little Rock Arkansas 72202
501-374-0747

B. J. Harris, Executive Director

348.

Arkansas State Chamber of Commerce
911 Wallace Building
Little Rock Arkansas 72201
501-374-9225

Bob Lamb, Executive Director

349.

Central City Chamber of Commerce
P.O. Box 6293
Pine Bluff Arkansas 71611
501-535-0110

Matthew Henry, Treasurer

350.

Black Business Exchange
1013 Pardee St
Berkeley California 94710-2627
510-644-2646

351.

**Black Chamber of Commerce
of Los Angeles County**
3860 Amberly Dr
Inglewood California 90305-2260
310-412-1991

352.

African American Business Association
8721 S Broadway
Los Angeles California 90003-3321
213-752-4300

353.

**African American Chamber
of Commerce**
1999 W Adams Blvd
Los Angeles California 90018-3514
213-766-0637

354.

Black Business Association of Los Angeles
3550 Wilshire Blvd, #816
Los Angeles California 90001
213-380-8803
213-380-9242—Fax

Mary Ann Mitchell

355.

African American Muslim Chamber of Commerce
5218 Foothill Blvd
Oakland California 94601-5431
510-532-4522

356.

Black Chamber of Commerce
117 Broadway
Oakland California 94607-3715
510-444-5741

357.

Oakland–Alameda County Black Chamber of Commerce
117 Broadway at Jack London Waterfront
Oakland California 94607-3715
510-444-5741

358.

U.S. African-American Chamber of Commerce Inc.
117 Broadway at Jack London Waterfront
Oakland California 94607-3715
510-444-5741
510-444-5866—Fax

Oscar J. Coffey Jr., L.L.D., President & CEO

359.

Afro American Chamber of Commerce
P.O. Box 7858
Oxnard California 93031
805-985-3369

Joyce Jones

360.

Contra Costa Black Chamber of Commerce
P.O. Box 1686
Richmond California 94802
415-235-3738

Willie L. Williams

361.

African-American Chamber of Commerce
P.O. Box 56237
Riverside California 92517
909-369-7190

James White, President

362.

Sacramento Black Chamber of Commerce
2251 Florin Rd
Sacramento California 95822
916-392-SBCC

Dan Powell, Executive Director

363.

Black Chamber of Commerce
1727 Euclid Ave
San Diego California 92105-5414
619-262-2121

364.

San Francisco Black Chamber of Commerce
1426 Filmore St, Suite 205
San Francisco California 94102
415-922-8720 or 415-931-3001

Frederick E. Jordan, President

365.

Black Chamber of Commerce
325 S 1st St
San Jose California 95113-2835
408-294-6583

366.

Black Business Alliance of Orange County
1202 Civic Center Dr W
Santa Ana California 92703-2252
714-547-2646

367.

Orange County Black Chamber of Commerce
2101 E 4th St, Suite A215
Santa Ana California 92705
714-547-3730
714-547-8030—Fax

Aaron Lovejoy

368.

Stockton–San Joaquin County Black Chamber of Commerce
40 S San Joaquin St
Stockton California 95202
209-466-7222

Margaret Burrough, President

369.

Vallejo–Solano County Black Chamber of Commerce
621 Tuolumne St
Vallejo California 94590

Matthew H. Dawson, President

370.

Colorado Black Chamber of Commerce
1564 Elmira St
Aurora Colorado 80010
303-341-1296

Neil Levy

371.

Colorado Springs Black Chamber of Commerce
P.O. Box 10287
Colorado Springs Colorado 80932
719-260-9535

James Stewart, President

372.

African American Business Association
9 Hawthorne Ct, NE
Washington DC 20017-1014
202-232-0570

373.

Black Business Council
1900 L St, NW
Washington DC 20036-5002
202-466-3490

374.

D.C. Chamber of Commerce
1310 Pennsylvania Ave, Suite 309
Washington DC 20004
202-347-7201

Kwasi Holman, Executive Vice President

375.

National African American Chamber of Commerce
2000 L St, NW
Washington DC 20036
202-416-1622

376.

Jacksonville Chamber of Commerce
3 Independent Dr
Jacksonville Florida 32202
904-366-6600

Glenda Washington, Director

377.

Black Business Association of Miami
6600 NW 27th Ave
Miami Florida 33147-7220
305-835-6220

378.

Black Economic Development Coalition
6255 NW 7th Ave
Miami Florida 33150-4319
305-751-8934

379.

Miami–Dade County Chamber of Commerce
9190 Biscayne Blvd, Suite 201
Miami Florida 33138
305-751-8648

Dorothy Baker, President/CEO

380.

West Florida Chamber of Commerce
2407 W Jordan St
Pensacola Florida 32505
904-438-3175

Jerry Hunter, President

381.

Minority Business Council Inc.
1201 E Atlantic Blvd
Pompano Beach Florida 33060-7405
305-942-1042

382.

Sun Coast Chamber of Commerce
P.O. Box 251
West Palm Beach Florida 33402
407-697-4522
407-697-4655—Fax

Ketly Blaise, President

383.

Federation of Southern Cooperatives
100 Edgewood Ave, Suite 1229
Atlanta Georgia 30303
404-524-6882

Ralph Paige, Executive Director

384.

Dekalb Black Chamber of Commerce
P.O. Box 831974
Stone Mountain Georgia 30083
404-469-2232
404-469-3406—Fax

Horace White

385.

**Minority Business & Professional
Association**
P.O. Box 447
Thomasville Georgia 31799
912-228-4345

Phillip Brown, President

386.

African Chamber of Commerce
70 W Madison St
Chicago Illinois 60602-4205
312-214-3236

387.

Cosmopolitan Chamber of Commerce
1326 S Michigan Ave
Chicago Illinois 60605
312-786-0212

Consuelo Pope, President & CEO

388.

**Hoosier Minority Chamber
of Commerce**
464 E Arch, P.O. Box 441411
Indianapolis Indiana 46244-1411
317-687-1903
317-687-8009—Fax

Kay Debow, Director of Administration

389.

**National Black Chamber of Commerce
Inc.**
2447 W 14th St, Suite 217, P.O. Box 441822
Indianapolis Indiana 46244-1822
317-263-6614
317-687-8009—Fax

Harry C. Alford, Chairman & CEO

390.

Grambling Chamber of Commerce
P.O. Box 608
Grambling Louisiana 71245

Ed Jones, President

391.

African Chamber of Commerce
3030 Gentilly Blvd
New Orleans Louisiana 70122-3808
504-948-9769

392.

Shreveport Negro Chamber of Commerce
3805 Lakeshore Dr
Shreveport Louisiana 71109-2003
318-635-7138

E. S. Harrison, President

393.

Black Economic Cluster
1300 Mercantile Ln
Landover Maryland 20785-5327
301-925-8640—Fax

394.

Metropolitan Chamber of Commerce Inc.
3306 Flushing Rd
Flint Michigan 48504
313-235-5514
313-235-4407—Fax

Jean L. Conyers

395.

Council of Minority Business Organizations
115 W Allegan St, #540
Lansing Michigan 48933
517-485-8775
517-485-0620—Fax

Marcus J. Gray

396.

Saginaw African-American Business Association
322 S 4th St
Saginaw Michigan 48607
517-752-6755

Norman Braddock

397.

Minority Business Owners of Washtenaw County
32 N Wash
Ypsilanti Michigan 48198
313-480-5505

398.

African American Chamber of Commerce
1121 Glenwood Ave
Minneapolis Minnesota 55405-1431
212-374-5787

399.

Central Mississippi Business Association
P.O. Box 2542
Jackson Mississippi 39201-2542

Malcolm Shepard

400.

Black Chamber of Commerce
1601 E 18th St
Kansas City Missouri 64108-1646
816-474-9901

401.

Kansas City Black Chamber of Commerce
P.O. Box 27254
Kansas City Missouri 64110
816-358-9444

Edward Pendleton, President

402.

African-American Chamber of Commerce
P.O. Box 23709
St. Louis Missouri 63121
314-381-0141

Evelyn Preston, President

403.

Nevada Black Chamber of Commerce
P.O. Box 4850
Las Vegas Nevada 89106
702-648-6222

Linda Bowie, President

404.

African-American Chamber of Commerce
909A Broad St, Suite 270
Newark New Jersey 07102
201-371-4518
201-399-6723—Fax

Wayne Smith, President

405.

Caribbean-American Chamber of Commerce
Brooklyn Navy Yard, Bldg 5
Brooklyn New York 11205
718-834-4544

406.

Buffalo African American Chamber of Commerce
120 Bickford Ave
Buffalo New York 14215
716-883-5752

Kevin Peterson

407.

Greater Harlem Chamber of Commerce & Harlem Week Inc.
1 W 125th St
New York New York 10027
212-427-7200

Lloyd Williams, President

408.

Dayton–Miami Valley Chamber of Commerce
2128 University Place
Dayton Ohio 45406
513-274-6878

Raymond O'Neal, Esq., President

409.

Lawton Chamber of Commerce
P.O. Box 1914
Lawton Oklahoma 73501
405-355-9547

William Lee

410.

Capital Chamber of Commerce Inc.
P.O. Box 18878
Oklahoma City Oklahoma 73118
405-848-8022

Patrick Paulden, President

411.

Greenwood Chamber of Commerce
130 N Greenwood, Suite H
Tulsa Oklahoma 74120
918-585-2084

Stephanie Chappelle

412.

National Chamber of Commerce
2000 L St, NW
Washington DC 20036
202-416-1622

413.

**African American Chamber
of Commerce**
1212 Market St
Philadelphia Pennsylvania 19107-3615
215-925-8510

414.

Black Business Association of Pittsburgh
P.O. Box 3502
Pittsburgh Pennsylvania 15230

Charles Reaves

415.

African American Concerted Enterprise
3134 Park Ave
Memphis Tennessee 38111-3003
901-323-0364

416.

Black Business Association of Memphis
555 Beale St
Memphis Tennessee 38103
901-526-9300
901-525-2357—Fax

Kenneth H. Porter, President

417.

Capital City Chamber of Commerce
5407 N I-35, Suite 304
Austin Texas 78723
512-459-1181
512-459-1183—Fax

Karen Box, Executive Director

418.

**North, East, West, South (News)
Chambers of Commerce**
105 N Gillard
Bayton Texas 77520
713-451-9606

Chauncey Bogan, President

419.

Dallas Black Chamber of Commerce
2828 Martin Luther King Jr. Blvd
Dallas Texas 75215
214-421-5200
214-421-5510—Fax

Thomas Houston, Executive Director

420.

Dennison Black Chamber of Commerce
404 W Parnell
Dennison Texas 75020
214-463-3116

Frank Harper, President

421.

Ennis Black Chamber of Commerce
P.O. Box 1036
Ennis Texas 75120
214-875-9222

Alfred Bennett, President

422.

Houston Business Council
6161 Savoy Dr, Suite 1030
Houston Texas 77036
713-974-0286
713-974-2437—Fax

Richard A. Huebner, Executive Director

423.

Houston Citizens Chamber of Commerce
2808 Wheeler
Houston Texas 77004
713-522-9745

Willie B. Williams, President

424.

Killeen Black Chamber of Commerce
207 N Gray St
Killeen Texas 76541

Eli Ellfour

425.

Black Chamber of Commerce
P.O. Box 8150
Longview Texas 75607
214-758-0027

Mark Pruitt

426.

**Texas Association of Black Chambers
of Commerce**
P.O. Box 50473
Midland Texas 79710-0473
915-684-2864
915-684-6422—Fax

Robbyne (Hocker) Fuller, President

427.

Odessa Black Chamber of Commerce
303 Curver St
Odessa Texas 79761
915-332-7215

Odel Crawford

428.

**African American Chamber
of Commerce**
400 N Loop, 1604 E
San Antonio Texas 78232-1243
210-490-1624

429.

Texarkana Black Chamber of Commerce
414 Texas Blvd
Texarkana Texas 75501
214-792-8931

Eldridge Robertson

430.

**Heart of Texas Black Chamber
of Commerce**
P.O. Box 1485
Waco Texas 76703
817-799-8615

Louis Banks

431.

Black Business Chamber of Commerce
P.O. Box 8033
St. Thomas Virgin Islands 00801
809-774-8784 or 809-774-5176

Eric Christian, President

432.

**African American Chamber of
Commerce**
5232 W Center St
Milwaukee Wisconsin 53210-2334
414-871-5838

433.

**Milwaukee Minority Chamber of
Commerce**
509 W Wisconsin Ave
Milwaukee Wisconsin 53203
414-226-4105
414-271-8841—Fax

J. Paul Jordan, President

❂ CHARITABLE ORGANIZATIONS ❂

434.

**Benevolent, Protective Order
Reindeer Inc.**
Grand Lodge Headquarters
842 E 28th St
Wilmington Delaware 19802
302-762-5880

Eugene Johnson, Grand Director

435.

International Benevolent Society Inc.
837 Fifth Ave P.O. Box 1276
Columbus Georgia 31902
706-322-5671

James O. Brown, Grand National President
The society presently has 165 chapters in 11
states. The society distributes annual scholar-

ships to qualifying high school seniors of the order. With many goals to advance the social and economic standard of its members and citizens, the main overall goal is to develop the society to the extent that it will become one of the premier self-help organizations in this country.

436.

Modern Free and Accepted Masons of the World Inc.
627 Fifth Ave
Columbus Georgia 31901
404-322-3326

Henry Williams, Supreme Grand Master
Founded in the city of Opelika, Alabama, this fraternal order encourages members to chart definite goals, to plan and work through the brotherhood method, and to train and educate leaders and specialists within the organization. It continues to pursue a strong economic base by pooling resources, investing in business, and providing employment for African Americans.

437.

African American National Charitable Trust
320 N Michigan Ave
Chicago Illinois 60639
312-237-6600

438.

African American Voters League
310 S Broad St
New Orleans Louisiana 70119-6416
504-822-2890

Colleen Johnson

Scholarship foundation, community service organization, and political organization. Sponsors a feed-the-needy program.

439.

Africa Cultural Center Inc.
13815 Marianna Dr
Rockville Maryland 20853
301-871-1397

Mohamed A. Khadar, Director and General Founder
A duly established, tax-exempt, nonprofit corporation that provides the public and members with cultural, educational, and information programs about Africa and the Caribbean. The center serves as a distributor of food and clothing to needy African families and as a contact point for those interested in conducting business in West Africa.

440.

Ancient Egyptian Arabic Order
Nobles Mystic Shrine Inc.
2211 Cass Ave
Detroit Michigan 48201
313-961-9148

Marion Cheatham, Imperial Recorder
A charitable and fraternal organization, whose main thrust is to provide funds for hospitals, schools, and educational grants.

441.

Africa Fund The
198 Broadway
New York New York 10038
212-962-1210

Jennifer Davis, Executive Secretary

Works to defend human and civil rights of needy Africans by providing or financing legal assistance, medical relief, rendering aid to indigent Africans in the United States or elsewhere who are suffering economic, legal, or social injustices, and providing educational aid or grants to Africans, particularly refugees; informs the American public about the needs of Africans, and engages in study, research, and analysis of questions relating to Africa.

442.

Grand United Order of Salem
1201 Castle St
Wilmington North Carolina 28401
910-762-6485

Ezzia Bryant, President; Ethel P. Gore, Secretary
"Salem" was organized in Wilmington and has expanded over the state of North Carolina. The purpose is to promote charity, benevolence, the relief of the sick, needy, and suffering among our members first; then others as circumstances will allow. Scholarships are available for juvenile members.

443.

Improved and Benevolent Protective Order of Elks of the World
P.O. Box 159
Winton North Carolina 27986
919-358-7661

Donald P. Wilson, Grand Exalted Ruler
The largest fraternal organization in the world, the order has contributed over $2.5 million in scholarships to youth of all races. Its purpose is to ensure that the welfare and happiness of its members be promoted and

enhanced, that nobleness of soul and goodness of heart be cultivated, that the principles of charity, justice, and brotherly love be inculcated, and that the spirit of patriotism be enlivened and exalted.

444.

Black United Fund of Central Ohio
815 E Mound St
Columbus Ohio 43205-2649
614-252-0888

445.

Most Worshipful National Grand Lodge Free and Accepted Ancient York Masons
735 Five Chop Rd
Orangeburg South Carolina 29115
803-531-1985 or 803-536-4019

Oscar Mack, National Grand Master
A Masonic fraternity of approximately 70,000 members whose primary purpose is the uplifting of humanity through contributions to charities and the teaching of fellowship through brotherhood.

446.

Federation of Masons of the World and Federation of Eastern Stars
P.O. Box 1296
Austin Texas 78767
512-477-5380

C.E. Gibson, President, Federation of Masons; Lucille McCants, President, Federation of Eastern Stars
Supporting projects that include research in multiple sclerosis and children's hospitals, the

Federation of Masons of the World and its sister society, the Federation of Eastern Stars, donate thousands of dollars to disadvantaged students aspiring to enter college and to the children of its members.

447.

United Order of Tents of J. R. Giddings and Jollifee Union
1620 Church St
Norfolk Virginia 23504

Dr. Lorine Cole McLeod, President; Minnie Gregg Madrey, Vice President; Dorothy Balley Rawls, Executive

The United Order of Tents was founded in Norfolk, Virginia. It is an organization of 8,000 women, representing four southern states and the District of Columbia. The organization has provided general benevolence to the minority community of the southeastern United States continuously for 125 years. These acts of benevolence, which were the dream of the founders, have taken many different forms over the past century and have addressed community needs appropriate to the times.

✪ CHILD WELFARE, YOUTH & FAMILY SERVICES ✪

448.

Black Family & Child Services Inc.
2323 N 3rd St
Phoenix Arizona 85004-1304
602-256-2948

449.

Black Family & Child Services–Teen Choice Center
1522 E Southern Ave
Phoenix Arizona 85040-3532
602-243-1773

450.

Black Women's Resource Center
518 17th St, Suite 202
Oakland California 94601
510-763-9501

Focuses on special needs of African-American women and youth. Information, referrals, job counseling, stress support, networking, and opportunities. Open to all who need assistance.

451.

Links Inc. The
1200 Massachusetts Ave, NW
Washington DC 20005
202-842-8686

Marion Schultz Sutherland, President
Founded as a public service organization; today over 8,000 members in 240 chapters in cities in the United States, Nassau, Bahamas, and Frankfurt, West Germany focus Links' activities around four program areas: the arts, services to youth, national trends and services, and international trends and services.
1946

452.

National Black Child Development Institute
1023 15th St, NW, Suite 600
Washington DC 20005
202-387-1281

Evelyn K. Moore, Executive Director
Dedicated to improving the quality of life for African-American children and families, NBCDI focuses on health, child welfare, education, and child care–early childhood education. NBCDI monitors public policy and educates the public. NBCD1's 41 affiliates provide direct services, including tutorial programs and culturally enriching activities.

453.

Black Family Project The
673 Beckwith St, SW
Atlanta Georgia 30314-4112
404-880-0679

454.

Minority Outreach Intervention Project
1579 N Milwaukee Ave
Chicago Illinois 60622-2009
312-276-5990

455.

African American Family Preservation
1631 E 17th St
Wichita Kansas 67200
316-269-0488

456.

African-American Youth Foundation
788 N Union St
Opelousas Louisiana 70570-6312
318-942-9648

457.

Minority Parents Coalition
47 W Elm
Brockton Massachusetts 02401
508-587-4366

Community outreach, working with schools, parents, and teachers.

458.

Black Child & Family Institute
835 W Genesee St
Lansing Michigan 48915-1899
517-487-3775

459.

Black Adoption & Foster Care Center
951 Jeanerette Dr
St. Louis Missouri 63130-2719
314-863-1321

460.

Associated Black Charities
105 E 22nd St
New York New York 10010
212-777-6060

Nonprofit federation of organizations in the five boroughs that offer health and human services to African Americans, including senior services and childcare.

461.

African American Parent Council
25 West St
Staten Island New York 10310-1920
718-447-5516

Denise Pedro

462.

African American Family Institute
617 N Summit Ave
Charlotte North Carolina 28216-5558

463.

Black Child Development Institute
1200 E Market St
Greensboro North Carolina 27401-3258
910-230-2138

Tutorial and mentoring service to children in the community. "Each one's spirit is excellent!" Matching students with volunteers.

464.

Black Child Development Institute—Akron
1310 Superior Ave
Akron Ohio 44307-1154
216-384-8188

465.

Minority Youth Concerns Action
4732 NE Garfield
Portland Oregon 97211
503-280-1050

466.

African-American Family Day Care
Memphis Tennessee 37501
901-353-7972

467.

African American Family Corporation
3940 N 21st St
Milwaukee Wisconsin 53206-1969
414-445-8481

468.

Minority Youth
2040 W Wisconsin Ave
Milwaukee Wisconsin 53208
414-933-9395

✿ CIVIL RIGHTS
& AFFIRMATIVE ACTION ✿

469.

Southern Poverty Law Center
400 Washington Ave
Montgomery Alabama 36104
205-264-0286

Joseph J. Levin, President
Seeks to protect and advance the legal and
civil rights of poor people, regardless of race,
through education, litigation, and subsequent
court decisions. Strives to defeat injustices
that keep poor people poor, including denial
of representation in government, deprivation
of municipal services, and discriminatory
abuse of civil rights. Does not accept fees
from clients.

470.

Western Center on Law and Poverty
1709 W 8th St
Los Angeles California 90017
213-483-1491

Legal services resources for the war on
poverty in Southern California.

471.

Black Christians Political Convention
P.O. Box 161659
Sacramento California 95816-1659
916-363-8583

472.

**Lawyer's Committee for Civil Rights
Under the Law**
1400 I St, NW, Suite 400
Washington DC 20005
202-371-1212

473.

Leadership Conference on Civil Rights
1629 K St, NW, Suite 1010
Washington DC 20036
202-667-1780

Benjamin L. Hooks, Chairperson; Ralph G.
Neas, Executive Director
The conference is a coalition of 165 national
organizations representing African Americans, Hispanics and Asian Americans, labor,
women, the handicapped, the aged, major
religious groups, minority businesses, and
professionals seeking to advance civil rights
through enactment and enforcement of federal legislation.

474.

**Minority Business Enterprise Legal
Defense and Education Fund Inc.**
220 I St, NE, Suite 280
Washington DC 20002
202-543-0040
202-543-4135—Fax

Warren J. Mitchell, Founder and Chairman; Anthony W. Robinson, Esq., President
The Fund's mission is to defend and uphold the legality of minority set-aside programs at the state, local, and national levels, to ensure the vigorous enforcement of these regulations, and to initiate legal action where they are clearly being violated.
1980

475.

National Association for Equal Opportunity
400 12th St, NE, #207
Washington DC 20002
202-543-9111

476.

National Catholic Conference for Interracial Justice
3033 4th St, NE
Washington DC 20017
202-529-6480

Jerome Ernst, Executive Director

477.

Southern Christian Leadership Conference
334 Auburn Ave, NE
Atlanta Georgia 30312
404-522-1420

Rev. Dr. Joseph Lowery, President
Nonsectarian coordinating and service agency for local organizations seeking full citizenship rights, equality, and the integration of African-Americans in all aspects of life in the United States and subscribing to the Ghandian phi-

losophy of nonviolence. Works primarily in 16 southern and border states to improve civic, religious, economic, and cultural conditions. Fosters nonviolent resistance to all forms of racial injustice, and conducts training programs on voting and registration, social projects, prejudice, and politics.

478.

American Association for Affirmative Action
200 N Michigan Ave
Chicago Illinois 60601
312-541-1271
312-541-1272—Fax

Everett Winters, National President
Equal opportunity/affirmative action officers at educational institutions and industrial firms. Its purposes are to foster the implementation of affirmative action and equal opportunity in employment and in education nationwide, and to provide formal liaison with federal, state, and local agencies involved with equal opportunity compliance in employment and education.

479.

National Black United Front
700 E Oakwood Blvd
Chicago Illinois 60653
312-268-7500, Ext. 144
312-268-5658—Fax

Dr. Conrad W. Worrill, National Chairman
The organization's principles of purpose are: to struggle for self-determination, liberation, and power for black people in the United States; to work in unity and common struggle with African liberation movements throughout the

world; to build a politically conscious, united black mass movement; to eliminate racism, colonialism, neo-colonialism, imperialism, and national oppression; and to maintain strict political and financial independence.

480.

**Operation PUSH
(People United to Serve Humanity)**
930 E 50th St
Chicago Illinois 60615
312-373-3366

Jesse Jackson, Founder
An organization founded to promote human rights, especially black self-empowerment. Now has a year-round exhibit on the civil rights movement, life-size statues of African-American heroes, and a civil rights library and audio archives.
1971

481.

**National Association for
the Advancement of Colored
People (NAACP)**
4805 Mt. Hope Dr
Baltimore Maryland 21215-3297
301-358-8900

Kweisi Mfume, CEO & Executive Director
The nation's oldest civil rights organization was founded in 1909 to improve race relations through direct action, legal advocacy, publicity, and moral persuasion. It has a total of 1800 branches, with over 500,000 members. It publishes the oldest African-American magazine in the country.

482.

National Urban Coalition
8601 Georgia Ave, #500
Silver Springs Maryland 20910
301-495-4999

483.

Congress of Racial Equality (CORE)
30 Cooper Sq, 9th Floor
New York New York 10003
212-598-4000

Roy Innis, National Chairman
A black nationalist organization whose philosophy is based on the tenets of Marcus Garvey.

484.

Minority Rights Group
169 E 78th St
New York New York 10021-0462
212-879-5489

485.

**NAACP Legal Defense and Education
Fund Inc.**
99 Hudson St, 16th Floor
New York New York 10021
212-310-9000

Julius L. Chambers, Director/Counsel

486.

**National Alliance Against Racist &
Political Repression**
11 John St
New York New York 10038-4009
212-406-3330

487.

National Urban Affairs Council
2350 Adam Clayton Powell Blvd
New York New York 10030
914-694-4000

488.

National Urban League Inc.
500 E 62nd St
New York New York 10021
212-310-9000
212-755-2026—Fax

Audrey Roe, Vice Chairman; Hugh Price, President/CEO
The league's mission is to secure equality of opportunity in every sphere of life for African Americans and other minorities. It provides direct services, serves as an advocate for minorities and the poor, engages in research into African America, and seeks to build bridges of understanding between the races.

489.

Office of Racial Justice National Board
600 Lexington Ave
New York New York 10022
212-753-4700

490.

Scholarship, Education and Defense Fund for Racial Equality Inc.
164 Madison Ave
New York New York 10016
212-532-8216

Develops leadership programs and community organization techniques, handles legal problems, engages in voter registration, and provides scholarship assistance with demonstrated leadership in civil rights activities.

❖ COLLEGES & UNIVERSITIES ❖

491.

Lawson State Community College
3060 Wilson Rd, SW
Birmingham Alabama 35221
205-925-2515

Dr. Perry W. Ward, President

492.

Miles College
P.O. Box 3800
Birmingham Alabama 35208
205-923-2771

Albert L. H. Sloan II, President
Carolyn Ray, Ph.D., Dean Of Students, 205-923-2771, Ext. 243

Founded by the Christian Methodist Episcopal church. Degrees: A.A., B.A., B.S. Dual degrees in engineering, veterinary medicine, and allied health.
1905

493.

J. F. Drake Technical College
3421 Meridian St N
Huntsville Alabama 35811
205-539-8161

Dr. Johnny L. Harris, President

494.

Oakwood College
Huntsville Alabama 35806
205-726-7000

Benjamin F. Reaves, President
1896

495.

Bishop State Community College
351 N Broad St
Mobile Alabama 36603
205-690-6801

Dr. Yvonne Kennedy, President

496.

Alabama State University
P.O. Box 271
Montgomery Alabama 36101-0271
205-293-4286 or 205-293-4284

Leon Howard, President
Office of Enrollment Management
205-293-4290

Founded as Lincoln Normal School, a private school for blacks. Reorganized as a state-supported institution in 1874. Degrees: A.A., B.A., B.S., M.S., Ed.S.
1866

497.

Trenholm State Technical College
1225 Air Base Blvd
Montgomery Alabama 36108
334-832-9000

Dr. Thad McClammy, President

498.

Alabama A & M University
P.O. Box 1027
Normal Alabama 35762
205-851-5000

David B. Henson, President; Ames Heyward, Director of Admissions
Public university. Degrees: B.A., B.S.. M.B.A., M.Ed., Ed.S., Ph.D. School originally established for the education of black teachers.
1875

499.

Concordia College
1804 Green St
Selma Alabama 36701
205-874-5700

Julius Jenkins, President
1922

500.

Selma University
1501 Lapsley
Selma Alabama 36701
205-872-2533

Willie Muse, President
1878

501.

Talladega College
Talladega Alabama 35160
205-362-0206

Joseph B. Johnson, President; Ardie Dial, Admissions Director.
Founded by freedmen William Savery and Thomas Tarrant as a private liberal arts college for blacks. Degrees: B.A.
1867

502.

Fredd State Technical College
205 Skyline Blvd
Tuscaloosa Alabama 35405
205-758-3361

Dr. Thomos Umphrey, President

503.

Stillman College
P.O. Box 1430
Tuscaloosa Alabama 35403
205-349-4240

Cordell Wynn, President
Barbara Smith, Director of Admissions
205-349-4240, Ext. 347

A private, four-year liberal arts college founded by the Presbyterian Church. Degrees: B.A., B.S.
1876

504.

Tuskegee University
317 Kresge Center
Tuskegee Alabama 36083
205-727-8011

Benjamin F. Rayton, President
Lee Young, Admissions Office, 205-727-8500.
Best-known historically black college in the United States. It was founded by Lewis Adams, and not Booker T. Washington as popularly believed.

505.

Arkansas Baptist College
1600 Bishop St
Little Rock Arkansas 72202
501-374-7856

W. Thomas Keaton, President
Founded by the Consolidated Missionary Baptist State Convention. Degrees: B.A., B.S.
1884

506.

Philander Smith College
812 W 13th St
Little Rock Arkansas 72202
501-375-9845

Myer L. Titus, President
Admissions Office, 800-446-6772
Founded by the Methodist Episcopal Church. Degrees: B.A., B.S.
1877

507.

Shorter College
604 Locust St
North Little Rock Arkansas 72114
501-374-6305

Dr. Katherine P. Mitchell, President
Private four-year college founded by the
African Methodist Episcopal Church.
Degrees: A.A., A.S.
1886

508.

University of Arkansas at Pine Bluff
400 S Main
Pine Bluff Arkansas 71601
501-536-0654

Lawrence A. Davis Jr., Chancellor
1873

509.

Compton Community College
1111 E Artesia Blvd
Compton California 90221
310-637-2660

Byron R. Skinner, President

510.

Minority & Women Doctoral Directory
10540 Barnett Valley Rd
Sebastopol California 95472
707-829-0765

Provides affirmative action and faculty
recruitment information to universities.

511.

African-American College Alliance
427 8th St, SE
Washington DC 20003-2833
202-543-3283

512.

Howard University
2400 6th St, NW
Washington DC 20059
202-806-6100

Franklin G. Jennifer, President
One of the nation's most prestigious historically black colleges, this institution actually
began as a multiracial school, composed
largely of young white women. The advent of
Jim Crow restrictions made this school a
magnet for black youth shut out of the educational system. Its Gallery of Art contains
impressive collections of African and African-
American art.

513.

**National Association for Equal
Opportunity in Higher Education**
400 12th St, NE, The Lovejoy Bldg, 2nd
Floor
Washington DC 20002
202-543-9111

A voluntary membership organization of 117
historically and predominantly African-
American colleges and universities founded to
express the need for a system of higher education where race, income, and previous education are not factors in attaining quality
higher education.
1969

514.

Office for the Advancement of Public Black Colleges
1 Dupont Circle, Suite 710
Washington DC 20036
202-778-0818
202-296-6456—Fax

Dr. Robert L. Clodius, Chairman of the Advisory Board; Dr. N. Joyce Payne, Director The Office for the Advancement of Public Black Colleges has endeavored to increase public awareness of the contributions of public African-American institutions, to influence state and national policies and programs, and to stimulate greater public and private support. In addition, OARBC procures technical assistance, monitors federal policies and programs, targets human and capital resources, and stimulates national support for the public African-American colleges as a primary source of exemplary talent.
1969

515.

University of the District of Columbia
4200 Connecticut Ave, NW
Washington DC 20008
202-282-7300

Miles Mark Fisher IV, Interim President
Alfred O. Taylor Jr, Assistant Provost for Student Services, 202-282-3200
Urban, land grant, commuter institution with two- and four-year academic programs.
Degrees: A.A., B.A.. M.S.
1976

516.

Delaware State College
Dover Delaware 19901-2275
302-736-4901

William B. DeLauder, President
Jethro Williams, Director of Admissions, 302-739-4917.
Degrees: B.A., B.S.
1891

517.

Bethune-Cookman College
640 Second Ave
Daytona Beach Florida 32115
904-255-1401

Oswald R. Bronson Sr., President
Bethune-Cookman College's excellent facilities, diverse academic programs, and concerned faculty make it one of the nation's most prestigious historically black colleges. Located on 52 acres just two miles from the Atlantic Ocean in Daytona Beach, Bethune-Cookman is a four-year, accredited, co-ed, liberal arts, United Methodist Church–related college, offering bachelor of arts and science degrees.
1904

518.

Black College Today
6721 NW 44th Ct
Fort Lauderdale Florida 33319-4030
305-749-4560

519.

Edward Waters College
1658 Kings Rd
Jacksonville Florida 32209
904-355-3030

Dr. Jesse L. Burns, President

520.

Florida Memorial College
15800 NW 42nd Ave
Miami Florida 33054
305-625-4141

Lee Everett Monroe, President
Office of Admissions, 305-625-4141
Founded as the Florida Baptist Institute for
Negroes. Degrees: B.A., B.S.
1879

521.

**Florida Agricultural & Mechanical
University**
S Adams St
Tallahassee Florida 32307
904-599-3000

Florida's oldest historically black college.
1887

522.

Albany State College
Albany Georgia 31705
912-430-4600

Billy C. Black, President
Degrees: B.A., B.S., M.A., M.S.
1903

523.

Atlanta Metropolitan Junior College
1630 Stewart Ave, SW
Atlanta Georgia 30310
404-756-4000

Dr. Edwin A. Thompson, President

524.

Atlanta University Center
James P. Brawley Center, SW
Atlanta Georgia 30314
404-522-8980

Amalgamation of the country's six most
important historically black colleges: Clark
Atlanta, Morris Brown, Morehouse, Morehouse School of Medicine, Interdenominational Theological Center, and Spelman.
Houses substantial African-American archival
material in library.

525.

Clark Atlanta University
111 James P. Brawley Dr
Atlanta Georgia 30314
404-880-8000

Thomas W. Cole Jr., President
Peggy D. Wade, Associate Director of Admissions, 404-880-8000.
Degrees: B.A., B.S., M.A., M.S., M.B.A.,
Ed.S., M.P.A., Ed.D., Ph.D. Historically black
college. Originally known as Clark College, it
merged with Atlanta University in 1988.

526.

Interdenominational Theological Center
671 Beckwith St, SW
Atlanta Georgia 30314
404-527-7700
404-527-0901—Fax

James H. Costten, President
Dr. Edith Thomas, Registrar, 404-527-7707
Founded as a consortium of six seminaries: Gammon Theological Seminary (United Methodist), Charles H. Mason Theological Seminary (Church of God in Christ), Morehouse School of Religion (Baptist), Phillips School of Theology (Christian Methodist Episcopal), Johnson C. Smith Seminary (Presbyterian Church USA), and Arnold Turner Theological Seminary (African Methodist Episcopal). Degrees: M.Div., M.A.C.Ecl.
1958

527.

Morehouse College
830 Westview Dr, SW
Atlanta Georgia 30314
404-681-2800

The nation's only historically black, all-male, four-year liberal arts college. Its alumni include Martin Luther King Jr. and Spike Lee.
1867

528.

Morehouse School of Medicine
720 Westview Dr, SW
Atlanta Georgia 30310
404-752-1500

Louis W. Sullivan, President

The #1 school in the nation for the highest percentage rate of graduates practicing as primary care physicians.

529.

Morris Brown College
643 Martin Luther King Jr. Dr, NW
Atlanta Georgia 30314
404-525-7831

Historically black college founded for African Americans by African Americans.
1881

530.

Spelman College
350 Spelman Lane, SW
Atlanta Georgia 30314-4399
404-681-3643

Johnetta B. Cole, President
Admissions Office, 404-681-3643, Ext. 2188
Private, four-year, historically black liberal arts college for African-American women.
Degrees: B.A., B.S.
1881

531.

Paine College
Augusta Georgia 30901
800-476-7703

Julius S. Scott Jr., President
Private four-year, liberal arts college established by the United Methodist Church and Christian Methodist Episcopal Church.
Degrees: B.A., B.S.
1882

532.

Fort Valley State College
Fort Valley Georgia 31030
912-825-6211

Oscar L. Prater, President
Degrees: A.A., B.A., B.S., M.A., M.S.
1895

533.

Savannah State College
Savannah Georgia 31404
912-356-2186

William E. Gardener Jr., Acting President
1890

534.

Chicago State University
9501 S King Dr
Chicago Illinois 60628
312-995-2000

Dolores E. Cross, President

535.

Kennedy-King College
6800 S Wentworth Ave
Chicago Illinois 60621
312-962-3200

Dr. Harold Pates, President

536.

Kentucky State University
Frankfort Kentucky 40601
502-227-6000

Mary L. Smith, President

Lyman Dale, Director Of Admissions, 502-227-6813, 800-633-9415 (inside Kentucky), 800-325-1716
Degrees: A.A., B.A., B.S., M.P.A., Teacher Certification Programs.
1886

537.

Simmons Bible College
1811 Dumesnil St
Louisville Kentucky 41210
502-776-1443

W. J. Hodge, President
1873

538.

Southern University
Harding Blvd
Baton Rouge Louisiana 70821
800-527-6843

Loyce Baucom, Chancellor
Melvin Hodges, Registrar, 504-286-5000
Originally established as a technical high school for African Americans, this university now serves as the parent campus of the largest predominantly black university system in the United States. Hosts the Black Heritage Exhibit Series.
1880

539.

Grambling State University
Grambling Louisiana 71245
314-247-2211

Harold W. Lundy, President
Admissions Office, 318-247-2435.

Degrees: A.A., A.S., B.A., B.S., B.S.W., M.A., M.A.T., M.A.I.S., M.B.A., M.S.W., Ed.S., Ed.D.
1901

540.

Dillard University
2601 Gentilly Blvd
New Orleans Louisiana 70122-3097
504-283-8822

Samuel Dubois Cook, President
Office of Admissions, 504-286-4670.
Dillard University offers over 30 majors in six academic divisions: business, education, humanities, natural sciences, nursing, and social sciences. Degrees: B.A., B.S., B.S.N.
1869

541.

Xavier University
7325 Palmetto St
New Orleans Louisiana 70125
504-483-7568

Norman C. Francis, President
The country's sole historically black Roman Catholic college, specializing in science education and known for sending a large number of its graduates to medical school.

542.

Southern University at Shreveport
Shreveport Louisiana 71107
318-674-3300

Jerome Green, Chancellor
Clifton Lones, Registrar, 318-674-3300
1964.

543.

Coppin State College
2500 W North Ave
Baltimore Maryland 21216
301-333-5990

Calvin W. Burnett. President
Allen Mosley, Director of Admissions, 301-333-5990.
Founded as a black teachers' training college. Named in honor of Fannie Jackson Coppin, who was among the first black women in the United States to earn a bachelor's degree.
Degrees: B.A., B.S., M.S., M.Ed.
1900

544.

Morgan State University
Baltimore Maryland 21239
410-319-3333

Earl S. Richardson, President
1867

545.

Sojourner-Douglass College
500 N Caroline St
Baltimore Maryland 21205
410-276-0306

Dr. Charles W. Simmons, President

546.

Bowie State University
Bowie Maryland 20175
301-464-3000

James E. Lyons Sr., President
University Admissions Office, 301-464-3000.

State-supported residential college. Degrees: B.A., B.S., M.A., M.Ed. 1865.

547.

University of Maryland at Eastern Shore
Princess Ann Maryland 21853
410-651-2200

William B. Hytche, President
1886

548.

Roxbury Community College
1234 Columbus Ave
Boston Massachusetts 21201
617-541-5310

Dr. Grace Carolyn Brown, President

549.

Lewis College of Business
17370 Myers Rd
Detroit Michigan 48235
313-862-6300

Dr. Marjorie Harris, President

550.

St. Augustine Seminary
199 Seminary Dr
Bay St. Louis Mississippi 39520
601-467-6414

America's first institute for training black Catholic seminarians.
1923

551.

Coahoma Community College
3240 Friars Point Rd
Clarksdale Mississippi 38614
601-627-2571

Dr. Vivian Presley, President

552.

Mississippi Industrial College
Holly Springs Mississippi 38835
601-252-2440

1905

553.

Rust College
Holly Springs Mississippi 38635-2328
601-252-8000

David L. Beckley, President
Jo Ann Scott, Director of Admissions & Recruitment, 601-252-8000, Ext. 4068.
Degrees: A.S., B.A., B.S. Mississippi's first institution of higher education for African Americans.
1866.

554.

Mississippi Valley State
Itta Bena Mississippi 38941
601-254-9041

William W. Sutton, President
1950

555.

Jackson State University
1400 Jon R. Lynch St
Jackson Mississippi 39217
601-968-2121

James E. Lyons Sr., President
Barbara J. Luckett, Director of Admissions &
Recruitment, 601-968-2100 or 800-682-5390
(within state)
Degrees: B.A., B.S., B.S.Ed., B.S.W., M.A.,
M.S., M.S.E., M.B.A., M.B., Ed.M., Ed.S.,
Ed.D., Ph.D. The sixth largest of the nation's
116 historically black colleges.
1877

556.

Alcorn State University
Hwy 552 at U.S. 61
Lorman Mississippi 39096
601-877-6100

Walter Washington, President
First black land grant agricultural college in
the United States.

557.

Natchez Junior College
1010 N Union St
Natchez Mississippi 39120
601-445-9702

Dr. Joseph Sutton, President

558.

Tougaloo College
500 Country Line Rd
Tougaloo Mississippi 39174
601-977-7700

Small school opened to educate freedmen
after the Civil War. Its students were active
participants in the civil rights struggles of the
1950s and 1960s.

559.

Hinds Junior College
P.O. Box 3
Utica Mississippi 39175
601-885-6062

Dr. George E. Barnes, President

560.

Mary Holmes College
P.O. Drawer 1257
West Point Mississippi 39773
601-494-6820

Sammy Potts, President
Natalie C. Raleigh, Admissions Counselor,
601-494-6820, Ext. 133-135.
The only private, accredited two-year historically black college in the United States.
Degrees: A.A., A.S.
1892

561.

Lincoln University
Jefferson City Missouri 65102-0029
314-681-5000

Wendell G. Rayburn, President
Office of Admissions, 314-681-5000
Founded at the close of the Civil War by sol-
diers and officers of the 62nd United States
Colored Infantry under the name Lincoln
Institute. Renamed Lincoln University in
1921. Degrees: A.A., A.A.S., B.A., B.S.,
B.S.Ed., B.M.E., M.A., M.Ed., M.B.A.
1866

562.

Harris-Stowe State College
3026 Laclede Ave
St. Louis Missouri 63103
314-340-3366

Dr. Henry Givens, Jr., President

563.

**Medgar Evers College
(City University of New York)**
1650 Bedford Ave
Brooklyn New York 11225
718-270-4900

Dr. Edison O. Jackson, President

564.

**African American Alumni Sporting
Association**
3076 Bailey Ave
Buffalo New York 14215-1617
716-837-2144

565.

Johnson C. Smith University
Charlotte North Carolina 28216
704-378-1000

Robert L. Albright, President
1867

566.

North Carolina Central University
Fayetteville and Lawson Sts
Durham North Carolina 27707
919-560-6100

Edward B. Fort, Chancellor

Admissions Office, 919-334-7946, or 800-443-8964 (within state)
Originally established as a school for the "Colored Race," this university now houses the James E. Shephard Memorial Library and its extensive collection of materials on African-American life and culture, and the NCCU Art Museum, which contains a collection of African-American art.

567.

Elizabeth City State University
Elizabeth City North Carolina 27909
919-335-3230

Jimmy R. Jenkins, Chancellor
Admissions Office, 131 Thorpe Hall, 919-335-3305
Founded as the State Colored Normal School. Renamed Elizabeth City State University in 1969, it is a state-assisted four-year liberal arts university. Degrees: B.A., B.S.
1891

568.

Fayetteville State University
1200 Murchison Rd
Fayetteville North Carolina 28301-4298
910-486-1141

Lloyd V. Hackley, Chancellor
Charles Darlington, Director of Admissions, 919-486-1141
State-assisted, four-year liberal arts university. Degrees: A.A., B.A., B.S., M.A., M.S., M.B.A.
1867

569.

Bennett College
900 E Washington St
Greensboro North Carolina 27401
910-273-4431

Gloria Randle Scott, President
Bennett College is a small, residential, liberal arts college for women in Greensboro, North Carolina, related to the United Methodist Church, educating and preparing women to be productive professionals, participating and informed active citizens, and the enlightened parents of the new millennium.
1873

570.

North Carolina Agricultural and Technical State University
1601 E Market St
Greensboro North Carolina 27401
919-334-7500 or 919-334-7946

Alma mater of Jesse Jackson and home to the H.C. Taylor Gallery and the Mattye Reed African Heritage Center, both of which have the finest collections of African arts, jewelry, and weaponry. Best known for four of its students who implemented a lunchtime sit-in at a local Woolworth's and sparked new militancy into the civil rights movement.

571.

Shaw University
Raleigh North Carolina 27611
919-546-8200

Talbert O. Shaw, President
1865

572.

St. Augustine's College
1315 Oakwood Ave
Raleigh North Carolina 27610-2298
919-516-4000

Prezell R. Robinson, President
Wanzo Hendrix, Office of Admissions, 919-516-4016, Ext. 207-358.
Degrees: B.A., B.S.
1867

573.

Livingstone College
701 W Monroe St
Salisbury North Carolina 28144
704-683-5500

Bernard W. Franklin, President
Admissions Office, 704-638-5502.
College named in honor of the famed abolitionist and explorer of Africa, David Livingstone. Also has collections and exhibits on African art, and African-American life, culture, religion, and history. Was the site of the first black intercollegiate football game.

574.

Winston-Salem State University
601 Martin Luther King Jr. Dr
Winston-Salem North Carolina 27110
910-750-2000

Cleon F. Thompson Jr., Chancellor
Admissions Office, 919-750-2070
Founded as Slater Industrial Academy. Currently a four-year, coeducational constituent institution of the University of North Carolina. Degrees: B.A., B.S., B.S.A.S.
1892

575.

Barber-Scotia College
143 Cabarrus Ave
Concord North Carolina 28025
704-786-5171

Joel O. Nwagbaraocha, President
Addie Butler, Director of Recruitment and
Admissions, 704-786-5171, Ext. 342/343/344.
Founded as a college of the Presbyterian
Church (USA).
1867

576.

Cuyahoga Community College
700 Carnegie Ave
Cleveland Ohio 44115
216-987-4000

Dr. Jerry Sue Owens, President

577.

Central State University
Wilberforce Ohio 45384-0001
513-376-6011

Arthur E. Thomas, President
Office of Admissions, 513-376-6348,
800-832-2222 (Ohio only)
Degrees: B.A., B.S.
1887

578.

Wilberforce University
Wilberforce Ohio 45384
513-376-2911

John L. Henderson, President
Office of Admissions, 800-367-8568

Wilberforce University is a private, four-year,
liberal arts university affiliated with the
African Methodist Episcopal Church and the
United Negro College Fund and accredited
by the North Central Association of Colleges
and Secondary Schools. Degrees: B.A., B.S.
1856

579.

Langston University
Hwy 33
Langston Oklahoma 73050
405-466-2231

Ernest L. Holloway, President
Admissions Office, 405-466-2980
Oklahoma's only historically black college or
university. It operates under both a land-grant
and urban mission, offering undergraduate
programs in thirty-six fields and graduate programs in four.
1897

580.

Cheyney University of Pennsylvania
Cheyney Pennsylvania 19319
215-399-2000

Leverne McCummings, President
Admissions Office, 215-399-2000.
Degrees: Associate in Electrical or Mechanical
Engineering Technology, B.A., B.S., B.S.Ed.
1837

581.

Allen University
Columbia South Carolina 29204
803-254-4165

Dr. Collie Coleman, President
1870

582.

Benedict College
Harden and Blanding Sts
Columbia South Carolina 29204
803-256-4220

Marshall C. Grigsby, President
Virginia McKee, Director of Admissions, 803-253-5143.
Co-ed private college. Degrees: B.A., B.S., B.S.W.
1870

583.

Denmark Technical College
P.O. Box 927
Denmark South Carolina 29042
803-793-3301

Dr. Joann R. G. Boyd-Scotland, President

584.

Voorhees College
Voorhees Rd
Denmark South Carolina 29042
803-793-3351

Leonard E. Dawson, President
Elizabeth Evelyn Wright, a protégée of Booker T. Washington, established this school for blacks because of her commitment to education as a form of liberation.

585.

West Virginia State College
Institute South Carolina 25112
304-766-3221

Hazo W. Carter Jr., President

Office of Admissions, 304-766-3221
Degrees: A.A., A.S., A.A.S., B.A., B.S.
1891

586.

Clafin College
700 College Ave
Orangeburg South Carolina 29115
803-534-2710

South Carolina's oldest historically black college.
1869

587.

South Carolina State University
300 College St NE
Orangeburg South Carolina 29117
803-536-7000

Dr. Barbara R. Hatton, President
Office of Enrollment Management,
803-536-7185
State supported, historically black. Degrees: B.A., B.S., M.A., M.S., M.Ed., Ed.S., Ed.D.
1896

588.

Clinton Junior College
P.O. Box 968
Rock Hill South Carolina 29731
803-327-7402

Reverend Cynthia Russell, President

589.

Morris College
100 W College St
Sumter South Carolina 29150-3599

Luns C. Richardson, President
Office of Admissions and Records,
803-775-9371.
Owned and operated by the Baptist
Educational and Missionary Convention of
South Carolina. Degrees: B.A., B.S.
1908

590.

Lane College
545 Lane Ave
Jackson Tennessee 38301-4598
901-426-7500

Dr. Wesley C. McCure, President
Ruth Maddox, Director of Admissions,
901-424-4600
A four-year, private liberal arts college, affiliated with the Christian Methodist Episcopal
Church. Degrees: B.A., B.S.
1882

591.

Knoxville College
901 College St
Knoxville Tennessee 37921
615-524-6500

Dr. Lois Williams, President

592.

Lemoyne-Owen College
807 Walker Ave
Memphis Tennessee 38126
901-774-9090

Burnett Joiner, President
Lemoyne-Owen is a four-year private liberal
arts, co-educational college, affiliated with the
United Church of Christ and the Tennessee

Baptist Missionary and Educational Convention.
1862

593.

Fisk University
1000 17th Ave N
Nashville Tennessee 37208
615-329-8500

Henry Ponder, President
Established to educate former slaves, its
library holds original manuscripts by Langston
Hughes, C. W. Chestnutt, W.E.B. Du Bois,
and others.
1866

594.

Meharry Medical College
1005 D. B. Todd Blvd
Nashville Tennessee 37208
615-327-6904

John Maupin, President
Office of Admissions, 615-327-6223
The largest private institution for the education of black health professionals. Degrees
offered by the School Of Medicine, School of
Dentistry, School of Graduate Studies, School
of Allied Health Professions.
1876

595.

Tennessee State University
Nashville Tennessee 37209-1561
615-320-3432

James A. Hefner, President
1912

596.

Huston-Tillotson College
Austin Texas 78702
212-505-3139

Joseph T. Mcmillan Jr., President
Affiliated with the United Methodist Church
and the United Church of Christ.
1876

597.

Paul Quinn College
3837 Simpson-Stuart Rd
Dallas Texas 75241
214-372-1951

Warren W. Morgan, President
Ralph Spencer Jr., Office of Admissions,
214-371-1312.
Degrees: B.A., B.S., B.S.Ed., B.S.W. Affiliated
with the African Methodist Episcopal Church.
1872

598.

Jarvis Christian College
P.O. Drawer G
Hawkins Texas 75765-9989
903-769-2174

Sebetha Lenkins, Interim President
Office of Admissions, 903-769-2174
Degrees: B.A., B.S., B.B.A.
1912.

599.

Texas Southern University
Houston Texas 77004
713-527-7011

William H. Harris, President
1947

600.

Wiley College
Marshall Texas 75670
903-927-3300

Dr. Lamore J. Carter, President/
Director of Admissions
Founded by the Methodist Episcopal Church.
Historically black, four-year coeducational
institution. Degrees: B.A., B.S.
1873

601.

Prairie View A&M University
Prairie View Texas 77446
409-857-2626

Julius Becton Jr., President
Linda S. Berry, Registrar and Director of Admissions & Records, 800-635-4859 (Texas) or
800-334-1807.
Degrees: B.A., B.D., M.A., M.S., M.B.A.

602.

Saint Phillip's College
1801 Martin Luther King Jr. Dr
San Antonio Texas 78203
210-531-3200

Dr. Hamice R. James, President

603.

Southwestern Christian College
P.O. Box 10
Terrell Texas 75160
214-524-3341

Dr. Jack Evans, President

604.

Texas College
2404 N Grand Ave
Tyler Texas 75702-2404
903-593-8311

Dr. Mitchell Ratton, President
Office of Admissions, 214-593-8311, Ext. 236.
Founded by the Christian Methodist Episcopal Church. Four-year liberal arts college.
Degrees: B.A., B.S.
1894

605.

Hampton University
Queen St
Hampton Virginia 23668
804-727-5000

William R. Harvey, President
The most renowned historically black college, also known for educating Native Americans, as well as for its sizable collection of papers from Booker T. Washington, George Washington Carver, Mary McLeod Bethune, and Dr. Martin Luther King Jr. African and Native American art are prominently displayed among the 9,000 works of art in the holdings of its museum. The site of annual jazz and African-American festivals, both held in June.
1868

606.

Saint Paul's College
406 Windsor Ave
Lawrenceville Virginia 23868
804-848-3111

Dr. Thomas M. Law, President

607.

Virginia Seminary & College
Lynchburg Virginia 24501
804-524-5000

Wesley Cornelius McClure, President
Karen Winston, Director of Admissions,
804-524-5902.
Founded under terms of bill sponsored by state general assemblyman, Alfred W. Harris, an African-American lawyer. Original name: Virginia Normal and Industrial Institute.
Degrees: B.S., M.A., M.S., M.Ed.
1882

608.

Norfolk State University
Norfolk Virginia 23504
804-683-8600

Harrison B. Wilson, President
Office of Admissions, 804-683-8396.
Degrees: A.A., B.A., B.S., B.S.W., M.A., M.S., M.S.W., Psy.D.
1935

609.

Virginia State University
One Hayden Dr
Petersburg Virginia 23806
804-524-5000

First state-supported African-American college in the country.
1882

610.

Virginia Union University
1500 N Lombardy St
Richmond Virginia 23220
804-257-5600

S. Dallas Simmons, President; Gil Rowell, Director of Admissions, 804-257-5881
A private, four-year institution with a Graduate School of Theology. Degrees: B.A., B.S., M.Div., D.M.
1865

611.

Bluefield State College
219 Rock St
Bluefield West Virginia 24701
304-327-4000

Dr. Robert E. Moore, President

612.

West Virginia State University
P.O. Box 399
Institute West Virginia 25112
304-766-3000

Dr. Hazo W. Carter, Jr., President

✪ COMMUNITY CENTERS ✪

613.

African Community Services of San Diego
7353 El Cajon Blvd
La Mesa California 91941-3412
619-466-4364

614.

African American Community Unity Center
5300 S Vermont Ave
Los Angeles California 90037-3530
213-778-7770

615.

Black Awareness Community Development Organization
4167 S Normandie Ave
Los Angeles California 90037-1736
213-291-7188

616.

African Community Health & Social Services
1212 Broadway
Oakland California 94612-1841
510-839-7764

617.

Black American Response to the African Community
127 N Madison Ave, Suite 400
Pasadena California 91102
818-584-0303

Frank E. Wilson, President

618.

National Association of Neighborhoods
1651 Fuller St, NW
Washington DC 20009
202-332-7766

Cleta Winslow, Chairperson; Deborah Crain, Executive Director
NAN represents 2,000 community groups across the country, providing technical assistance, training, and workshops in areas of economic development, social service delivery, and small business development.

619.

African American Home Finders Program
Chicago Illinois 60640
312-728-9088

620.

African Resource Center
3874 Martin Luther King Dr
St. Louis Missouri 63113
314-652-0889

621.

Interreligious Foundation for Community Organization (IFCO)
402 W 145th St
New York New York 10031
212-926-5757

Rev. Lucius Walker Jr., Executive Director
The IFCO is a nonprofit, ecumenical agency that coordinates church and community action programs for social justice. IFCO seeks to forward the struggles of oppressed people for justice and self-determination by supporting their community organizing efforts, through education programs, training, problem identification, conflict resolution, fundraising, and fiscal agent service.

622.

African Resource Center
1515 Linn St
Cincinnati Ohio 45214-2606
513-241-6638

623.

African Community Center
13828 St. Clair Ave
Cleveland Ohio 44110-3551
216-851-3933

624.

Karamu House
2355 E 89th St
Cleveland Ohio 44106-9990
216-795-7070

Taking its name from the Kiswahili word for "place of joyful gathering," this community

center dates back over 75 years and fosters multicultural perspectives in the arts.
1915

625.

African American Community Center
684 Oakwood Ave
Columbus Ohio 43205-2823
614-252-5297

626.

Black Community Solutions Inc.
1300 E Livingston Ave
Columbus Ohio 43205-2854
614-253-3335

627.

Crispus Attucks Community Center
605 S Duke St
York Pennsylvania 17403
717-848-3610

628.

Black Community Development Program
1746 Ohio Ave
Knoxville Tennessee 37921-1721
615-522-1543

629.

Knights of Pythias Temple
2551 Elm St
Dallas Texas 75215

For decades this was the social, cultural, and professional center of Texas's black community under Jim Crow. The building was designed by W. S. Pittman, Booker T. Washington's son-in-law.

⊙ COMPUTERS, ELECTRONICS & TECHNOLOGY ⊙

630.

Bingwa Software Co.
Mathematical Heritage Series
800-404-MATH

Produces a multicultural math program.

631.

Minority Electronics
5445 Oceanus Dr
Huntington Beach California 92649-1007
714-898-6400

632.

African Electrification Foundation
5100 W Goldleaf Cir
Los Angeles California 90056-1271
213-298-1040

633.

African Agricultural Systems Inc.
1278 Sacramento St
San Francisco California 94108-1911
415-775-2115

634.

Bid Whist Pro Conquest Systems
P.O. Box 44139
Washington DC 20026

Educational software developed by African-American engineers.

635.

African American Natural Gas Company
312 N Laflin St
Chicago Illinois 60607-1013
312-733-5656

636.

Metamorphosis
8775-M Centre Park Dr
Columbia Maryland 21045

410-494-3667
410-715-4365
mstudios@mstudios.com

Developer of interactive multimedia content for promotions, marketing, and advertising; producer of original interactive entertainment products.

637.

African Technology Forum
Massachusetts Institute of Technology
Cambridge Massachusetts 02139
617-255-0339
http://web.mit.edu/africantech/www

Marlon L. Buchanan
ATF publishes a unique magazine on science and technology in Africa and provides consulting services and networking opportunities for technical and business professionals involved in African development. Articles and organization information can be found on-line.

638.

Minority Technology Council of Michigan
506 E Liberty St
Ann Arbor Michigan 48104-2210
313-998-6222

✪ COMPUTERS, ON-LINE SERVICES & SITES ✪

639.

African American Studies WWW
http://www.sas.upenn.edu/African_Studies/AS.html

A World Wide Web site for those interested in African-American studies.

640.

African Education Research Network (AERN)
gopher://gopher.ohiou.edu:70/00/dept.servers/aern

A gopher site for practitioners of African studies.

641.

AfriInfo
ftp://ftp.netcom.com/pub/amcgee/African/my_African_related

FTP site for African and African-American related resources on the Internet.

642.

Afro-Amer History
ftp://ftp.msstate.edu/pub/docs/history/USA/Afro-Amer

An ftp resource for African-American history.

643.

alt.music.African
alt.music.African

Usenet discussion group for African music: "It's not just Afropop for breakfast!"

644.

alt.music.black-metal
alt.music.black-metal

Usenet discussion group about black metal music.

645.

aol.neighborhood.nation.central-african-republic
aol.neighborhood.nation.central-african-republic

Central African Republic national newsgroup.

646.

ASA-L: African-American Students Association
listserv@tamvm1.tamu.edu

An internet discussion list for discussion and networking between African-American student organizations.

647.

bit.tech.africana
bit.tech.africana

Usenet discussion forum for information technology and Africa.

648.

Black/African Related Resources
Art McGee
sisskind@sas.upenn.edu

A list of online information storage sites (ftp, gopher, telnet, WWW, BBS, database, etc.) that contain a significant amount of information relating to or of concern to black or African people, culture, and issues around the world.

649.

BLACKLIB: Conference of Black Librarians
listserv@guvm

An Internet discussion list for black librarians.

650.

BTO: Black Technical Organizations
listserv@arizvm1.ccit.arizona.edu

An Internet discussion list for discussion and networking between black technical organizations.

651.

CLNet's Diversity Page on the Web
http://latino.sscnet.ucla.edu/diversity1.html

Romelia Salinas, CLNet Manager

A World Wide Web site that provides information on listservs, gophers, and Web sites as well as news groups for African, Asian, and Native Americans as well as Latinos. There is also some information on multicultural Internet resources.

652.

Collected Articles of Frederick Douglass, a Slave
ftp://mrcnet.cso.uiuc.edu/etext/etext94/dug12 10x.xxx

All of the articles written by Frederick Douglass, on-line.

653.

DOWNLOW-L: Hip-Hop and Its Influences
listkeeper@hmc.edu

An Internet discussion list about hip-hop music.

654.

DRUM: Issues Facing Black/African Communities

An Internet discussion list about issues facing the black/African community. This list is semi-private. In order to subscribe to DRUM and its related lists, you must be referred by a current member.

655.

ECONDEV: Black Economic Development
econdev-request@blackx.alexhart.com

An Internet discussion list about issues of economic development in the black community.

656.

EJAS-L: Electronic Journal for Africana Studies
listserv@kentvm or listserv@kentvm.kent.edu

An electronic journal for those interested in Africana studies.

657.

EJBLACK: Electronic Journal of Black Librarianship
listserv@kentvm or listserv@kentvm.kent.edu

An electronic journal devoted to issues of black librarianship.

658.

FUTURE: The Future of Black Communities
future-request@blackx.alexhart.com

An Internet discussion group for discussion of the future of black communities.

659.

Interracial Voice
http://www.webcom.com/~intvoice/

Published every other month as an independent, information-oriented, networking news journal serving the mixed-race/interracial community in cyberspace.

660.

JALAS&L: Journal of African-Latin Studies & Literature
rmvieira@cldc.howard.edu

An electronic journal for those interested in the study of the African diaspora in Latin America.

661.

KALIMBA: Black/African Issues and Culture
kalimba@casbah.acns.nwu.edu

An Internet discussion group for discussion of black/African issues and culture. Access to this group is by invitation only: must be invited by a current list member.

662.

Martin Luther King Jr. Bibliography
gopher://soundgarden.micro.umn.edu:9001/7?mlk%20biblio

Lists approximately 2,700 bibliographic citations to works by or about Martin Luther King Jr. and the civil rights movement.

663.

MELALINK: The MELANET Resource Center
New Perspective Technologies Company

Web page for other Afrocentric WWW sites and home pages.

664.

MILES: Discussion on Jazz Trumpeter Miles Davis
listserv@hearn.nic.surfnet.nl

An Internet discussion group for discussion about the jazz trumpeter Miles Davis.

665.

MOLIS: Minority On-Line Information Service
gopher://gopher.fie.com or
ftp://ftp.fie.com or telnet://fedix.fie.com or
http://WWW.FIE.COM

Latest information on black and Hispanic colleges' and universities' missions, strengths, and emerging capabilities, including scholarships and fellowships and annual federal plans of assistance for HBCUs. The collection of data is ongoing, and updated as additional institutional information becomes available. All information appearing in the database has been reviewed and approved by participating institutions.

666.

PennInfo—African Studies
gopher://gopher.upenn.edu/PennInfo/
Gateway/PennInfo/Inte

Information servers at the University of Pennsylvania devoted to research in African studies.

667.

soc.culture.African.American
soc.culture.African.American

Discussions about African-American issues.

668.

Yahoo
http://www.yahoo.com/society and culture/
cultures/African American/
admin@yahoo.com

Maintains a WWW page with Internet resources for African Americans.

669.

Africa Commercial
P.O. Box 122
Cape Town 7975
27-21-788-2248
27-21-788-6613—Fax

Webmaster@africa.com
The Africa Commercial WWW service provides information on the tourism industry and business in South Africa.

670.

Internet Africa
6 Thicket Rd
Western Cape South Africa 7700
27-21-683-4370
27-21-683-4695—Fax

info@iafrica.com
Africa's gateway to the internet, providing all types of access from anywhere in South Africa as well as providing access in Zimbabwe and Zambia.

671.

Africana Conference Paper Index (AFRC)
Northwestern University Library
Evanston Illinois 60208-2300
874-491-7658
874-491-8306—Fax
Africana@nwu.edu
(IP 129.105.54.2)
On-line index to individual papers presented at Africana conference proceedings.

672.

Kokobar
59 Lafayette Ave
Brooklyn New York 11217
212-343-1779
212-343-1779—Fax

Angel Williams, President
The first African-American-owned espresso bar/cafe with in-house bookstore and "Cyberlounge," located in historic Fort Greene, Brooklyn. Features a full coffee/espresso/tea bar; healthy soup, salad, and sandwiches with fine wines and beers. Book lovers will find 100–150 great titles on everything from urban culture to Zen Buddhism, as well as a wide assortment of magazines. Internet access through the Cyberlounge.

673.

Griot Online
http://www.afrinet.net/~griot

On-line collection of discussions, research, and original work about African life, culture, and history. Offers maps, narrative, pictures, and a time line.

674.

Book The
http://www.blackhistory.com

Web site by Image Interactive about black history.

675.

African American Pioneers in Kentucky Law
http://www.louisville.edu/groups/law-www/legacy

Web site offering background information about African-American pioneers of law in Kentucky.

676.

Womanist Theory and Research
Institute for African-American Studies
Athens Georgia 30602
706-542-5197
http://www.uga.edu/~womanist

WTR provides a forum for exchanging feminist research, theory, and ideas among women-of-color scholars and students in the humanities, social sciences, education, theology, law, medicine, politics, librarianship, journalism, art, information technologies, and telecommunications.

677.

The Faces of Science: African Americans in the Sciences
http://www.lib.lsu.edu/lib/chem/display/faces.html

Web site profiles African-American men and women who have contributed to the advancement of science and engineering.

678.

Pan-African Political and Organizational Information
http://www.panafrican.org/panafrican

Web site offers information about Pan-African states.

679.

W. E. B. Du Bois Institute for Afro-American Research
26 Church St
Cambridge Massachusetts 02138
617-495-1000
http://web-dubois.fas.harvard.edu

The institute is the nation's oldest research center dedicated to the study of the history, culture, and social institutions of African Americans. Founded in 1975, the institute serves as the site for research projects, fellowships for emerging and established scholars, publications, conferences, and working groups. Offers a web site with a calendar of events and other information.

680.

Virtual Africa
http://africa.com

Web site offers infromation about South African business and travel services.

681.

African Technology Forum
Massachusetts Institute of Technology
Cambridge Massachusetts 02139
617-225-7477
http://web.mit.edu/africantech/www

Marlon L. Buchanan

ATF publishes a unique magazine on science and technology in Africa and provides consulting services and networking opportunities for technical and business professionals involved in African development. Articles and organization information can be found online.

682.

FRS Associates
2750 Market St
San Francisco California 94114-1987
415-626-9796
415-626-9793—Fax
http://www.frsa.com/frsbiz/shtml

FRS offers a variety of web site creation and maintenance services as well as business listings for individuals, businesses, and organizations who want to promote themselves on the Internet. They also provide software programming for ad hoc systems.

❂ CRAFTS ❂

683.

Freedom Quilting Bee
Route 1, Box 43-A
Alberta Alabama 36720
205-573-2225

Inspired by the civil rights movement, this all-black women's cooperative is nationally recognized for the quality of their quilts, the designs of which are drawn from a 140-year-old tradition.
1966

684.

African Fashions, Gifts & Crafts
2229 San Pablo Ave
Berkeley California 94702-1829
510-843-2821

685.

Heritage Enterprises
P.O. Box 5056
Long Beach California 90805
714-826-6946

Black heritage dolls and art. Color brochure, $2.00.

686.

African Imports & Exports
1474 W Martin Luther King Jr. Blvd
Los Angeles California 90062-1225
213-290-9879

687.

African Outlet The
505 Divisadero St
San Francisco California 94117-2212
415-776-3576

688.

Black Ethnic Collectibles
Temple Hills Maryland 20748
301-630-6698

689.

Africana Business Inc.
21 Boardwalk
Atlantic City New Jersey 08401-5001
609-344-8183

Sells African artifacts, clothing, figurines, crafts, books.

690.

African Heritage Products Co.
3388 Bailey Ave
Buffalo New York 14215-1133
716-838-5617

691.

Black Heritage Products
1315 Headquarters Dr
Greensboro North Carolina 27405-7919
910-379-7505

692.

Afro-Centric Boutique
Milwaukee Wisconsin 53200
414-462-9567

❖ CULTURAL ORGANIZATIONS ❖

693.

African American Weddings
718-655-3489
718-655-3489—Fax

Adaeze Agu, Owner and Designer
Wedding consultations, including groom, traditional or contemporary African-American weddings. Custom design and make outfits.
Jewelry. By appointment only.
1994

694.

**W. C. Handy Birthplace, Museum
& Library**
620 W College St
Florence Alabama 35630
205-760-6434

Tribute to the legendary blues musician. Also
houses a resource center for black history and
culture, and is the site of an annual music festival.

695.

African American Cultural Center
2560 W 54th
Los Angeles California 90043
213-299-6124

Dr. Karenga, Director

696.

Brockman for the Cultural Arts
3401 W 43rd St
Los Angeles California 90008
213-294-5201

Dale Davis, Co-Owner
Nonprofit organization that sponsors festivals
in Los Angeles that celebrate the African-
American heritage.

697.

African Cultural Center
4113 Macdonald Ave
Richmond California 94805-2333
510-234-8822

William Lewis, Director

698.

Black Cultural Enterprises
2 Bueno Ct
Sacramento California 95823-2822
916-392-9212

699.

**San Francisco African-American
Historical and Cultural Society**
Buchanan St at Marina Blvd
San Francisco California 94123
415-441-0640

Memorabilia of Mary Ellen Pleasant, prominent 19th-century abolitionist, compliment the paintings of Sargent Johnson and the West African wooden and soapstone carvings and baskets in the main holdings of this museum. Facilities also include: listening room, research library, gift shop. Affiliated with the Center for African & African-American Art and Performing Arts Workshops and Theater Productions of Wajumbe Dancers.

700.

**African American Cultural Education
Foundation**
4203 10th St, NE
Washington DC 20017-2122
202-832-9712

Offers cultural programs and free weekend programs that teach children math, reading, and responsibility on the Howard University campus.

701.

African American Holiday Foundation
410 8th St, NW
Washington DC 20004-2103
202-737-1670

702.

African Cultural Link
1747 Pennsylvania Ave, NW
Washington DC 20036
202-223-2338

703.

African Cultural Organization
1474 Columbia Rd, NW
Washington DC 20009-4773
202-667-5775

704.

Links Inc. The
1200 Massachusetts Ave, NW
Washington DC 20005
202-842-8686

Marion Schultz Sutherland, President
Founded as a public service organization; today over 8,000 members in 240 chapters in cities in the United States, Nassau, Bahamas, and Frankfurt, West Germany focus Links' activities around four program areas: the arts, services to youth, national trends and services, and international trends and services.
1946

705.

Martin Luther King Jr. Celebration
P.O. Box 8728
Washington DC 20005

706.

African American Caribbean Cultural Center
1601 S Andrews Ave
Fort Lauderdale Florida 33316-2509
305-467-4056—Fax

707.

Black Cuban Foundation
900 SW 1st St
Miami Florida 33010
305-325-8711

Lucia Rojas, President
An organization seeking the unification and integration of all segments of the exile community, incorporating black Cubans and their families in exile. Other goals include the desire to unify and preserve our roots, highlighting at the same time both influences (African and Spanish) in our culture. Encourages the diverse communities in Miami to practice ethnic and cultural awareness, tolerance, and acceptance.

708.

African American Heritage Society
400 S Jefferson St
Pensacola Florida 32501-5902
904-469-1299

Objectives are to enhance the development of society by the infusion of multiculturalism, to increase the public's awareness of and appreciation for African-American culture and heritage, and to enhance self-esteem and cultural literacy among disadvantaged youth. Programs include Partners in Education, Literature and Writing Project, Summer Festival of African-American Culture, Cultural Program Series.

709.

Center for African American Culture
210 S Woodward, B-105
Tallahassee Florida 32303
904-644-3252

710.

Afro-American Cultural Center
698 Echo St, NW
Atlanta Georgia 30318-6717
404-875-8082

711.

Mind, Body & Soul Enterprises
Southeast Regional Office:
1150 Collier Road NW, K-14
Atlanta Georgia 30318
404-355-4586

Mind, Body & Soul Enterprises is a multifaceted company that combines educational services with retail sales of audio and video merchandise. The company's mission is to engineer a better community by encouraging and promoting the mental, physical, and spiritual development of youths and adults. Its educational division offers workshops, lectures, seminars, and conferences concentrating on areas of holistic development.

712.

African American Heritage 7 Co.
3011 Rainbow Dr
Decatur Georgia 30034-1643
404-243-0511

713.

Afro-American-Japanese International
560 Fayetteville Rd SE
Decatur Georgia 30030
404-378-8266

714.

African American Community Trust
320 N Michigan Ave
Chicago Illinois 60639
312-237-6600

715.

African American Heritage Tours
240 W Randolph St
Chicago Illinois 60606-1812
312-443-9575
312-443-9575—Fax

Gregory Sims
Offers group tours related to African-American history in Chicago and nationwide.

716.

Black Expo Chicago & National Black Expo
10 W 35th St, 4th Floor
Chicago Illinois 60616
312-949-9440
312-949-9456—Fax

Sponsors conventions in Columbus, Chicago, Birmingham, and Nashville that attract hundreds of thousands of people from across the country.

717.

Black Heritage Coin Inc.
606 E Oakwood Blvd
Chicago Illinois 60653-2310
312-373-3500

718.

Chicago Historical Society
Clark St at North Ave
Chicago Illinois 60610
312-642-4600

"A House Divided: America in the Age of Lincoln" examines a tumultuous time in American history of critical significance to African Americans. Also chronicles important black figures in Chicago's history.

719.

African Cultural Center
1121 Emerson St
Evanston Illinois 60201-3131
708-864-8021

720.

Black Culture Center
315 University St
Lafayette Indiana 47906-2897
317-494-3092

Renee Thomas

721.

Kansas Fever Committee
3730 Truman
Topeka Kansas 66609
913-267-5381

Dedicated to making known the numerous contributions of African Americans in the region, including the sponsorship of African-American festivals and informal tours of heritage sites.

722.

African Heritage Foundation
1683 N Claiborne Ave
New Orleans Louisiana 70116-1326
504-949-5610

Sponsors the annual African Heritage Festival International.

723.

New Orleans Jazz & Heritage Festival
1205 N Rampart St
New Orleans Louisiana 70153
800-535-8747 or 504-522-4786 or
504-561-8747

Splendid regional food, African-American arts and crafts, and almost every variety of jazz around.

724.

Maryland Commission on Afro-American History and Culture
84 Franklin St, Suite 101
Annapolis Maryland 21401
301-269-2893

Serve as a historical body and also works with other state and governmental agencies, civil and professional organizations, and the black community. Seeks to preserve the heritage of black America and to encourage greater appreciation of that role.

725.

Office of Multicultural Affairs
American International College
Springfield Massachusetts 01109
413-747-6400 or 413-737-7000
413-737-2803—Fax

Naomi Inniss
Deals with people of color through cultural programs, guidance, books, and literature. Focuses on the college but also sponsors events within the community.

726.

African American Heritage Association
2648 W Grand Blvd
Detroit Michigan 48208-1237
313-875-0656

727.

Museum of African-American History
301 Frederick Douglass St
Detroit Michigan 48202
313-833-9800

Spans the entire history of African Americans, from the beginnings of slavery to contemporary statements about African Americans today. Sponsors the annual Africa World Festival.

728.

Sedalia Ragtime Archives
State Fair Community College
Sedalia Missouri 65301
816-826-7100

Original memorabilia of Scott Joplin, the "father of ragtime," are the highlights. Organizes the annual June Ragtime Festival.

729.

Vaughn Cultural Center
524 N Grand
St. Louis Missouri 63103
314-535-9227

Cultural center with programs focusing on African-American history, poetry, and culture. Also has an art gallery and is affiliated with the Urban League.

730.

Mind, Body & Soul Enterprises
Northeast Regional Office:
35 Bennington Dr
East Windsor, New Jersey 08520
609-443-5621

Mind, Body & Soul Enterprises is a multifaceted company that combines educational services with retail sales of audio and video merchandise. The company's mission is to engineer a better community by encouraging and promoting the mental, physical, and spiritual development of youths and adults. Its educational division offers workshops, lectures, seminars, and conferences concentrating on areas of holistic development.

731.

Afro-American Historical and Cultural Society Museum
1841 Kennedy Blvd
Jersey City New Jersey 07305
201-547-5262

Exploration of the lives of prominent African Americans of New Jersey.

732.

NAACP Historical & Cultural Project
441 Bergen Ave
Jersey City New Jersey 07304
201-547-6562

733.

African American Heritage Parade
1020 Broad St
Newark New Jersey 07102-2400
201-642-5051

734.

African Culture Inc.
82 Dover St
Newark New Jersey 07106-2310
201-371-9313

735.

African Culture & Fashion House
581 Vanderbilt Ave
Brooklyn New York 11238-3014
718-638-5803 or 800-704-9345 or
718-638-5553

Manufactures African *addreel* (clothing), bags, shoes, jewelry, hair braids.

736.

International African Arts Festival
451A Nostrand Ave
Brooklyn New York 11216-1904
718-638-6700

A big five-day festival that focuses on African-American history. Features family and children's programs, African-American vendors, and a women's history program at Boys & Girls High School.

737.

African American Village
1373 Main
Buffalo New York 14200
716-882-4267

738.

African Cultural Center Inc.
350 Masten Ave
Buffalo New York 14209-1792
716-884-2013
716-884-2013—Fax

Agnes Bain
Production company that imports and manufacturers African products.

739.

Negro Benevolent Society
220-13 Merrick Blvd
Jamaica New York 11413-1925
718-978-4126·

740.

African American Better Cultural Society
P.O. Box 195
New York New York 10000
212-722-4900

741.

African American Day Parade
1 Dr. Martin Luther King Jr. Blvd
New York New York 10027-4524
212-348-3080

742.

African Voices Communications
270 W 96th St
New York New York 10025
212-865-2982

Cultural arts organization, nonprofit. Promotes literature, art, and poetry readings, by and for African Americans. Publishes a bimonthly newspaper. Accepts written work for publication. A referral service available to match up creative persons with clients.

743.

Studio Museum of Harlem
144 W 125th St
New York New York 10027
212-865-2420

America's most renowned institution for the display of works by artists of color. Also has a concert hall, lecture hall, and assembly hall to complement its art collections.

744.

Afro-American Cultural Foundation
Westchester Community College
Valhalla New York 10585
914-285-6600

745.

Young Men's Institute Cultural Center
39 S Market St
Asheville North Carolina 28801
704-252-4614

Sponsors programs and services for youths, economic development, cultural awareness, and educational advancement.

746.

Afro American Cultural Center
401 N Myers St
Charlotte North Carolina 28202-3091
704-374-1565
704-374-9273—Fax

Wanda Montgomery, Director
Art gallery and performance space featuring local and national African-American art performances throughout the year.

747.

Hayti Heritage Center
804 Old Fayetteville St
Durham North Carolina 27702
919-687-0288

Houses the William Tucker African-American Archive (a collection devoted to the famous author and illustrator of children's books) as well as an art gallery and dance studio.

748.

Afro Centric
108 E Henderson St
Salisbury North Carolina 28144-3630
704-637-2499

749.

Black Cultural Center
The University of Akron
Akron Ohio 44325
216-972-7030

750.

African American Events
2012 W 25th St
Cleveland Ohio 44113-4131
216-241-5727

751.

African Heritage
5750 Broadway Ave
Cleveland Ohio 44127-1715
216-429-2955

752.

Black Unity House Inc.
1167 Hayden Ave
Cleveland Ohio 44110-3557
216-681-5927

753.

Karamu House
2355 E 89th St
Cleveland Ohio 44106-9990
216-795-7070

Taking its name from the Kiswahili word for "place of joyful gathering," this community center dates back over 75 years and fosters multicultural perspectives in the arts.
1915

754.

Emancipation Celebration
Gallia County Fairgrounds
Gallipolis Ohio 45631
614-245-5418 or 614-245-5418

The huge two-day festival celebrating the end of slavery, which has been held almost every year since President Lincoln's Emancipation Proclamation. The highlight of this Christian-oriented two-day celebration of fun, games, parades, food, and music (occurring on the weekend closest to Sept. 22) is a countywide, multidenominational service.

755.

National Afro-American Museum and Cultural Center
1350 Brush Row Rd
Wilberforce Ohio 45384
513-376-4944

Contains a museum, art gallery, library, and archives. Programs include an oral and visual history project, joint degree offerings in archival and administration and museology, and exhibit loans. Publishes a quarterly journal.

756.

Boley Historic District
c/o Boley Chamber of Commerce
Boley Oklahoma 74829
918-667-3477

An all-black town that drew its settlers from the descendants of slaves held by the Creek Indians. All of its public and prominent officials were black. Now a National Historic Landmark, it serves to give a glimpse of the African-American presence in the American West, as well as the site of an annual Black Rodeo held on Memorial Day weekend.

757.

Negro Cultural Association Inc.
321 Ridge Ave
Allentown Pennsylvania 18102-5325
610-439-9498

758.

African Royal Prince's Fund for Culture Exchange
1401 Arch St
Philadelphia Pennsylvania 19102-1525
215-569-3140

Sponsors cultural and educational programs to promote understanding between African and African-American peoples.

759.

Afro-America Historical and Cultural Museum
Seventh and Arch Sts
Philadelphia Pennsylvania 19107
215-574-0380

Traces the importance of black America's presence in the arts and life of the nation. Art galleries, performance spaces, multimedia presentations, changing exhibitions, permanent exhibitions, and a 22-site African-American heritage tour of Philadelphia.

760.

**African Heritage Federation
of the Americas**
P.O. Box 3833
Pittsburgh Pennsylvania 15230
412-361-8425

A. Ndubsi Ezekoye, President
Individuals of African ancestry working to
promote knowledge and understanding of
African heritage. Conducts educational programs, sponsors charitable programs, maintains speakers' bureau.

761.

Rhode Island Black Heritage Society
46 Aborn St
Providence Rhode Island 02903
401-751-3490

Creates an environment and understanding
about the contributions of African Americans
and the importance of African-American culture to the development of American culture.
Dedicated to discovering, preserving, interpreting, and exhibiting black history and culture and to educating the public at large.
1974

762.

Gullah Festival
c/o Gullah Festival Inc.
Beaufort South Carolina 29901
803-525-0628

Festival that celebrates the unique African-
American subculture that emerged along the
southeast coast of the United States from the
mixture of English and various West African
languages.

763.

African American Calendar
2321 Main St
Columbia South Carolina 29201-1955
803-254-8362

764.

Greenville Cultural Exchange Center
P.O. Box 5482, Station B
Greenville South Carolina 29606
803-232-9162

Documents the local African-American heritage and houses the Jesse Jackson Hall of
Fame, which honors the Greenville native.

765.

Oyuntunji African Village
U.S. 17-21
Sheldon South Carolina 29941
803-846-8900 or 803-846-9939

A replica of a Yoruba village, this place offers
a glimpse of what life is like in southeastern
Nigeria, including arts and crafts, religious
iconography, and yearly festivals.

766.

**Africa in April Cultural Awareness
Festival Inc.**
P.O. Box 111261
Memphis Tennessee 38111
901-947-2133
901-947-2414—Fax

David L. Acey, Executive Director
A nonprofit sponsoring an annual four-day
outdoor event focusing on Afrocentric culture, history, education, music, and art. Each

year they honor an African or Caribbean country. Vendors, crafts, displays, along with 30,000–40,000 people, flock to historic Beale Street. Also sponsors anticrime, antidrug programs, scholarships, celebrations for African American History Month, Martin Luther King's birthday, and Kwanzaa.

767.

Center for Southern Folklore
152 Beale St
Memphis Tennessee 38101
901-525-3655

Chronicles the heritage of the South through exhibits, photographs, tours, festivals, and films, with African-American contributions prominently displayed.

768.

African American Cultural Center The
2209 Buchanan St
Nashville Tennessee 37208-1911
615-330-6628

769.

African American Cultural Heritage Center
3434 S.R.L. Thornton Freeway
Dallas Texas 75224

770.

Museum of African-American Life and Culture
1620 First Ave
Dallas Texas 75226
214-565-9026

Artifacts and folk art from Africa and the diaspora, supplemented by occasional lectures, exhibits, and festivals that celebrate the black heritage.

771.

Newsome House Museum and Cultural Center
2803 Oak St
Newport News Virginia 23607
804-247-2380

Joseph Thomas Newsome, a son of former slaves, rose up to become the editor of the *Newport News Star* and was licensed to practice law before the Virginia Supreme Court. His restored home now offers programs and exhibits on African-American history and culture.

772.

African Drumming and Dance Camp/ African Cultural Camp
Camp Sealth
6716 Rainier Ave S
Seattle, WA 98118

Seven days and six nights of hands-on participation in playing traditional drums and percussion, song and dance folkloric presentations. Songs, plays, games, and social greetings.

773.

Camp Washington-Carver Museum
HC 35, Box 5
Clifftop West Virginia 25831
304-438-3005

At the site of the nation's first State Negro 4-H Camp (now on the National Register of

Historic Places), this organization is now primarily devoted to exploring black culture through arts camps for youth, photographs, and artifacts.

774.

African Cultural Building
4411A N 60
Milwaukee Wisconsin 53225
414-536-6148

775.

African World Festival Limited
316 N Milwaukee
Milwaukee Wisconsin 53202
414-347-0444

776.

Black Buffalo Soldiers
2000 N 31st St
Milwaukee Wisconsin 53208-1961
414-442-0117

❂ DIET & NUTRITION ❂

777.

Afrikan-Amerikan Institute for Positive Living
3011 Oakridge Dr
Dayton Ohio 45417-1568
513-263-7800

❂ DOMESTIC VIOLENCE ❂

778.

African-American Women's Clergy Association
P.O. Box 1493
Washington DC 20013
202-797-7460

The Rev. Imagene Bigham Stewart, National Chairwoman
The association's 26 local affiliates operate the only African-American shelter for homeless families and satellite centers for battered men and battered women in the nation's capital.
1969

❂ EDUCATIONAL ORGANIZATIONS ❂

779.

African American Studies WWW
http://www.sas.upenn.edu/African_Studies/
AS.html

A World Wide Web site for those interested in African-American studies.

780.

African Education Research Network (AERN)
gopher://gopher.ohiou.edu:70/00/dept.servers/aern

A gopher site for practitioners of African studies.

781.

Afro-Amer History
ftp://ftp.msstate.edu/pub/docs/history/USA/Afro-Amer

An ftp resource for African-American history.

782.

ASA-L: African-American Students Association
listserv@tamvm1.tamu.edu

An Internet discussion list for discussion and networking between African-American student organizations.

783.

EJAS-L: Electronic Journal for Africana Studies
listserv@kentvm or listserv@kentvm.kent.edu

An electronic journal for those interested in Africana studies.

784.

EJBLACK: Electronic Journal of Black Librarianship
listserv@kentvm or listserv@kentvm.kent.edu

An electronic journal devoted to issues of black librarianship.

785.

JALAS&L: Journal of African-Latin Studies & Literature
rmvieira@cldc.howard.edu

An electronic journal for those interested in the study of the African diaspora in Latin America.

786.

Birmingham Civil Rights Institute
Sixth Ave and 16th St N
Birmingham Alabama 35203
205-328-9696

Collections and exhibits on segregation, black culture, and the civil rights movement.

787.

Black Progress Review
3010 Wilshire Blvd
Beverly Hills California 90210
310-285-0112

Publication for minority recruitment at corporations and school districts.

788.

African Center for Religious Education
5225 Wilshire Blvd
Los Angeles California 90036-4301
213-932-0082

789.

African Children Advanced Learning Center
896 Isabella St
Oakland California 94607-3430
510-839-7727

790.

African Scientific Institute
P.O. Box 12161
Oakland California 94604
510-653-7027

Lee O. Cherry, Executive Director
Encourages minority youth to pursue careers in science or engineering. Serves as a forum for the exchange of technical information and expertise. Sponsors programs to assist people in feeling comfortable with science and technology.

791.

Black Scholar Magazine
P.O. Box 2869
Oakland California 94609
510-547-6633

Robert Crisman, Publisher

792.

Black Women Organize for Educational Development
518 17th St
Oakland California 94601
510-763-9501

793.

African-American Historical & Cultural Society
Fort Mason Center, Building C-165
San Francisco California 94123
415-441-0640 or 415-292-6172

Julian Haile, Director
Interested in the role of the African American in art and history. Houses a museum and gallery.

794.

Minority Educational Information
94 Elmwood Pl
Bridgeport Connecticut 06605-1406
203-367-0009

795.

African-American College Alliance
427 8th St, SE
Washington DC 20003-2833
202-543-3283

796.

Bethune-DuBois Fund
600 New Hampshire Ave, NW
Washington DC 20037
202-625-2900

797.

Black Alumni Network Development
Washington DC 20011
202-726-1020

798.

Black Education & Employment Network
Washington DC 20007

799.

Booker T. Washington Foundation
4324 Georgia Ave, NW
Washington DC 20011
202-829-4634—Fax

800.

Black Man's Development Center
1703 W 4th St
Wilmington Delaware 19805-3547
302-429-0206

Community service organization specializing in providing housing for low- and no-income individuals. Exclusively charitable, nonprofit educational program.

801.

Black Employment & Education
2625 Piedmont Rd, NE
Atlanta Georgia 30324-3012
404-469-5891

802.

Mind, Body & Soul Enterprises
Southeast Regional Office:
1150 Collier Road NW, K-14
Atlanta GA 30318
404-355-4586

Mind, Body & Soul Enterprises is a multifaceted company that combines educational services with retail sales of audio and video merchandise. The company's mission is to engineer a better community by encouraging and promoting the mental, physical, and spiritual development of youths and adults. Its educational division offers workshops, lectures, seminars, and conferences concentrating on areas of holistic development.

803.

National Black College Alumni Hall of Fame
38 Washington St, #E18
Atlanta Georgia 30315
404-658-8155

804.

African American Studies Program
19 S La Salle St
Chicago Illinois 60603-1401
312-443-0929

805.

African-American Images
1909 W 95th St
Chicago Illinois 60643
312-445-0322
312-445-9844—Fax

Dr. Jawanza Kunjufu, Chief Executive
Officer; Rita Kunjufu, Executive Director
African-American Images is a full-service
communications company that offers a bookstore, gift shop, video, publishing, curriculum
materials, and tutorial services for children.

806.

Black Education Network
Chicago Illinois 60621
312-224-0202

807.

Career Communications Group
729 E Pratt St, Suite 504
Baltimore Maryland 21202
410-244-7101
410-752-1837—Fax

Tyrone D. Taborne, President/CEO
The country's largest minority-owned media
services company producing information
about education and careers for black and
Hispanic professionals.

808.

Black College Satellite Network
619 Hampton Park Blvd
Capital Heights Maryland 20743-4926
301-350-0056

809.

A Better Chance Inc.
419 Boylston St
Boston Massachusetts 02116
617-421-0950
617-421-0965—Fax

Judith Berry Griffin, President
A Better Chance Inc. (ABC) is the oldest and
only nationwide academic talent search
agency for minority youth. ABC seeks out talented and motivated children of color, from
all economic levels and every part of the country, and provides them with access to college
preparation, academic enrichment, and
career options. In addition, ABC offers access
to enrichment programs in such fields as academic and leadership skills.
1963

810.

**W. E. B. Du Bois Institute for Afro-
American Research**
26 Church St
Cambridge Massachusetts 02138
617-495/1000
http://web-dubois.fas.harvard.edu

The institute is the nation's oldest research
center dedicated to the study of the history,
culture, and social institutions of African
Americans. Founded in 1975, the institute
serves as the site for research projects, fellowships for emerging and established scholars,
publications, conferences, and working
groups. Offers a web site with a calendar of
events and other information.

811.

Minority Employment Program
2345 Main St
Springfield Massachusetts 01107-1907
413-736-8470

Job training and educational services.

812.

Black Scholar
2514 Pittsfield Blvd
Ann Arbor Michigan 48104-5241
313-677-2230

813.

Black Child & Family Institute
835 W Genesee St
Lansing Michigan 48915-1899
517-487-3775

814.

African American Academy
Minneapolis Minnesota 55408
612-827-3727

815.

Inroads
1221 Locust St, Suite 410
St. Louis Missouri 63103
(314) 241-7330

Reginald D. Dickson, CEO & President
A program that encourages corporations to sponsor internships for minority students and pledge to develop career opportunities for the interns. Prepares black, Hispanic, and Native American high school and college students for leadership positions within major American corporations in their own communities.

816.

Mind, Body & Soul Enterprises
Northeast Regional Office:
35 Bennington Dr
East Windsor   New Jersey 08520
609-443-5621

Mind, Body & Soul Enterprises is a multifaceted company that combines educational services with retail sales of audio and video merchandise. The company's mission is to engineer a better community by encouraging and promoting the mental, physical, and spiritual development of youths and adults. Its educational division offers workshops, lectures, seminars, and conferences concentrating on areas of holistic development.

817.

African American Institute
833 United Nations Plaza
New York New York 10017-3581
212-994-9566
212-682-6174—Fax

Vivian Lowery Derryck, President
Works to further development in Africa, improve African-American understanding, and inform Americans about Africa. Offers fellowships for students.
1954

818.

African Heritage Studies Association
P.O. Box 1733
New York New York 10037
212-795-2096
212-795-6674—Fax

Dr. John Henrik Clarke, Founder/President
Organization of scholar-activists (Ph.D.s and professors) throughout the world who specialize in Africans in the continent and the diaspora. Conferences, seminars, colloquia.

819.

Africana Publishing
160 Broadway
New York New York 10038
212-374-0100
212-374-1313—Fax

Miriam J. Holmes, Managing Director
Academic, scholarly, publishing press for books about Africana subjects. Publishes several journals as well for research in Africa.

820.

Assault on Illiteracy Program
231 W 29th St, Suite 1205
New York New York 10001
212-967-4008
212-971-4682—Fax

Earl Gray, President
AOIP is a process whereby more than 90 of the most effective organizations (with a membership and family reach of well over 16 million deeply concerned consumer citizens) in black America can work together to (1) achieve the absolutely necessary community-building AOIP year 2000 goals and beyond, and (2) vastly increase—and guarantee—the sales action of those corporations that support those goals by advertising in the AOIP, participating media, and the National Black Monitor. This advertising is the "indirect" funding source for AOIP.

821.

Black Child Development Institute
1200 E Market St
Greensboro North Carolina 27401-3258
910-230-2138

Tutorial and mentoring service to children in the community. "Each one's spirit is excellent!" Matching students with volunteers.

822.

Black Child Development Institute— Akron
1310 Superior Ave
Akron Ohio 44307-1154
216-384-8188

823.

Afrikids
108 William Howard Taft Rd, Suite 2
Cincinnati Ohio 45219
513-569-8286
513-569-8284—Fax

Keena Mcdowell-Smith, CEO
Afrikids offers educational books, games, toys and resources for African-American children ranging from preschool through junior high school as well as parenting books. All materials available by mail order.

824.

Concerned Educators of Black Students
473 Marathon Ave
Dayton Ohio 45406
513-275-9133

825.

American Foundation for Negro Affairs
117 S 17th St, Suite 1200
Philadelphia Pennsylvania 19103
215-854-1470

Samuel L. Evans, President and National Chairman
The AFNA Program recruits students at the end of 10th grade and supplies them with specialized educational experience that leads them through college and professional school. This is accomplished by placing students in an intensive, coordinated, advanced educational environment that supplements their academic experience to enable them to meet the standards of each level.

826.

Negro Education Emergency Drive
643 Liberty Ave
Pittsburgh Pennsylvania 15123
412-566-2760

NEED is a voluntary organization that provides financial assistance for Negro students to continue their education beyond the high school level. Volunteers work directly with secondary schools and also with higher education institution to obtain supplemental financial aid. They provide a link between individual students, secondary schools, colleges, and universities.

827.

Penn Center
Box 126
St. Helena Island South Carolina 29920
803-838-2432 or 803-838-2235

School was founded by Laura Towne, Ellen Murray, and Charlotte Forten Grimke to educate the 10,000 formerly enslaved African Americans on the island. Its mission is to preserve the Gullah culture on Sea Island by serving as a local, national, and international educational resource center.

828.

Black Issues in Higher Education
10520 Warwick Ave
Fairfax Virginia 22030-3100
703-385-2981

❂ ENVIRONMENTAL ORGANIZATIONS ❂

829.

African American Environmental Organization
733 6th St, SE
Washington DC 20003-2753
202-543-2649

830.

African Wildlife Foundation
1717 Massachusetts Ave, NW
Washington DC 20036-2001
202-265-8394

831.

Minority Environmental Association
119 E Court Sq
Decatur Georgia 30030-2522
404-373-4771

832.

African Society for Animal Protection Inc.
175 W 79th St
New York New York 10024-6450
212-769-2727

❂ FAMILY PLANNING & ABORTIONS ❂

833.

African American Life Alliance of Maryland
4467 Old Branch Ave
Temple Hills Maryland 20748-1854
301-249-1153

Anti-abortion organization.

❂ FASHION INDUSTRY ❂

834.

African American Weddings
718-655-3489
718-655-3489—Fax

Adaeze Agu, Owner and Designer
Wedding consultations, including groom, traditional or contemporary African-American
weddings. Custom design and make outfits.
Jewelry. By appointment only.
1994

835.

Black Ethnic Hair Stylist
Phoenix Arizona 85012
602-285-5534

836.

J. M. Products Company
2501 State St
Little Rock Arkansas 72206
501-371-0040

Ernest Joshua, Chairman; Michael Joshua,
President

837.

African Fashions, Gifts & Crafts
2229 San Pablo Ave
Berkeley California 94702-1829
510-843-2821

838.

W.O.C. Products Inc.
17145 S Margay Ave
Carson California 90746
213-636-5033

Frank Davie, President

839.

Kizure Professional Products
1950 N Central
Compton California 90222
310-604-0032

Jerry White, President
Manufactures cosmetics and hair care products designed especially for women of color.

840.

Hightime Products Inc.
1605 W 14th St
Long Beach California 90813
310-436-4842

H. R. Phillips, President

841.

African Clothing by Sade
3209 W 17th St
Los Angeles California 90000
213-737-2557

842.

Ethnic Appeal
408 Canoe Court
Redwood Shores California 94065
415-654-0961

Offers multicultural products created by people of color for people of color. Collection includes products chosen to reinforce positive self-images.

843.

African Eye Inc.
2134 Wisconsin Ave, NW
Washington DC 20007
202-625-2552

844.

Black Fashion Museum
2007 Vermont Ave, NW
Washington DC 20001-4029
202-667-0744

845.

African Fashions
3033 NW 79th St
Miami Florida 33010
305-835-6255

846.

Black Models Network
3850 NE Miami Ct
Miami Florida 33137-3636
305-571-9224

847.

Afro Centric Network
576 Lee St, SW
Atlanta Georgia 30310-1928
404-756-0200

Andega Silas
Sells Afrocentric clothing wholesale nationwide.

848.

Bronner Bros.
903 Martin Luther King Jr. Dr
Atlanta Georgia 30314
404-577-4323

Bernard Bronner Sr., President

849.

McBride Research Laboratories Inc.
2500 Park Central Blvd, Suite A-6
Decatur Georgia 30035
404-981-8722

Cornell McBride Sr., President
Manufactures cosmetics and hair care products for women of color.

850.

AFAM Concepts, Inc.
1736 S Michigan Ave
Chicago Illinois 60616
312-939-6377

Al Washington, President

851.

Afro-centric Fashions Men's & Women's Clothing
Chicago Illinois 60617
312-978-7412

852.

Alaion Products Co.
P.O. Box 19606
Chicago Illinois 60619
312-978-0980

Mary Brooks, General Manager

853.

American Health and Beauty Aids Institute
401 N Michigan Ave, 24th Floor
Chicago Illinois 60611
312-644-6610
312-527-6658—Fax

Frank Davie, Chairman; Geri Duncan Jones, Executive Director
AHBAI has established itself as the authority in the ethnic health and beauty aids (HBA) industry. A national organization representing the leading manufacturers of beauty products, AHBAI promotes the image of the category, fosters communication between members and industry partners: contributes to economic development of black communities.
1981

854.

Luster Products Inc.
1625 S Michigan Ave
Chicago Illinois 60616
312-431-1150

Jory Luster, President

855.

Soft Sheen Products Inc.
1000 E 87th St
Chicago Illinois 60619
312-978-0700

Edward G. Gardner, Chairman; Gary Gardner, President

856.

Negro League Baseball Apparel
P.O. Box 25
Brentwood Maryland 20722
800-255-2289

Free catalog.

857.

African American Fashion
29 Roxbury St
Roxbury Massachusetts 02119-1720
617-445-4484

858.

A. W. Curtis Laboratories
46 Seldon Ave
Detroit Michigan 48201
313-833-6797

Dr. Austin W. Curtis, President
Produces a line of cosmetics for women of color.

859.

Afro World Hair Company
7276 Natural Bridge Rd
St. Louis Missouri 63121
314-389-5194

Russ B. Little Sr., President

860.

Oran's International
1234 S 13th St
Omaha Nebraska 68108
402-346-2929

Oran Belgrave, President

861.

African Fabric, Food & Cosmetics
140 Somerset St
Plainfield New Jersey 07060-4830
908-668-0260

862.

African Culture & Fashion House
581 Vanderbilt Ave
Brooklyn New York 11238-3014
718-638-5803 or 800-704-9345 or
718-638-5553

Manufactures African *addreel* (clothing), bags, shoes, jewelry, hair braids.

863.

African International Fashion Center
707 Fulton St
Brooklyn New York 11217-1213
718-243-1768

864.

African Shine Products
95 5th Ave
Brooklyn New York 11217-3201
718-857-9796

865.

African American International
110 W 40 St
New York New York 10018
212-398-1237

Sewing for wholesale and retail clothing.

866.

African Fabric and Clothing Wholesale
50 W 34th St
New York New York 10001
212-695-9144
212-268-4956—Fax

African clothing, T-shirts, hats, scarves, jewelry, and more.

867.

Black Fashion Museum
155-57 W 126th St
New York New York 10027
212-666-1320

The contributions of African Americans to fashion are celebrated here, from Elizabeth Keckley to contemporary designers.

868.

African American Apparel Inc.
2917 Central Ave
Charlotte North Carolina 28205-0444
704-563-8204

869.

Dudley Products Inc.
7856 McCloud Rd
Greensboro North Carolina 27409
910-668-3000

Joe L. Dudley Sr., President

870.

American Beauty Products Company
1623 E Apache
Tulsa Oklahoma 74106
918-428-2577

Chapman R. Cannon Jr., President

871.

Ashaway Products
1543 Junior Dr
Dallas Texas 75208
214-948-8837

Charles B. Johnson, President

872.

PRO—Line Corporation
2121 Panoramic Circle
Dallas Texas 75212
214-631-4247

Comer Cottrell, President

873.

BW Hair Enterprises Inc.
P.O. Box 111184
Houston Texas 77293
713-442-8562

Bernice Wadley, CEO

874.

Pride & Power Inc.
3901 0 St
Houston Texas 77021
713-748-2591

Rudolphus Johnson, President

❂ FILM & BROADCAST MEDIA ❂

875.

WAGG-AM
Booker T. Washington Broadcasting
Company
Birmingham Alabama 35201
205-328-5454
205-254-1833—Fax

A. G. Gaston, President; Kirkwood Balton,
General Manager
Religious format.

876.

WATV-AM
Birmingham Ebony Broadcasting Inc.
Birmingham Alabama 35208
205-780-4034

Shelley Stewart; Erskine R. Faush
Black, urban contemporary. ABC affiliate.

877.

WAYE-AM
1408 Third Ave
Birmingham Alabama 35208
205-786-9293

Bishop L. E. Willis, President; Cheryl
Thomas, General Manager
Religious.

878.

WEUP-AM
Broadcast One
2609 Jordan Lane
Huntsville Alabama 35806
205-837-9387
205-837-9404—Fax

Huntley Batts, President; Virginia Caples,
General Manager
Urban contemporary, religious. American
urban affiliate.

879.

WZZA-AM
1570 Woodmont Dr
Tuscumbia Alabama 35674
205-381-1862

Bob Carl Bailey, President & General
Manager
Black, religious, urban contemporary.

880.

WBIL-AM/FM
New World Communications
P.O. Box 666
Tuskegee Alabama 36083
205-727-2100
205-727-2969—Fax

George H. Clay, President
Urban contemporary.

881.

WSFU-FM
2402 E Clarence Ave
Tuskegee Alabama 36083
205-738-5101

Bishop L. E. Willis, President

882.

WAPZ-AM
J&W Promotions Inc.
Route 6, Box 43
Wetumpka Alabama 36092
205-567-2251

Johnny Roland, President; John Knight,
General Manager

883.

KSNE-FM
Highway 65
Marshall Arkansas 72650
501-448-5800
501-448-2425—Fax

Bishop L. E. Willis, President; Corey Horton,
General Manager
Country.

884.

KCLT-FM
307 Hwy, 49 Bypass
West Helena Arkansas 72390
501-572-9506

L.T. Simes II
Black, urban contemporary.

885.

KBLX-AM/FM
Inner City Broadcasting Corporation
601 Ashby Ave
Berkeley California 94710
510-848-7713
510-658-0894—Fax

Pierre M. Sutton, President
Adult contemporary.

886.

Tinsel Townsend
9830 Wilshire Blvd
Beverly Hills California 90212
310-288-4545

Robert Townsend, President
Motion pictures and television. Producers of
*Hollywood Shuffle, 5 Heartbeats, Meteor
Man, The Parenthood.*

887.

Verdon-Cedric Productions
9350 Wilshire Blvd, Suite 310
Beverly Hills California 90212
213-274-7253

Sidney Poitier, President
Motion picture and television production
company.

888.

Arsenio Hall Communications
c/o Sony Entertainment
Culver City California 90232
310-280-6833

Arsenio Hall, President

Motion pictures, television, syndication, special interest video.

889.

Black & White Productions
Sony Pictures Plaza
Culver City California 90232
310-280-5204
310-280-2062—Fax

Jasmine Guy, President
Motion pictures, television.

890.

Lenox-Greene Films
Columbia Studios
10202 West Washington
Culver City California 90232
213-280-8239

Dennis Greene, President

891.

New Deal Productions
Tri-Star 15
10202 West Washington
Culver City California 90232
310-280-7700

John Singleton, President
Motion pictures, television, music videos, interactive multimedia.

892.

Minority Media Services Inc.
69 Rockford Ave
Daly City California 94015-4725
415-992-4001

893.

KRGO-FM
Frontier Communications Inc.
P.O. Box 129
Fowler California 93625
209-834-5337

Dr. Carlton Goodlett, President; Woodie Miller, General Manager
Talk radio.

894.

Masai Films
6922 Hollywood Blvd, Suite 401
Hollywood California 90028
213-466-5451

Fritz Goode, President

895.

Whoop Inc.
5555 Melrose Ave, Wilder Building, Suite 114
Hollywood California 90038
213-956-5673

Whoopi Goldberg, President

896.

African Network Television
8510 S Broadway
Los Angeles California 90003-3335
213-752-1100

897.

Black Movie Channel
6362 Hollywood Blvd
Los Angeles California 90028-6330
213-469-9485

898.

Communications Bridge Institute
1968 W Adams Blvd
Los Angeles California 90018
213-766-9815

Brock Peters, President

899.

De Rasse Entertainment Inc.
5750 Wilshire Blvd, Suite 610
Los Angeles California 90036
213-965-2580
213-965-2598—Fax

Suzanne De Rasse, CEO

900.

Future Agency
4311 Wilshire Blvd, Suite 314
Los Angeles California 90010
310-388-9602

Sonny Porter, President

901.

Juice
3600 Wilshire Blvd, Suite 832
Los Angeles California 90010
213-384-9811

J. Melvin Muse, President

902.

KGFJ-AM
East-West Broadcasting Inc.
Los Angeles California 90019
213-930-9090
213-930-9056—Fax

William Shearer, President
Oldies.

903.

KILH-FM
Taxi Productions Inc.
3847 S Crenshaw Blvd
Los Angeles California 90008
213-299-5960

Stevland Morris, President; Karen Slade,
General Manager

904.

Logo Entertainment
11601 Wilshire Blvd, 21st Floor
Los Angeles California 90025
213-276-6700
213-445-1191—Fax

Louis Gossett Jr., President
Motion pictures, television, documentaries,
syndication, features direct to video.

905.

Reuben Cannon Productions
1640 S Sepulveda, 4th Floor
Los Angeles California 90025
213-575-1257

Reuben Cannon, President

906.

Underdog Films
1396 S Orange Dr
Los Angeles California 90019
213-936-3111
213-936-9421—Fax

Carl Craig, President
Motion pictures, television, and music videos. Producers of *Hollywood Shuffle, House Party 3, Snoop Doggy Dog.*

907.

United Image Entertainment
1640 S Sepulveda Blvd, Suite 311
Los Angeles California 90025
310-479-1640
310-479-4843—Fax

Tim Reid, President
Motion picture and television production company responsible for *Race for Freedom: The Underground Railroad* and *Out of Sync.*

908.

2 Tuff-E-Nuff Productions Inc.
7677 Oakport St, #1030
Oakland California 94621
415-635-7496
415-632-9798—Fax

Toni McElroy-Granberry, President & CEO

909.

Bust It Productions
80 Swan Way, Suite 130
Oakland California 94621
510-569-8475

Louis K. Burrell, President

910.

KDIA-AM
384 Embarcadero, W
Oakland California 94607
510-251-1400
510-633-0414—Fax

Priscilla Watts, General Manager
Urban contemporary.

911.

Yaga Productions Inc.
P.O. Box 609
Pacific Palisades California 90272
310-454-3643
310-454-3703—Fax

Bill Duke, President

912.

KMAX-FM
3844 E Foothill Blvd
Pasadena California 91107
213-681-2486

N. John Douglas, President

913.

KWWN-FM
Douglas Broadcasting Inc.
Placerville California 95567
916-621-0921

N. John Douglas, President; Len Allen, General Manager

914.

KFOX-FM
KFOX Radio Inc.
Redondo Beach California 90277
310-374-9796
310-318-2578—Fax

B.J. Howell, President; Tom McCulloch,
General Manager
Talk radio.

915.

KEST-AM
Douglas Broadcasting Inc.
San Francisco California 94103
415-626-5585
415-978-5380—Fax

N. John Douglas, President; Allen Schultz,
General Manager
Foreign language/ethnic, talk, New Age.

916.

KPOO-FM
Poor Peoples Radio
San Francisco California 94101
415-346-5373

Terry Collins, President; Joe Randolph,
General Manager

917.

KNTV-TV
Granite Broadcasting
San Jose California 95110
408-286-1111
408-295-5461—Fax

W. Don Cornell, President; Stewart Park,
General Manager
VHF. ABC affiliate.

918.

Enleyetning Concepts Inc.
1223 Wilshire Blvd, Suite 141
Santa Monica California 90403
310-821-4677
310-821-4996—Fax

919.

Longridge
15250 Ventura Blvd, Suite 800
Sherman Oaks California 91403
818-783-6251

Robert Guillaume, President
Television production company.

920.

Kolbeco
11112 Ventura Blvd
Studio City California 91604
818-753-4330
818-753-5109—Fax

Robert Johnson & Marc Kolbe, Presidents

921.

Midwest Group Inc.
23460 Hatteras
Woodland Hills California 91367
818-704-5568

Barry Hankerson, President; Flo Allen,
President

922.

WKND-AM
Hartcom Inc.
Windsor Connecticut 06095
203-688-6221
203-688-0711—Fax

Marion Thornton-Anderson, General Manager
Urban contemporary.

923.

Black Entertainment Television
1899 9th St, NE
Washington DC 20018
202-608-2300 or 818-566-9948
818-566-1655—Fax

Robert Johnson, President
Television.

924.

Black Entertainment Television (BET)
1232 31st St, NW
Washington DC 20007
202-337-5260

Robert L. Johnson, President

925.

Black Film Review
2025 I St, NW
Washington DC 20006-1902
202-466-2753

926.

**National Association of Black-Owned
Broadcasters**
1730 M St, NE, #412
Washington DC 20036
202-463-8970

927.

On the Potomac Productions Inc.
1221 11th St, NW
Washington DC 20001
202-898-0899
202-898-1498—Fax

Thomas A. Hart Jr., President

928.

WHMM-TV
Howard University
2600 4th St, NW
Washington DC 20059
202-806-3200

Ed Jones, General Manager

929.

WHUR-FM
Howard University
Washington DC 20059
202-806-3500

James Watkins, General Manager

930.

WKYS-FM
Albimar Communications Inc.
Washington DC 20016
202-686-9300
202-686-2028—Fax

Skip Finley, President & General Manager
Urban contemporary.

931.

WMMJ-FM
Almic Broadcasting Company
400 H St, NW
Washington DC 20002
202-675-4800

Cathy Hughes, President; J.J. Starr, General Manager, WOL; Tom Gauger, General Manager, WMMJ
Black. ABC affiliate.

932.

WOL-AM
Almic Broadcasting Company
400 H St, NW
Washington DC 20002
202-675-4800

Cathy Hughes, President; J.J. Starr, General Manager, WOL; Tom Gauger, General Manager, WMMJ
Black. ABC affiliate.

933.

WYCB-AM
National Press Building
Washington DC 20045
202-737-6400

Howard Sanders, President; Karen Jackson, General Manager
Adult contemporary, gospel. American Urban affiliate.

934.

WRBD-AM
Sunao Broadcast Company Inc.
4431 Rock Island Rd
Ft. Lauderdale Florida 33319
305-731-4800

John Ruffin Jr., President & General Manager

935.

WBSF-TV 43
Black Star Communications
4450-L Enterprise Court
Melbourne Florida 32935
407-254-4343
407-242-0863—Fax

John Oxendine, President; Ed Parker, General Manager
UHF.

936.

WPUL-AM
2598 S Nova Rd
S Daytona Beach Florida 32121
904-767-1131
904-254-7510—Fax

Charles Cherry, Chairman
Jazz, oldies. American Urban affiliate.

937.

WRXB-AM
1700 34th St S
St. Petersburg Florida 33711
813-864-1515

Jake E. Danzey, President

938.

WTVT—Channel 13
P.O. Box 31113
Tampa Florida 33631-3113
813-876-1313
813-875-8329—Fax

Clarence V. McKee, President
VHF. CBS affiliate.

939.

WJIZ-FM
Silver Star Communications
P.O. Box 5226
Albany Georgia 31706
912-432-7447
912-439-7239—Fax

Dr. John Robert E. Lee, President
Urban contemporary. American Urban
affiliate.

940.

WXAG-AM
Common Share Stock
Athens Georgia 30605
404-549-1470

Larry Blount, President
Urban contemporary, gospel. American
Urban affiliate.

941.

African Media Services
300 Peachtree St, NE
Atlanta Georgia 30308-3210
404-577-7250

942.

Black Family Television Network
52 Walton St, NW
Atlanta Georgia 30303-2326
404-577-9444

943.

Black Media
2258 Cascade Rd, SW
Atlanta Georgia 30311-2825
404-756-9658

944.

Geechee Girls Production Inc.
c/o Moore Little Inc.
Atlanta Georgia 30309
404-872-5115

Angela Moore, Publicist; Julie Dash, President

945.

WIGO-AM
Brunson Broadcasting of Georgia 1526
Howell Mill Rd
Atlanta Georgia 30318
404-352-3943

Dorothy Brunson, President
Black, oldies.

946.

WFXA-FM
Davis Broadcasting Company Inc.
P.O. Box 1584
Augusta Georgia 30903
803-279-2330
803-279-8149—Fax

Gregory A. Davis, President; Bill Jaeger, General Manager
News/talk. American Urban affiliate.

947.

WRDW-AM/FM
Val-Tel Inc.
1480 Eisenhower Dr
Augusta Georgia 30904
404-722-9797

Henry Brigham, President
Urban contemporary. NBC, American Urban affiliate.

948.

WTHB-AM
Davis Broadcasting Company Inc.
P.O. Box 1584
Augusta Georgia 30903
803-279-2330
803-279-8149—Fax

Gregory A. Davis, President; Bill Jaeger, General Manager
News/talk. American Urban affiliate.

949.

DDL Entertainment Inc.
332 Westwood Place, Suite 7, P.O. Box 50374
Austeel Georgia 30001
404-732-0986
404-593-3960—Fax

Darryl D. Lassiter, President

950.

WFXE-FM
Davis Broadcasting Inc.
P.O. Box 1100
Columbus Georgia 31994
706-576-3565
706-576-3683—Fax

Gregory A. Davis, President
Urban contemporary. ABC affiliate.

951.

WOKS-AM
Davis Broadcasting Inc.
P.O. Box 1998
Columbus Georgia 31994
706-576-3565
706-576-3683—Fax

Gregory A. Davis, President
Black. American Urban affiliate.

952.

WFAV-FM
P.O. Box 5766
Cordele Georgia 31015
912-273-1404

Dr. John Robert E. Lee, President; Fred Suttles, General Manager

953.

WMJM-AM
P.O. Box 5766
Cordele Georgia 31015
912-273-1404

Dr. John Robert E. Lee, President; Fred Suttles, General Manager

954.

Paragon
2527 Park Central Blvd
Decatur Georgia 30035
404-322-9181

Lou Walker
Motion picture production, public relations, management consulting, miscellaneous publishing.

955.

WTJH-AM
Willis Broadcasting
2120 Dodson Dr
East Point Georgia 30344
404-549-1470
404-346-0647—Fax

Bishop L. E. Willis, President; Valencia Williams, General Manager
Religious.

956.

WFXM-FM
Davis Broadcasting Inc.
Macon Georgia 31201
912-742-2505
912-742-8299—Fax

Gregory A. Davis, President; William Chatman, General Manager
Urban contemporary. American Urban affiliate.

957.

WGXA-TV 24
Russell Rowe Communications
P.O. Box 340
Macon Georgia 31297
912-745-2424

Herman J. Russell, President

958.

WIBB-FM
Davis Broadcasting Inc.
Macon Georgia 31201
912-742-2505
912-742-8299—Fax

Gregory A. Davis, President; William Chatman, General Manager
Urban contemporary. American Urban affiliate.

959.

WBCP-AM
WBCP Inc.
Champaign Illinois 62706
217-359-1580

J. W. Pirtle

960.

African-American Images
1909 W 95th St
Chicago Illinois 60643
312-445-0322
312-445-9844—Fax

Dr. Jawanza Kunjufu, CEO; Rita Kunjufu, Executive Director
African-American Images is a full-service communications company that offers a book-

store, gift shop, video, publishing, curriculum materials, and tutorial services for children.

961.

Harpo Inc.
110 N Carpenter St
Chicago Illinois 60607
312-633-T000
312-633-1111—Fax

Oprah Winfrey, Chairman/CEO; Jeffrey Jacobs, President/COO
Motion pictures and television; produces *The Oprah Winfrey Show.*

962.

Internetwork Ltd.
505 N Lake Shore Dr, Suite 3204
Chicago Illinois 60611
312-527-9781

963.

Johnson Communications Inc.
820 S Michigan Ave
Chicago Illinois 60605
312-322-9200

John H. Johnson, Chairman/CEO; Linda Johnson Rice, President/COO

964.

Minorities in Cable and New Technologies
1900 E 87th St
Chicago Illinois 60617
(312) 721-7500

Will Horton, Founder/Executive Director

Goals are to educate and inform minorities about the widening world of cable and new technologies; to enhance the recruitment, placement, and networking of minorities in these industries; to aid in the promotion of cable and new technologies as a vehicle for creative community and individual expression; and to create a forum for minority individuals to communicate and share ideas and experiences germane to minority interests.

965.

Paradise Group Video Products
1737 S Michigan Ave, Suite 1N
Chicago Illinois 60616
312-427-4011

Carolyn Sartor, President

966.

Third Wave Productions Inc.
30 E Huron, Suite 5304
Chicago Illinois 60611
312-649-1164
312-649-1383—Fax

967.

Tribune Central City, Productions
One E Erie, Suite 540
Chicago Illinois 60611
312-664-5900
312-664-5894—Fax

Don Jackson, President

968.

WJPC-AM/FM
820 S Michigan Ave
Chicago Illinois 60605
312-322-9400

John H. Johnson, President
Urban contemporary. American Urban affiliate.

969.

WVON-AM
Midway Broadcasting Corporation
Chicago Illinois 60623
312-247-6200

Wesley W. South, President & General
Manager

970.

WEEK-TV
Granite Broadcasting Inc.
East Peoria Illinois 61617
309-698-2525

W. Don Cornwell

971.

WESL-AM
149 S 8th St
East St. Louis Illinois 62201
618-271-1490

Bishop L. E. Willis, President
Gospel. American Urban affiliate.

972.

WBEE-AM
Mariner Broadcasters Inc.
Harvey Illinois 60426
708-331-7840
708-333-2560—Fax

Charles R. Sherrell, President
Jazz, blues.

973.

WLTH-AM
Inter Urban Broadcasting
Gary Indiana 46409
219-884-1370
219-980-0483—Fax

Lorenza Butler, Chairman/CEO
News/talk, sports. NBC, CNN affiliate.

974.

WWCA-AM
Willis Broadcasting
Gary Indiana 46402
219-886-9171

Bishop L. E. Willis, President
Religious.

975.

WFBM-TV 11
4625 N Keystone Ave
Indianapolis Indiana 46205
317-254-1511

Lee Jackson, President

976.

KBBG-FM
Afro-American Community Broadcasting
Waterloo Iowa 50703
319-234-1441

Jimmie Porter, Founder & President

977.

KTPK-FM
Shawnee Broadcasting, Inc.
Topeka Kansas 66611
913-267-2300
913-267-5875—Fax

Dr. Marvin Wilson, President
Country. ABC affiliate.

978.

WLOU-AM
Johnson Communications
Louisville Kentucky 40208
502-636-3535
502-637-7943—Fax

John H. Johnson, CEO
Black, urban contemporary. American Urban
affiliate.

979.

KTRY-AM/FM
North Delta Broadcasting
Bastrop Louisiana 71220
318-381-3656

Henry Cotton
Black. American Urban affiliate.

980.

KQLZ-FM
City Wide Broadcasting Corporation
Baton Rouge Louisiana 70806
504-926-1106

Peter Moncrief, President

981.

WXOK-AM
Winnfield Life Broadcasting
P.O. Box 66475
Baton Rouge Louisiana 70896
504-927-7060
504-928-1606—Fax

Ben D. Johnson, President; Matt Horton,
General Manager
Black, news. ABC affiliate.

982.

KBCE-FM
Trinity Broadcasting
Boyce Louisiana 71409
318-793-2923
318-793-8888—Fax

Gus E. Lewis, President
Urban contemporary. American Urban
affiliate.

983.

KJCB-AM
Jackson & Company
Lafayette Louisiana 70501
318-223-4262

Joshua Jackson, President
Urban contemporary. ABC affiliate.

984.

WBOK-AM
Willis Broadcasting Company
New Orleans Louisiana 70119
504-943-4600
504-944-4662—Fax

Bishop L. E. Willis, President
Religious.

985.

WCCL-TV 49
Crescent City Communications
New Orleans Louisiana 70117
504-945-4949

Barbara LaMont, President
UHF.

986.

WNOL-TV Fox 38
Quincy Jones Broadcasting Inc.
New Orleans Louisiana 70112-28262
504-525-3838
504-569-0908—Fax

Quincy Jones, President
UHF. Fox.

987.

WYLD-AM/FM
InterUrban Broadcasting of New Orleans
Inc.
2228 Gravier
New Orleans Louisiana 70119
504-822-1945
504-826-7723—Fax

Thomas P. Lewis, Chairman; James J.
Hutchinson, General Partner; Penny Brazile,
Vice President/General Manager
Gospel. ABC affiliate.

988.

WVII-TV
Seaway Communications
Bangor Maine 04401
207-945-6457
207-942-0511—Fax

Dr. James Buckner, President; Barbara Cyr,
General Manager
VHF. ABC affiliate.

989.

Career Communications Group
729 E Pratt St, Suite 504
Baltimore Maryland 21202
410-244-7101
410-752-1837—Fax

Tyrone D. Taborne, President & CEO
The country's largest minority-owned media
services company, producing information
about education and careers for black and
Hispanic professionals.

990.

WEBB-AM
Brunson Broadcasting Corp.
3000 Druid Park Dr
Baltimore Maryland 21216
301-367-9322

Dorothy Brunson, President

991.

WWIN-AM/FM
200 S President St
Baltimore Maryland 21202
410-332-8200
410-752-2252—Fax

Ragan Henry, President
Religious, gospel. ABC affiliate.

992.

WILD-AM
90 Warren St
Boston Massachusetts 02119
617-427-2222

Bernadine Foster Nash, President
Urban contemporary. ABC affiliate.

993.

Black Awareness in Television
13217 Livernois St
Detroit Michigan 48238
313-931-3427

994.

WGPR-FM
WGPR Inc.
3146 E Jefferson St
Detroit Michigan 48207
313-259-8862

George Matthews, President
Urban contemporary. American Urban affiliate.

995.

WGPR-TV
WGPR Inc.
3146 E Jefferson St
Detroit Michigan 48207
313-259-8862

George Matthews, President
Urban contemporary. American Urban affiliate.

996.

WJZZ-FM
Bell Broadcasting Corp.
Detroit Michigan 48202
313-871-0591
313-871-8770—Fax

Mary Bell, President; Robert Bass, General Manager
Jazz.

997.

WDZZ-FM
1 E First St, Suite 1830
Flint Michigan 48502
810-767-0130

Scott Williams, Programming Director
Urban contemporary.

998.

WCXT-FM
Waters Broadcasting Corp.
220 Polk Rd
Hart Michigan 49420
616-873-7129
616-873-7120—Fax

Nancy Waters, President; Ruth Nalley, General Manager
Adult contemporary.

999.

WCHB-AM
Bell Broadcasting Corp.
32790 Henry Ruff Rd
Inkster Michigan 48141
313-278-1440

Mary Bell, President; Dr. Wendell Cox, General Manager
Gospel. American Urban, Westwood One affiliate.

1000.

WKWM-AM
P.O. Box 828
Kentwood Michigan 49508
616-676-1237
616-676-2329—Fax

Richard Culpepper
Urban contemporary. American Urban affiliate.

1001.

WXLA-AM
Diamond Broadcasters Inc.
5920 S Logan
Lansing Michigan 48911
517-393-6397

Helena DeBose, President; Robert Williams, General Manager

1002.

WKSG-FM
850 Stephenson Hwy
Troy Michigan 48083
313-589-7900

Ragan Henry, President

1003.

KBIR-TV
Granite Broadcasting Corp.
230 E Superior St
Duluth Minnesota 55802
218-727-8484

W. Don Cornwell

1004.

WBFL-AM
1000 Blue Meadow Rd
Bay St. Louis Mississippi 39520
601-467-5243

William E. Thrasher Jr., President/CEO

1005.

WBSL-AM
1000 Blue Meadow Rd
Bay St. Louis Mississippi 39520
601-467-5243
601-467-5295—Fax

William E. Thrasher Jr., President/CEO
Country.

1006.

WACR-AM/FM
T8.W Communications
Columbus Mississippi 39701
601-328-1050
601-328-1054—Fax

Bennie Turner, President; Charles Penson,
General Manager
Religious.

1007.

WBAD-FM
Interchange Communications
7 Oaks Rd
Greenville Mississippi 38701
601-355-9265

William Jackson, President

1008.

WESY-AM
Interchange Communications
7 Oaks Rd
Greenville Mississippi 38701
601-355-9265

William Jackson, President

1009.

WLBT-TV 3 Inc.
715 S Jefferson St
Jackson Mississippi 39202
601-948-3333
601-960-4435—Fax

Frank E. Melton, President
VHF. NBC affiliate.

1010.

WLTD-FM
J. Scott Communications
Route 1, Box 288 E
Lexington Mississippi 39095
601-843-1103

Philip Scott, General Manager

1011.

KCXL-AM
Kansas City Communications, Inc.
Kansas City Missouri 64110
816-333-2583

Elbert Anderson, President

1012.

KPRS-AM/FM
KPRS Broadcasting Corporation
Kansas City Missouri 64137
816-763-2040
816-966-1055—Fax

Michael Carter, President
Gospel (AM) and urban contemporary (FM).

1013.

KIRL-AM
3713 Hwy 94 N
St. Charles Missouri 63301
314-946-6600

William White, General Manager
Jazz, religious.

1014.

KATZ-AM/FM
InterUrban Broadcasting
1139 Olive St
St. Louis Missouri 63101
314-241-6000
314-241-7498—Fax

Thomas P. Lewis, Chairman; Charles Richardson, General Manager
Blues, black.

1015.

WHSL-TV 46
Roberts Broadcasting Inc.
St. Louis Missouri 53113
314-367-4600

Michael Roberts, Chairman

1016.

WNIR-AM
Sound Radio Inc.
Hillside New Jersey 07205
908-688-5000

Daniel Robinson, Chairman; Elizabeth Satchell, General Manager

1017.

Harambee Productions
P.O. Box 25578
Newark New Jersey 07101
201-642-0132
201-754-8859—Fax

Wayne Slappy, President

1018.

WCMC-AM
3010 New Jersey Ave
Wildwood New Jersey 08260
609-522-1416
609-729-9264—Fax

Ragan Henry, President
Big band. SMN affiliate.

1019.

WZXL-FM
3010 New Jersey Ave
Wildwood New Jersey 08260
609-522-1416
609-729-9264—Fax

Ragan Henry, President
Big band. SMN affiliate.

1020.

40 Acres & a Mule Filmworks Inc.
124 DeKalb Ave
Brooklyn New York 11217
718-624-3703
718-624-2008—Fax

Spike Lee, President
Motion picture company whose movies include *Crooklyn, Mo' Better Blues, Do the Right Thing, Jungle Fever, Malcolm X.*

1021.

WKBW-TV
Queen City Broadcasting
Buffalo New York 14202
716-845-6100

Bruce Llewellyn, Chairman
VHF. ABC affiliate.

1022.

WUFO-AM
Sheridan Broadcasting
89 LaSalle Ave
Buffalo New York 14214
716-834-1080

Lenore Williams, President; Jesse Key, General Manager

1023.

WEIF-FM
P.O. Box 86
Clayville New York 13322
315-839-5375

Christopher & Clara Crocco

1024.

African Heritage Movie Network
238 Greenwich St
New York New York 10007
212-227-0494
212-227-8391—Fax

Frank Mercado Valdez, President
Syndicates and produces black movies.

1025.

American Urban Radio Network (AURN)
463 Seventh Ave
New York New York 10018
212-714-1000
212-714-2349—Fax

Sydney Small & Rodney R. Davenport, Co-Chairmen
AURN was formed as a result of a partnership consummated between the nation's two black-owned network radio companies—Sheridan Broadcasting Networks and National Black Network. It covers almost 92 percent of all black Americans each week through over 600 radio station affiliates.

1026.

Black Filmmakers Foundation
375 Greenwich St, #600
New York New York 10013
212-941-3944

1027.

Black & White Television
73 Spring St, Suite 504
New York New York 10012
212-777-2300
212-966-5475—Fax

Joel Hinman & Paris Barclay, Presidents
Television, music videos, commercials.

1028.

Block & Chip Inc.
353 W 56th St, Suite 10F
New York New York 10019
212-489-6570

Melvin Van Peebles, President

1029.

Classic Concepts
444 W 35th St
New York New York 10001
212-268-3849
212-268-3879—Fax

Lionel C. Martin, President

1030.

Drop Squad Pictures
594 Broadway, Suite 405
New York New York 10012
212-925-9303
212-431-8093—Fax

Butch Robinson & David Johnson, Co-Owners

1031.

Eddie Murphy Productions Inc. & Eddie Murphy Television Enterprises Inc.
152 W 57 St, 47th Floor
New York New York 10019
212-399-9900 or 213-956-4545
212-399-0555 or 213-956-8602—Fax

Eddie Murphy, Chairman & President
Motion pictures include *Boomerang, Beverly Hills Cop II*.

1032.

Hudlin Bros. Inc.
Tribeca Film Center
New York New York 10013
212-941-4004

Warrington Hudlin, President

1033.

Minority Pictures
205 Lexington Ave
New York New York 10016-6022
212-679-3226

1034.

Minority Telecommunications Corporation
166 Madison Ave
New York New York 10016
212-686-6850

Roy Thompson, President
The parent company of the Black Radio Network.

1035.

Think Again Productions Ltd.
54 E 3rd St, Suite 10
New York New York 10003
212-674-5928

Darnell Martin, President

1036.

Time Shift
7 Bond St
New York New York 10012
212-533-4945

David Daniel, President

1037.

WBLS-FM
Inner City Broadcasting
New York New York 10017
212-661-3344
212-922-9460—Fax

Pierre M. Sutton, President
Black, news/talk. ABC affiliate.

1038.

WLIB-AM
Inner City Broadcasting
New York New York 10017
212-661-3344
212-922-9460—Fax

Pierre M. Sutton, President
Black, news/talk. ABC affiliate.

1039.

Yeah Inc.
353 W 56th St, Suite 10F
New York New York 10019
212-489-6570

Melvin Van Peebles, President

1040.

WGNY-AM/FM
P.O. Box 2307
Newburgh New York 12550
914-561-2131

Sharon MacWilliams, President & General
Manager
Adult contemporary.

1041.

WDKX-FM
Monroe County Broadcasting
683 E Main St
Rochester New York 14605
716-262-2050
716-262-2626—Fax

Andrew Langston, Chairman
Urban contemporary.

1042.

WWRL-AM
NBN Broadcasting Inc.
41-30 58th St
Woodside New York 11377
718-335-1600

Sydney Small, Chairman

1043.

Black Conscience Syndication
21 Bedford St
Wyandanch New York 11798
516-491-7774

Clyde Davis, President
Buys 1,000 features annually. Uses material
for magazines, newspapers, radio, and television.

1044.

WVOE-AM
Ebony Enterprises Inc.
Route 3, P.O. Box 328
Chadbourn North Carolina 28431
919-654-5621

Willie J. Walls, President
Urban contemporary, black, gospel.

1045.

WGSP-AM
4209 F. Stuart Andrew
Charlotte North Carolina 28217
704-527-9477

Bishop L. E. Willis, President; Laurence
Means, General Manager
Gospel.

1046.

WSRC-AM
3202 Guess Rd
Durham North Carolina 27705
919-477-7999

Bishop L. E. Willis, President
Religious.

1047.

WBXB-FM
P.O. Box 0
Edenton North Carolina 27932
919-482-3200
919-482-5290—Fax

Bishop L. E. Willis, President; Dave Eldridge,
General Manager
Gospel.

1048.

WOKN-FM
Eastern Regional Broadcasting
P.O. Box 804
Goldsboro North Carolina 27533
919-734-4213

Bob Swinson, President

1049.

WLLE-AM
522 E Main St, P.O. Box 26836
Raleigh North Carolina 27611
919-833-3874

Henry & Prentice Jr. Monroe
Black.

1050.

WQOK-FM
8601 Six Forks Rd, Suite 609
Raleigh North Carolina 27615
919-848-9736

Ragan Henry, President

1051.

WRSV-FM
Radio Station WEED Inc.
P.O. Box 2666
Rocky Mount North Carolina 27802
919-442-9776

Charles O. Johnson, President
Black, adult contemporary. ABC affiliate.

1052.

WTNC-AM
Willis Broadcasting
725 Salem St
Thomasville North Carolina 27360
919-472-0790

Bishop L. E. Willis, President
Gospel, religious. American Urban affiliate.

1053.

WBMS-AM
Brunson Broadcasting of North Carolina
Wilmington North Carolina 28403
919-763-4633

Dorothy Brunson, President; Tony Gray,
General Manager
Urban contemporary. MBS affiliate.

1054.

WGTM-AM
P.O. Box 3837, Hwy 42
Wilson North Carolina 27893
919-243-2188

Bishop L. E. Willis, President; Thomas Ward,
General Manager
Gospel.

1055.

WAAA-AM
Evans Broadcasting Corp.
P.O. Box 11197
4950 Indiana
Winston-Salem North Carolina 27106
919-767-0430

Mutter D. Evans, President
Black.

1056.

WSMX-AM
P.O. Box 16049
Winston-Salem North Carolina 27115
919-761-1545

Willie J. Walls, President; Al Martin, General
Manager
Religious, gospel.

1057.

WAKR-AM
1735 S Hawkins
Akron Ohio 44320
216-869-9800

Ragan Henry, President
Adult contemporary. Moody affiliate.

1058.

WONE-FM
1735 S Hawkins
Akron Ohio 44320
216-869-9800

Ragan Henry, President
Adult contemporary. Moody affiliate.

1059.

WCIN-AM
ACI Inc.
106 Glenwood Ave
Cincinnati Ohio 45217
513-281-7180

Ernest L. James, President
Classical, oldies, black. Unistar affiliate.

1060.

WIZF-FM
InterUrban Broadcasting of Cincinnati Inc.
7030 Reading
Cincinnati Ohio 45237
513-351-5900

Thomas Lewis, Chairman

1061.

WCKX-FM
LDH Communications of Ohio
510 E Mound St
Columbus Ohio 43215
614-464-0020

Jack Harris, President

1062.

WXLE-FM
1150 Morse Rd
Columbus Ohio 43229
614-436-1040

Ragan Henry, President

1063.

WDAO-AM
Johnson Communications Inc.
4309 W 3rd St
Dayton Ohio 45417
513-263-9326

Jim Johnson, General Manager
Urban contemporary.

1064.

WJTB-AM
Taylor Broadcasting Company
105 Lake Ave
Elyria Ohio 44035
216-327-1844

James Taylor, President
Urban contemporary.

1065.

WHAT-AM
KBT Communications Inc.
2471 N 54th St
Philadelphia Pennsylvania 19131
215-581-5161
215-581-5185—Fax

Cody Anderson, President
Black, talk, jazz.

1066.

WURD-AM
5301 Tacony St, Building #10
Philadelphia Pennsylvania 19137
215-533-8900
215-533-5679—Fax

Bishop L. E. Willis, President; Celestine
Willis, General Manager
Gospel. MBS affiliate.

1067.

WAMO-AM/FM
Sheridan Broadcasting Corporation
960 Penn Ave, Suite 200
Pittsburgh Pennsylvania 15222
412-471-2181

Ronald Davenport, Chairman/President;
Anthony Rizza, General Manager
Urban contemporary, middle-of-the-road.
American Urban affiliate.

1068.

WRAW-AM
1265 Perkiomen Ave
Reading Pennsylvania 19602
215-376-7173

Ragan Henry, President
Middle-of-the-road, contemporary hits/top
40. CBS affiliate.

1069.

WRFY-FM
1265 Perkiomen Ave
Reading Pennsylvania 19602
215-376-7173

Ragan Henry, President
Middle-of-the-road, contemporary hits/top 40. CBS affiliate.

1070.

WVGB-AM
Vivian Broadcasting
Beaufort South Carolina 29902
803-524-4700

Vivian M. Galloway, President; Donzella Hendrix, General Manager
Adult contemporary, religious, oldies.

1071.

WTGH-AM
Midland Communications Inc.
1303 State St
Cayce South Carolina 29033
803-796-9533

Isaac Heyward, President; Raleigh Williams, General Manager
Religious. American Urban affiliate.

1072.

WBUB-FM
Lowcountry Media Inc.
4995 LaCross Rd, Suite 1600
Charleston South Carolina 29418
803-566-1100

Ronald E. Hoover, President; Charles A. Barton, General Manager

1073.

WPAL-AM
WPAL Inc.
1717 Wappo Rd
Charleston South Carolina 29417
803-763-6330

William Saunders, President
Black, gospel.

1074.

WQIZ-AM
Lowcountry Media Inc.
4995 LaCross Rd, Suite 1600
Charleston South Carolina 29418
803-566-1100

Ronald E. Hoover, President; Charles A. Barton, General Manager

1075.

WWWZ-FM
Wicks Communications of Charleston, South Carolina
2045 Spaulding Dr
Charleston South Carolina 29417
803-308-9300

Cliff Fletcher, President

1076.

WWPD-FM
American Legion Rd
Marion South Carolina 29571
803-423-5971

Bishop L. E. Willis, President
Country, religious.

1077.

WNCI-AM
314 Rembert Dennis Blvd
Moncks Corner South Carolina 29461
803-761-6010

Clary Butler, President; Dorothy Mitchell, General Manager

1078.

WBOL-AM
Shaw Broadcasting Company
P.O. Box 191
Bolivar Tennessee 38008
901-658-3690

Johnny Shaw & Opal Shaw
Gospel.

1079.

WFKX-FM
425 E Chester
Jackson Tennessee 38301
901-427-9616

James Wolf, President/General Manager

1080.

WDIA-AM
112 Union Ave
Memphis Tennessee 38103
901-529-4300

Ragan Henry, President; Rick Caffey, General Manager
Black, adult contemporary, news/talk. CBS affiliate.

1081.

WHRK-FM
112 Union Ave
Memphis Tennessee 38103
901-529-4300

Ragan Henry, President; Rick Caffey, General Manager
Black, adult contemporary, news/talk. CBS affiliate.

1082.

WLOK-AM
Gilliam Communications Inc.
P.O. Box 69
Memphis Tennessee 38101
901-527-9565

Art Gilliam, President; H. A. Gilliam Jr., General Manager
Black. American Urban and NBC affiliate.

1083.

WMDB-AM
Babb Broadcasting Company
3051 Stokers Lane
Nashville Tennessee 37218
615-255-2876
615-255-2876—Fax

Morgan Babb, President; Michael Babb, General Manager
Black, religious.

1084.

WQQK-FM
Phoenix of Nashville Inc.
1320 Brick Church Pike
Nashville Tennessee 37207
615-227-1470

Samuel Howard, President; Jay Childress, General Manager

1085.

WVOL-AM
Phoenix of Nashville Inc.
1320 Brick Church Pike
Nashville Tennessee 37207
615-227-1470

Samuel Howard, President; Jay Childress, General Manager

1086.

KAZI-FM
KAZI Community Radio
4700 Loyola Lane, #014
Austin Texas 78723
512-926-0275

Thomas Ybarra, General Manager

1087.

KWWJ-AM
4638 Decker Dr
Baytown Texas 77520
713-424-7000

Darrell E. Martin, General Manager
Religious. American Urban affiliate.

1088.

KIUS-AM
Forward Press Ministries
4925 Fanett Rd
Beaumont Texas 77720
409-842-1979

Albert Armstrong

1089.

KGLF-FM
1227 Hwy 332, Suite 9
Clute Texas 77531
409-265-5453

Ragan Henry, President

1090.

WPTA-TV
Granite Broadcasting Inc.
3401 Butler Rd
Fort Wayne Texas 46808
219-483-0584

W. Don Cornwell, President; Barbara Wigham, General Manager

1091.

KCOH-AM
KCOH Inc.
Houston Texas 77004
713-522-1001

Mike Petrizzio, General Manager

1092.

KSAQ-FM
Inner City Broadcasting Corporation
San Antonio Texas 78205
512-271-9600

Pierre M. Sutton, President; Charles Andrews,
General Manager
Rock, contemporary hit/top 40. ABC, CBS,
NBC, Westwood One affiliate.

1093.

KSJL-AM
Inner City Broadcasting Corporation
San Antonio Texas 78205
512-271-9600

Pierre M. Sutton, President; Charles
Andrews, General Manager
Rock, contemporary hit/top 40. ABC, CBS,
NBC, Westwood One affiliate.

1094.

K101-FM
29801 I-45 North
Spring Texas 77381
713-367-0107

Ragan Henry, President

1095.

WPAK-AM
Great Sports Inc.
P.O. Box 4940
Farmville Virginia 23901
804-392-8114

Rick Darnell
Urban contemporary

1096.

WARR-AM
553 Michigan Dr
Hampton Virginia 23669-3899

Eleanor Reynolds, General Manager

1097.

WTJZ-AM
553 Michigan Dr
Hampton Virginia 23669
804-723-3391

Eric Reynolds, President

1098.

WIMG-FM
Circuit Broadcasting Company
1204 Graveline Rd
Hattiesburg Virginia 39401
601-544-1941

Vernon C. Floyd, President

1099.

WORV-AM
Circuit Broadcasting Company
1204 Graveline Rd
Hattiesburg Virginia 39401
601-544-1941

Vernon C. Floyd, President

1100.

WBSK-AM/FM
645 Church St, Suite 400
Norfolk Virginia 23510
804-627-5800

Ragan Henry, President

1101.

WSVV-FM
P.O. Box 1878
Petersburg Virginia 23805

Dr. Walton M. Belle, President

1102.

WFTH-AM
Willis Broadcasting
Richmond Virginia 23227
804-262-8624

Bishop L. E. Willis, President; Jack Johnson, General Manager
Gospel.

1103.

WREJ-AM
6001 Wilkinson Rd
Richmond Virginia 23227
804-264-1540

Dr. Walton M. Belle, President; Herbert Pollard, General Manager
News, talk. BRN and USA affiliate.

1104.

Minority Media Network Agency
1108 S 11th St
Tacoma Washington 98424
206-926-0410

1105.

KUJ-AM
KUJ Ltd. Partnership
Route 5, P.O. Box 513
Walla Walla Washington 99362

509-529-8000
509-525-3727—Fax

Patrick Prout, President; Dianne Sapp, General Manager
Oldies. Unistar affiliate.

1106.

WLUM-FM
All Pro Broadcasting Company
Milwaukee Wisconsin 53216
414-444-1290
414-444-1409—Fax

William D. Davis, President
Adult contemporary, black, contemporary hit/top 40. CBS and SMN affiliates.

1107.

WMVP-AM
All Pro Broadcasting Company
Milwaukee Wisconsin 53216
414-444-1290
414-444-1409—Fax

William D. Davis, President
Adult contemporary, black, contemporary hit/top 40. CBS and SMN affiliates.

1108.

WNOV-AM
Courier Communications
Milwaukee Wisconsin 53206
414-449-9668
414-449-9945—Fax

Jerrel W. Jones, President
Black. American Urban affiliate.

1109.

WVMP-AM
All Pro Broadcasting Company
Milwaukee Wisconsin 53216
414-444-1290

1110.

WJJA-TV 49
TV-49, Inc.
4311 E Oakwood Rd
Oak Creek Wisconsin 53154
414-764-4953

Joel Kinlow Sr., President

1111.

WAEO-TV
Seaway Communications
Rhinelander Wisconsin 54501
715-369-4700

Dr. James Buckner, Chairman; Marie
Platteter, General Manager

❂ FINANCE & INVESTMENTS ❂

1112.

**National Association of Investment
Companies**
1111 14th St, NW, Suite 700
Washington DC 20005
202-289-4336
202-289-4329—Fax

JoAnn H. Price, President
This is an alliance of small business investment companies licensed by the Small
Business Administration to provide capital to
businesses owned by socially or economically
disadvantaged Americans. Total private capital investment in the MESBIC program
exceeds $100 million.

1113.

Black Financial Empowerment
3400 Enon Rd
Atlanta Georgia 30349-1234
404-349-6522

1114.

Ariel Mutual Funds
Ariel Capital Management Inc.
307 N Michigan Ave
Chicago Illinois 60601
800-BY-ARIEL

1115.

Minority Investment Development
15 Westminster St
Providence Rhode Island 02903-2424
401-351-2999

1116.

African Financiers Fund Association
6125 Airport Fwy
Fort Worth Texas 76117-5358
817-834-5584

❄ FOOD & RESTAURANTS ❄

1117.

African Marketplace
2560 W 54th St
Los Angeles California 90000
213-299-6124

1118.

African Market The
San Jose California 95135
408-270-5882

1119.

A Taste of Heritage Foundation
627 Glyrita Circle
Reistertown Maryland 21136
410-526-3655

Chef Joseph Randall, Founder

Raises scholarship funds for minority students
going into the culinary profession.

1120.

African Food & Peace Foundation
75 Croton St
Wellesley Massachusetts 02181-3134
617-237-2382

1121.

African Fabric, Food & Cosmetics
140 Somerset St
Plainfield New Jersey 07060-4830
908-668-0260

1122.

African & American Restaurant
1987 Dr. Martin Luther King Jr. Blvd
Bronx New York 10453-4404
718-731-8595

1123.

African Food Products
5 E 167th St
Bronx New York 10452-8224
718-293-5668

1124.

African & American Market
643 Rogers Ave
Brooklyn New York 11226-1501
718-282-0711

Specializes in groceries, foodstuffs, and spices
for African, Caribbean, and African-American
cuisine.

1125.

Africa Restaurant
247 W 116 St
New York New York 10019
212-666-9400

1126.

African Caribbean American Food Mart
640 Flatbush Ave
Brooklyn New York 11225-5606
718-693-0261

Market specializing in fruits, vegetables, and
other foods from Africa and the Caribbean.

1127.

African International Market Inc.
234 4th Ave
Brooklyn New York 11215-1060
718-260-9078

Specializing in food and other groceries from
Africa.

1128.

African Market Center
2718 Frederick Douglass Blvd
New York New York 10030-3706
212-283-2419

African groceries.

1129.

Sylvia's Restaurant
328 Malcolm X Blvd
New York New York 10027
212-996-0660

1130.

African American Cafe
244 Warburton Ave
Yonkers New York 10701-2226
914-963-9746

1131.

African Roots Restaurant
1011 NW 16th Ave
Portland Oregon 97209-2303
503-226-1258

❂ FOOTBALL ❂

1132.

Pro Football Hall of Fame
2121 George Halas Dr
Canton Ohio 44708
216-456-8207

Contains tributes to the greatest pro football athletes ever to play the game, most of whom are of African-American descent. Also chronicles the struggle of black football players before they were readily accepted into the league.

❂ FRATERNITIES & SORORITIES ❂

1133.

Iota Phi Lambda Sorority Inc.
P.O. Box 11609
Montgomery Alabama 36111-0609
205-284-0203

Dorethea Hornbuckle, President
Iota Phi Lambda seeks to unite qualified business and professional women for the following purposes: promoting increased interest in business education among young women in high school and college; encouraging the development of leadership skills through educational opportunities; and establishing and promoting civic and social service activities for youths and adults.

1134.

Chi Eta Phi Sorority Inc.
3029 13th St, NW
Washington DC 20009
202-232-3858

Mary Helen Morris, Supreme Basileus
Chi Eta Phi Sorority Inc. is an international professional nursing organization. This organization has over 6,000 members in 60 graduate and 18 undergraduate chapters located throughout the United States, the District of Columbia, St. Thomas, Virgin Islands, and the Republic of Liberia in West Africa. An international sanitation project is underway in Malawi, Africa, with AFRICARE.

1135.

Delta Sigma Theta Sorority Inc.
1701 New Hampshire Ave, NW
Washington DC 20009
202-986-2400
202-986-2513—Fax

Dr. Bertha M. Roddey, President; Roseline McKinney, Executive Director
This public service organization was founded at Howard University. Today the organization has over 185,000 members in 850-plus chapters in the United States, Germany, Haiti, Liberia, Bermuda, the Bahamas, the Virgin Islands, the Republic of Korea, and Japan. Delta Sigma Theta encourages academic excellence through scholarship assistance and endowments for distinguished professorships.

1136.

Omega Psi Phi Fraternity Inc.
2714 Georgia Ave, NW
Washington DC 20001
202-667-7158
202-667-7159—Fax

Founded at Howard University, this social action and leadership development fraternity provides service to mankind through its mandated programs. Its 661 chapters organized into 11 districts and international chapters focus on achievements, youth, and community uplift. The fraternity also offers scholarships to individuals for undergraduate and graduate educations.

1137.

Phi Beta Sigma Fraternity Inc.
National Headquarters
145 Kennedy St, NW
Washington DC 20011
202-726-5434
202-882-1681—Fax

Carter D. Womack, National President
This 90,000-member collegiate, business, and professional fraternity was founded at Howard University. The goals of the fraternity are twofold: to promote brotherhood and community service and to pursue scholastic excellence. Specific program support is given to education, African-American business development, and social welfare projects. Members of the fraternity assisted in the founding of Zeta Phi Beta Sorority.

1138.

Zeta Phi Beta Sorority Inc.
1734 New Hampshire Ave, NW
Washington DC 20009
202-387-3103

Jylla Moore-Foster, National President
Established on the campus of Howard University, the purpose of the sorority is to promote education by encouraging the highest standards of academic achievement; by supporting worthwhile college and community projects; by providing training scholarships, counseling services, and grants; and by implementing improvement in every area of community life through programs and volunteer services.

1139.

Alpha Kappa Alpha Sorority Inc.
5656 S Stony Island Ave
Chicago Illinois 60637
312-684-1282

Mary Shy Scott, National President; Alison Harris Alexander, Executive Director
Over 121,000 college-educated women hold membership in this service-oriented organization founded in 1908 at Howard University. The more than 820 chapters are located throughout the United States, Germany, the Virgin Islands, West Africa, the Bahamas, and Seoul, Korea. The organization is dedicated to improve social, economic, health, and cultural conditions of African-American communities around the world.

1140.

National Sorority of Phi Delta Kappa Inc.
8233 S King Dr
Chicago Illinois 60619
312-783-7379

Marguerite McClelland, Supreme Basileus; Edna McClain Murray, Executive Director
The National Sorority of Phi Delta Kappa Inc. is a professional organization of educators for the purpose of promoting educational advancement. It was chartered in New Jersey. We now have a membership of over 5,000 members emphasizing education working with youths and giving over $50,000 in scholarships.

1141.

Sigma Gamma Rho Sorority Inc.
8800 S Stony Island Ave
Chicago Illinois 60617
312-873-9000
312-731-9642—Fax

Corine J. Green, Grand Basileus
The only African-American sorority founded on the campus of Butler University. "Greater Service, Greater Progress" is its slogan, and the thrust of its national programs is aimed at community service, academic achievement, and the cultural and educational development of youth. Over 72,000 members found in over 400 chapters in the United States, Bermuda, the Virgin Islands, and the Bahamas. Publishes *The Aurora*.

1142.

National Pan-Hellenic Council Inc.
Suite 30, IMU
Bloomington Indiana 47405
812-855-8820
812-855-5381—Fax

Carter D. Womack, National President; Dr. Michael V. W. Gordon, Exec. Dir.
The NC is the coordinating agency for eight historically black international fraternities and sororities, comprising nearly 1.5 million members. Its major purpose is to help advance and strengthen the black fraternity and sorority movement. The NC assists in the establishment and development of undergraduate councils at American colleges and universities and graduate councils in locations throughout the world.

1143.

Alpha Phi Alpha Fraternity Inc.
2313 St. Paul St
Baltimore Maryland 21218-5234
(410) 554-0054

Milton C. Davis, Esq., General President; James B. Blanton III, Executive Director Founded at Cornell University, the fraternity sponsors voter registration drives, provides scholarships for undergraduate and high school students, and is involved in various educational and community projects. It has more than 650 college and alumni chapters throughout the Caribbean, Europe, Asia, and Africa.

1144.

Alpha Pi Chi Sorority
P.O. Box 255
Kensington Maryland 20895

Magoline Carney, President
A service sorority of business and professional women. Conducts fund-raising activities for civil rights organizations and black charities and sponsors a charity showcase for young amateurs.

1145.

Groove Phi Groove Social Fellowship Inc.
P.O. Box 8337
Silver Springs Maryland 20907-8337

Victor Henderson, First National Vice President
This fraternity was founded at Morgan State College. Its primary mission is to promote academic awareness and good ethical stan-

dards among college and graduate level men. In keeping with the mission, Groove actively supports various positive community services, including UNCF, the Center for Missing and Exploited Children, youth mentoring, tutorial and career development programs.

1146.

Eta Phi Beta Sorority Inc.
16815 James Couzens
Detroit Michigan 43235
313-862-0600

Mildred Harpole, Esq., National President A national business and professional women's organization founded in Detroit. Its purpose is to sponsor, foster and promote programs and activities designed to improve the standards of business and professional women.

1147.

Kappa Alpha Psi Fraternity Inc.
2322-24 N Broad St
Philadelphia Pennsylvania 19132-4590
215-228-7184
215-228-7181—Fax

Atty. Robert L. Harris, Grand Polemarch; Samuel C. Hamilton, Grand Keeper of Records and Exchequer
The fraternity's national service program, "Guide Right," mandates each of its approximately 338 undergraduate chapters and 337 graduate chapters to administer service and tutorial aid to serving the elderly.

❂ GAY & LESBIAN ORGANIZATIONS ❂

1148.

AMASSI (African-American AIDS Support Services & Survival Institute)
3419 Martin Luther King Jr. Way
Oakland California 94609
510-601-9066

This human and social services center was designed to provide an affirming and safe place of care and support for diverse sexual communities with emphasis on people of color, primarily African American. Not only an AIDS organization, AMASSI focuses on the importance of self-love, empowerment, and affirmation, both in AIDS prevention and healing and in living in a racist/homophobic society in general.

1149.

Coalition of Black Lesbians & Gays
1517 U St, NW
Washington DC 20009
202-265-7117

1150.

Committee of Black Gay Men
P.O. Box 7209
Chicago Illinois 60680
312-248-5188

Larry Baker, Executive Secretary

Purposes are to disseminate information concerning problems that affect black members of the gay community and to provide services through outreach programs and networking with similar organizations. Attempts to gain recognition and understanding within the church in the black community and offers social services such as food pantries, counseling, support groups, and education.

1151.

African American Gay & Lesbian Inc.
604 W Lexington St
Baltimore Maryland 21201
410-625-8830

An organization serving black gays and lesbians.

1152.

Dallas Gay Black Coalition
3920 Cedar Springs
Dallas Texas 75201

⚙ GENEALOGIES & FAMILY HISTORIES ⚙

1153.

Afro-American Historical & Genealogical Society
P.O. Box 73806
Washington DC 20056

Sylvia Cooke Martin, President
Encourages scholarly research in African-American history and genealogy as it relates to American history and culture. Collects, maintains, and preserves relevant material, which the society makes available for research and publication.

1154.

Afro American Genealogical & Historical Society of Chicago
740 E 56th Place
Chicago Illinois 60637
312-947-0600

An organization concerned with the roots of black Americans. Publishes the *AAGS Newsletter*.

1155.

Tarrant County Black Historical & Genealogical Society
1020 E Humbolt
Fort Worth Texas 76104

Don Williams, President

❂ GOVERNMENT AGENCIES & OFFICIALS, NATIONAL & INTERNATIONAL ❂

1156.

World Conference of Mayors Inc.
101 Fonville St
Tuskegee Alabama 36083
205-727-0065
205-727-4820—Fax

Hon. Johnny Ford, Founder & President Emeritus
Established at the National Conference of Mayors Inc.'s 10th annual convention, WCM is a worldwide network composed of mayors from cities in Africa, the Near & Far East, the Caribbean and the U.S.A., whose objectives are to stimulate trust, trade, technology transfer, tourism and twin-city relationships among its members.
1984

1157.

Black American Response to the African Community
127 N Madison Ave, Suite 400
Pasadena California 91102
818-584-0303

Frank E. Wilson, President

1158.

Black Advocates in State Service
1529 I St
Sacramento California 95814-2016
916-456-2277

1159.

African American Labor Center
1925 K St, NW
Washington DC 20006
202-778-4600

Works with trade unions in continental Africa to build sound national labor organizations that will be of lasting value to workers and the community, institutions that contribute to the economic and social development of their countries. Workers' education and leadership training, vocational training, cooperatives and credit unions, union medical and social service programs, administrative support, and communication and information.

1160.

Africare
1601 Connecticut Ave, NW
Washington DC 20009
202-462-3614

Dedicated to improving the quality of life in rural Africa through the development of water resources, increased food production, the delivery of health services, and the provision of emergency refugee assistance.

1161.

Association of Black American Ambassadors
440 R St
Washington DC 20001

1162.

Conference of Minority Public Administrators
1120 G St, NW
Washington DC 20005
202-398-7878

1163.

Congressional Black Associations
U.S. House of Representatives, Room 1979
Washington DC 20515
202-225-5865

1164.

Congressional Black Caucus
2244 Rayburn House Office Building
Washington DC 20515
202-225-3436
202-225-4160—Fax

Donald Payne, Chairman; Earl Hilliard, Vice Chairman; Barbara Rose Collins, Vice Chairman
This organization, composed of the African-American members of the U.S. Senate and House of Representatives, serves as a catalyst for the economic, educational, and social concerns of African-Americans and other underrepresented Americans. The organization draws up a yearly legislative agenda outlining the major policies it supports: full employment, national health care, education, minority business assistance, urban redevelopment, welfare reform, and international relations.
1970

1165.

Congressional Black Caucus Foundation Inc.
1004 Pennsylvania Ave, SE
Washington DC 20003
202-675-6730

Hon. Alan Wheat (D-MO), President; LeBaron Taylor, Vice President
The Congressional Black Caucus Foundation Inc. was incorporated to support and conduct nonpartisan research, technical assistance, training, education, and informational activities, and programs to advance political participation by blacks and other minority group members. The foundation sponsors a Graduate Internship Program and conducts the Congressional Black Caucus Legislative Weekend, an annual event bringing black leaders to Washington to investigate issues of mutual concern.
1976

1166.

Embassy of Algeria
2137 Wyoming Ave, NW
Washington DC 20008
202-265-2800

His Excellency Yazki Zerhouni, Ambassador

1167.

Embassy of Angola
1899 L St, NW, Suite 400
Washington DC 20036
202-785-1156

His Excellency Antonio Esparanza, Ambassador

1168.

Embassy of Antigua & Barbuda
3400 International Dr, NW
Washington DC 20008
202-362-5122

His Excellency Patrick Lewis, Ambassador

1169.

Embassy of Barbados
2144 Wyoming Ave, NW
Washington DC 20008
202-939-9200
202-332-7467—Fax

His Excellency Dr. Rudi Valentine Webster, Ambassador

1170.

Embassy of Benin
2737 Cathedral Ave, NW
Washington DC 20008
202-232-6656

His Excellency Candide Ahouansou, Ambassador

1171.

Embassy of Botswana
Suite 7M, 3400 International Dr, NW
Washington DC 20008
202-244-4990

His Excellency Archibald M. Mogwe, Ambassador

1172.

Embassy of Burkina Faso
2340 Massachusetts Ave, NW
Washington DC 20008
202-332-5577

His Excellency Thomas Yara Kambou, Charge d'Affaires

1173.

Embassy of Burundi
2233 Wisconsin Ave, NW
Washington DC 20007
202-342-2574

His Excellency Severin Npahomvukiye, Ambassador

1174.

Embassy of Cameroon
2349 Massachusetts Ave, NW
Washington DC 20008
202-265-8790

His Excellency Paul Pondi, Ambassador

1175.

Embassy of Cape Verde
3415 Massachusetts Ave, NW
Washington DC 20007
202-965-6820

His Excellency Carlos Alberto Santos Silva, Ambassador

1176.

Embassy of Central African Republic
1618 22nd St, NW
Washington DC 20008
202-483-7800

His Excellency Jean-Pierre Sohahong-Kombet, Ambassador

1177.

Embassy of Chad
2002 R St, NW
Washington DC 20009
202-462-4009

His Excellency Laournaye Koumbairia, Ambassador

1178.

Embassy of Cote D'Ivoire
2424 Massachusetts Ave, NW
Washington DC 20008
202-797-0300

His Excellency Louis Koumoue, Ambassador

1179.

Embassy of Djibouti
1156 15th St, NW, Suite 515
Washington DC 20005
202-331-0270

His Excellency Robel Olhaye, Ambassador

1180.

Embassy of Egypt
2310 Decatur Place, NW
Washington DC 20008
202-232-5400

His Excellency Ahmed Maher El Sayed, Ambassador

1181.

Embassy of Ethiopia
2134 Kalorama Rd, NW
Washington DC 20008
202-234-2281

His Excellency Berhana Gebre-Christos, Ambassador

1182.

Embassy of Gambia
1155 15th St, NW, Suite 1000
Washington DC 20005
202-785-1399

His Excellency Ousman Ahmadou Sallah, Ambassador

1183.

Embassy of Ghana
3512 International Dr, NW
Washington DC 20008
202-686-4520

His Excellency Ekwow Spio-Garbrah, Ambassador

1184.

Embassy of Grenada
1701 New Hampshire Ave, NW
Washington DC 20009
202-265-2561

His Excellency Harold Denneth Modeste, Ambassador

1185.

Embassy of Guinea
2112 Leroy Place, NW
Washington DC 20008
202-483-9420

His Excellency Elhadj Barry, Ambassador

1186.

Embassy of Guinea-Bissau
918 16th St, NW, Mezzanine Suite
Washington DC 20006
202-872-4222

His Excellency Alfredo Lopes Cabral, Ambassador

1187.

Embassy of Haiti
2311 Massachusetts Ave, NW
Washington DC 20008
202-332-4090

Harold Joseph, Charge d'Affaires

1188.

Embassy of Jamaica
1850 K St, NW
Washington DC 20006
202-452-0660

His Excellency Richard Bernal, Ambassador

1189.

Embassy of Kenya
2249 R St, NW
Washington DC 20008
202-387-6101

His Excellency Denis D. Afande, Ambassador

1190.

Embassy of Lesotho
2511 Massachusetts Ave, NW
Washington DC 20008
202-797-5533

His Excellency Dr. Eunice M. Bulane, Ambassador

1191.

Embassy of Liberia
5201 16th St, NW
Washington DC 20011
202-723-0437

Konah K. Blackett, Charge d'Affaires

1192.

Embassy of Libya
3000 K St, NW, Suite 600
Washington DC 20007
202-338-6500

1193.

Embassy of Madagascar
2374 Massachusetts Ave, NW
Washington DC 20008
202-265-5525

His Excellency Pierrot Rajaonarivelo, Ambassador

1194.

Embassy of Malawi
2408 Massachusetts Ave, NW
Washington DC 20008
202-797-1007

His Excellency W. Chokani, Ambassador

1195.

Embassy of Mali
2130 R St, NW
Washington DC 20008
202-332-2249

His Excellency Siragatou Ibrahim, Cisse

1196.

Embassy of Mauritania
2129 Leroy Place, NW, Suite 441
Washington DC 20008
202-232-5700

His Excellency Mohamed Fali Ainina, Ambassador

1197.

Embassy of Mauritius
4301 Connecticut Ave, NW
Washington DC 20008
202-244-1491

His Excellency Anund Neewoor, Ambassador

1198.

Embassy of Morocco
1601 21st St, NW
Washington DC 20009
202-462-7979—Fax

His Excellency Mohamed Benaissa, Ambassador

1199.

Embassy of Mozambique
1900 M St, NW, Suite 570
Washington DC 20036
202-293-7146

1200.

Embassy of Namibia
1605 New Hampshire Ave, NW
Washington DC 20009
202-293-7146

His Excellency Tuliameni Kalomoh, Ambassador

1201.

Embassy of Niger
2204 R St, NW
Washington DC 20008
202-483-4224

His Excellency Amadou Seydou, Ambassador

1202.

Embassy of Nigeria
1333 16th St, NW
Washington DC 20036
202-986-8400

His Excellency Zubair Kazaure, Ambassador

1203.

Embassy of Rwanda
1714 New Hampshire Ave, NW
Washington DC 20009
202-232-2882

His Excellency Aloy Uwimana, Ambassador

1204.

Embassy of Senegal
2112 Wyoming Ave, NW
Washington DC 20008
202-234-0540

His Excellency Ibra Deguene Ka, Ambassador

1205.

Embassy of Sierra Leone
1701 19th St, NW
Washington DC 20009
202-939-9261

His Excellency Thomas Kargbo, Ambassador

1206.

Embassy of South Africa
3051 Massachusetts Ave, NW
Washington DC 20008
202-232-4400

His Excellency Harry Ranklin Sonn, Ambassador

1207.

Embassy of St. Lucia
2100 M St, NW
Washington DC 20037
202-463-7378

His Excellency Dr. Joseph Edsel Edmunds, Ambassador

1208.

Embassy of Sudan
2210 Massachusetts Ave, NW
Washington DC 20008
202-338-8565

His Excellency Ahmed Suliman, Ambassador

1209.

Embassy of Swaziland
3400 International Dr, NW
Washington DC 20008
202-362-6683

Her Excellency Mary M. Kanya, Ambassador

1210.

Embassy of Tanzania
2139 R St, NW
Washington DC 20008
202-939-6125

His Excellency Charles M. Nyirabu, Ambassador

1211.

Embassy of the Bahamas
2220 Massachusetts Ave, NW
Washington DC 20008
202-319-2660

His Excellency Timothy B. Richardson, Ambassador

1212.

Embassy of the Dominican Republic
1715 22nd St, NW
Washington DC 20008
202-332-6280

His Excellency Jose Ariza, Ambassador

1213.

Embassy of the Gabon
2034 20th St, NW
Washington DC 20009
202-797-1000

His Excellency Paul Boundoukou Latha, Ambassador

1214.

Embassy of Togo
2208 Massachusetts Ave, NW
Washington DC 20008
202-234-4212

His Excellency Edem F. Hegbe, Charge d'Affaires

1215.

Embassy of Trinidad & Tobago
1708 Massachusetts Ave, NW
Washington DC 20036
202-467-6490

His Excellency Angus Albert Khan, Ambassador

1216.

Embassy of Tunisia
1515 Massachusetts Ave, NW
Washington DC 20005
202-862-1850

His Excellency Ismail Khell Marengo, Ambassador

1217.

Embassy of Uganda
5909 16th St, NW
Washington DC 20011
202-726-7100

His Excellency Stephen Katenta-Apull, Ambassador

1218.

Embassy of Zaire
1800 New Hampshire Ave, NW
Washington DC 20009
202-234-7690

His Excellency Mukende Tombo R. Kabela, Charge d'Affaires

1219.

Embassy of Zambia
2419 Massachusetts Ave, NW
Washington DC 20008
202-265-9717

His Excellency Dunstan W. Kamana, Ambassador

1220.

Embassy of Zimbabwe
1608 New Hampshire Ave, NW
Washington DC 20009
202-332-7100

His Excellency Amos B.M. Midzi, Ambassador

1221.

National Forum for Black Public Administrators
777 North Capitol St, NE, #807
Washington DC 20002
202-408-9300

1222.

Transafrica Inc.
1744 R St, NW
Washington DC 20009
202-797-2301

Foreign policy lobbying organization for issues involving Africa and the Caribbean.

1223.

Embassy of Equatorial Guinea
c/o Permanent Mission of Equatorial Guinea
to the United Nations
57 Magnolia Ave
Mount Vernon New York 10553
914-667-6913

His Excellency Tastor Micha, Ambassador

1224.

African National Congress of South Africa
801 Second Ave
New York New York 10017-4706
212-838-3650

1225.

Embassy of Sao Tome & Principe
c/o Permanent Mission of Sao Tome &
Principe to the United Nations
122 E 42nd St, Room 1604
New York New York 10168
212-697-4211

1226.

Embassy of Seychelles
820 Second Ave, Suite 900F
New York New York 10017
212-687-9766

His Excellency Marc Michael Rogers Marengo, Ambassador

1227.

Minority Rights Group International
866 United Nations Plaza
New York New York 10017-1822
212-758-3201—Fax

1228.

African Human Rights Committee
1701 N Bryan St
Arlington Virginia 22201-4015
703-525-6989

1229.

Black Public Elected & Appointed Officials
101 Municipal Building
Seattle Washington 98104

❋ GOVERNMENT AGENCIES & OFFICIALS, STATE & LOCAL ❋

1230.

Alabama Legislative Black Caucus
11 Union St
Montgomery Alabama 36130
205-859-2234

1231.

Black American Political Association of California
2408 28th
Sacramento California 95815
916-737-1901

1232.

California Legislative Black Caucus
State Capitol, Rm 4040
Sacramento California 95814
916-445-7486

1233.

National Association of Black County Officials
440 1st St, NW, #500
Washington DC 20001
202-347-6953

1234.

National Black Caucus of Local Elected Officials
1301 Pennsylvania Ave, 6th Floor
Washington DC 20004
202-626-3120
202-626-3043—Fax

Wilbert Minter, President; Thomas McCloud, Director of the Center for Public Affairs
NBC-LEO is designed as a vehicle for African-American elected officials to accelerate broader acceptance of the goals and priorities important to minorities. It operates as an affiliate of the National League of Cities, and as an independent coalition concerned with the permanent interests of African Americans.
1970

1235.

National Black Caucus of State Legislators Inc.
602 Hall of the States Building
444 N Capitol St
Washington DC 20001
202-624-5457
202-737-1069—Fax

Sen. Regis F. Groff (Colorado), President; Charles Bremer, Executive Director
NBCSL represents a broad-based, nonpartisan political force with 450 members in 45 states and the U.S. Virgin Islands. The caucus offers a national network whereby lawmakers can exchange information, share expertise, foster interstate communication and cooperation, and ensure a strong cohesive voice for its constituency of over 26 million African Americans.
1977

1236.

Florida Caucus of Black State Legislators
14251 NW 41st Ave
Opa-Locka Florida 33054

1237.

Georgia Legislative Black Caucus
P.O. Box 38028
Atlanta Georgia 30334

1238.

National Conference of Black Mayors Inc.
1430 West Peachtree St, NW, Suite 700
Atlanta Georgia 30309
404-892-0127

Hon. Henry Espy, Mayor of Clarksdale, Mississippi, and President; Michelle D. Kourouma, Executive
With a membership of 355 African-American mayors, representing cities and towns ranging in population from less than 100 to 6 million, NCBM seeks to assist its members in solving numerous problems associated with municipal management, growth, and development. Incorporated as the Southern Conference of Black Mayors Inc., the organization has grown in size and services.
1974

1239.

Illinois Legislative Black Caucus
P.O. Box 641255
Chicago Illinois 60664

1240.

Indiana Black Legislative Caucus
Indiana State House
Indianapolis Indiana 46204
317-232-9646

Rep. William Crawford, Chairperson

1241.

Iowa Legislative Black Caucus
2500 Harding Rd, #4
Des Moines Iowa 50310
515-281-5129

1242.

Kansas Black Legislative Caucus
3736 Weaver Dr
Kansas City Kansas 66104

1243.

Louisiana Legislative Black Caucus
P.O. Box 44003
Baton Rouge Louisiana 70804
504-342-7342
504-342-3384—Fax

Sen. Diana E. Bajoie, Chairperson
To provide equal opportunities for all blacks,
to assist blacks in recognizing the need to
repeal, enact, or reenact laws affecting their
lives, to strengthen black economic development, and to intercede and bridge the gap
between government and blacks.
1977

1244.

Maryland Legislative Black Caucus
3518 Everest Dr
Temple Hills Maryland 20748
410-841-3328

1245.

Massachusetts Legislative Black Caucus
State House, Room 127
Boston Massachusetts 02133
617-722-2680

1246.

Black Caucus Foundation of Michigan
11000 W McNichols
Detroit Michigan 48200
313-863-3006

1247.

Michigan Legislative Black Caucus
State Capitol
Lansing Michigan 48913

1248.

Minneapolis Department of Civil Rights
239 City Hall
Minneapolis Minnesota 55415
612-673-3012

Mary Emma Hixson, Executive Director

1249.

Mississippi Legislative Black Caucus
735 Campbell St
Jackson Mississippi 39203

1250.

Missouri Legislative Black Caucus
House Post Office
Jefferson City Missouri 65101
314-751-6500

1251.

New Jersey Legislative Black Caucus
State House
Trenton New Jersey 08625
609-292-2121

1252.

Black & Puerto Rican Legislative Body
P.O. Box 30
Albany New York 12220
518-427-8363

1253.

North Carolina Legislative Black Caucus
Legislative Office Building, Room 522
Raleigh North Carolina 27603

1254.

Black Elected Democrats of Ohio
37 W Broad St, #430
Columbus Ohio 43215
614-341-6912

1255.

Oklahoma Legislative Black Caucus
417-A State Capitol
Oklahoma City Oklahoma 73105
405-521-2711

1256.

Rhode Island Caucus of Black State Legislators
1453 Broad St
Providence Rhode Island 02905
401-941-1660 or 401-272-0112

1257.

South Carolina Legislative Black Caucus
207 Solomon Blatt Building
Columbia South Carolina 29211
803-734-3041
803-734-8711—Fax

Sen. Maggie W. Glover, Chairperson
Serves the members of the Black Caucus and their constituents and the Corporate Roundtable. Legislative and advocacy body, which sponsors workshops on legislative issues and voting rights and related issues.

1258.

Tennessee Black Caucus of State Legislators
209 War Memorial Building
Nashville Tennessee 37219

1259.

Texas Legislative Black Caucus
P.O. Box 2910
Austin Texas 78768

1260.

Virginia Legislative Black Caucus
256 W Freemason St
Norfolk Virginia 23510

❂ HEALTH ADVOCACY GROUPS ❂

1261.

African American Donor Task Force
P.O. Box 51315
East Palo Alto California 94303-0721
415-322-9418

1262.

Minority Biomedical Research
1301 Avenida Cesar Chavez
Monterey Park California 91754-6001
213-265-0678

1263.

African Community Health & Social Services
1212 Broadway
Oakland California 94612-1841
510-839-7764

1264.

Bay Area Black Women's Health Project
P.O. Box 10529
Oakland California 94610
510-533-6923
510-532-0104—Fax

1265.

Black Americans Against Cancer Inc.
1614 X St
Sacramento California 95818-2334
916-446-9549

1266.

Association of Black Psychologists
P.O. Box 55999
Washington DC 20040
(202) 722-0808

Dennis E. Chestnut, Ph.D., President
Purposes are to enhance the psychological well-being of black people in America, to define mental health in consonance with newly established psychological concepts and standards, and to develop policies for local, state, and national decision-making bodies that have an impact on the health of the black community.

1267.

National Association of Health Services Executives
50 F St, NW, #1040
Washington DC 20001
202-628-3953

1268.

National Black Nurses' Association Inc.
1012 10th St, NW
Washington DC 20001
202-393-6870
202-347-3808—Fax

Linda Burnes Bolton, Ph.D., President
The association's philosophy is "to investigate, define and determine what the health care needs of African Americans are and to imple-

ment changes to make available to African Americans and other minorities health care commensurate to that of the larger society." 1971

1269.

African American Hospital Foundation
1635 Campbellton Rd, SW
Atlanta Georgia 30311-4009
404-755-2979

1270.

Minority Doctors Referrals
3480 Greenbriar Pkwy, SW
Atlanta Georgia 30331-3121
404-346-3627

1271.

Minority Health Professions Foundation
20 Executive Park Dr, NE
Atlanta Georgia 30329-2206
404-634-1993

1272.

National Black Women's Health Project
1237 Gordon St, SW
Atlanta Georgia 30310
404-753-0916

Byllye Y. Avery, Director
Encourages mutual and self-help activism among women to bring about a reduction in health care problems prevalent among black women such as high blood pressure, obesity, breast and cervical cancers, diabetes, kidney disease, arteriosclerosis, and teenage pregnancy and infant mortality.

1273.

Black Mental Health Alliance
2901 Druid Park Dr
Baltimore Maryland 21215-8104
410-523-6670

1274.

Black Womens Health Council Inc.
311 68th Pl
Capital Heights Maryland 20743-2108
301-808-0786

1275.

Black Psychologists
22250 Providence Dr
Southfield Michigan 48075-4825
810-552-0360

1276.

African Medical & Research Foundation Inc.
19 W 44th St, Rm 1708
New York New York 10036
212-768-2440
212-768-4230—Fax

Organization for development of health care in Africa. Fund-raising.

1277.

Minority Health Education Development
325 W 26th St
Erie Pennsylvania 16508-1701
814-453-6229

1278.

Minority Health Education System
218 E 11th St
Erie Pennsylvania 16503-1010
814-455-9931—Fax

❂ HOMELESSNESS ❂

1279.

Black History Tours
1721 W 85th St
Chicago Illinois 60620-4738
313-233-8907

1280.

Operation PUSH (People United to Serve Humanity)
930 E 50th St
Chicago Illinois 60615
312-373-3366

Jesse Jackson, Founder
An organization founded to promote human rights, especially black self-empowerment. Now has a year-round exhibit on the civil rights movement, life-size statues of African-American heroes, and a civil rights library and audio archives.
1971

1281.

African-American Women's Clergy Association
P.O. Box 1493
Washington DC 20013
202-797-7460

The Rev. Imagene Bigham Stewart, National Chairwoman
The association's 26 local affiliates operate the only African-American shelter for homeless families and satellite centers for battered men and battered women in the nation's capital.
1969

1282.

Minority Services Fair Housing Council of Suburban Philadelphia
Philadelphia Pennsylvania 19100
610-352-4075

❂ IMMIGRATION SERVICES ❂

1283.

African Refugee Center
6399 Wilshire Blvd
Los Angeles California 90048-5703
213-966-5537

1284.

African Visitors Centre The
1212 Broadway
Oakland California 94612-1841
510-238-5170

1285.

**African American Immigration
Services Inc.**
1424 Sheepshead Bay Rd
Brooklyn New York 11235-3814
718-743-5844

1286.

African Peoples Council Inc.
6 Maiden Ln, 6th Floor
New York New York 10038-4047
212-346-9750
212-346-9863—Fax

Immigrant services, including job readiness,
English language skills, voter registration, and
other social services.

1287.

**Minority and Nationalities Service
Center**
Philadelphia Pennsylvania 19092
215-893-8400

❂ INSURANCE ❂

1288.

**Booker T. Washington Insurance
Company**
1728 Third Ave N
Birmingham Alabama 35203
205-328-5454
205-251-6873—Fax

Louis J. Willie, Chairman, President/CEO

1289.

**Protective Industrial Insurance
Company of Alabama Inc.**
2300 11th Ave
North Birmingham Alabama 35234
205-323-5256
205-251-7614—Fax

Paul E. Harris, President & CEO

1290.

Golden State Mutual Life Insurance Company
1999 W Adams Blvd
Los Angeles California 90018
213-731-1131
213-733-0320—Fax

Larkin Teasley, President/CEO

1291.

Curtis Moring Insurance
3905 National Ave
San Diego California 92113
800-321-0677 or 619-262-7519
619-262-8459—Fax
e-mail: thinkcmi@sierra.net

CMI has been involved in insurance since 1963. In addition to writing personal lines and providing financial planning services, CMI also has an extensive background in the areas of mainstream commercial insurance and nonprofit, governmental, and specialty risks. CMI produces an on-line newsletter where guests can get instant auto insurance quotes by hyperlinking to CMI's *CMI Quick Quote Auto Insurance Application.*

1292.

Atlanta Life Insurance
100 Auburn Ave, NE
Atlanta Georgia 30312
404-659-2100

Jesse Hill Jr., Chairman/CEO
America's second largest African-American-owned insurance firm.

1293.

Pilgrim Health & Life Insurance Company
1143 Laney Walker Blvd
Augusta Georgia 30901
404-722-5517
404-724-6349—Fax

Jesse Hill Jr., Board Chairman/CEO

1294.

Chicago Metropolitan Assurance Company
4455 Martin Luther King Jr. Dr
Chicago Illinois 60653-3395
312-285-3030
312-285-0064—Fax

Josephine King, President/CEO

1295.

American Woodmen's Life Insurance Company
1021 N. 7th, #107
Kansas City Kansas 66101
913-371-6140

Lillie Anne Owens, President/CEO

1296.

Mammoth Life & Accident Insurance Company
608 W Muhammad Ali Blvd
Louisville Kentucky 40203
502-585-4137
502-581-1689—Fax

Edwin Chestnut Sr., President

1297.

Reliable Life Insurance Company
718 Jackson St
Monroe Louisiana 71201
318-387-1000

Joseph H. Miller Jr., Esq., President

1298.

Gertrude Geddes Willis Life Insurance Company
2128 Jackson Ave
New Orleans Louisiana 70113
504-522-2525

Joseph O. Misshore Jr., Board Chairman/ President

1299.

National Service Industrial Life Insurance Company
1716 N Claiborne Ave
New Orleans Louisiana 70116
504-943-6621
504-942-5076—Fax

Dr. Joan Rhodes Brown, President

1300.

Peoples Progressive Insurance Company
109 Harrison St
Rayville Louisiana 71269
318-325-6389

Marion Gundy Hill, President

1301.

Benevolent Life Insurance Company
1624 Milam St
Shreveport Louisiana 71103
318-425-1522

Granville L. Smith, President/CEO

1302.

Lighthouse Life Insurance Company
1544 Milam St
Shreveport Louisiana 71103
318-221-5292

Bunyan Jacobs Founder, President/CEO

1303.

Wright Mutual Insurance Company
2995 E General Motors Blvd
Detroit Michigan 48202
313-871-2112

Wardell C. Croft, FLMI Board Chairman/ CEO

1304.

Peoples Assured Family Life Insurance Company
886 Farish St
Jackson Mississippi 39202
601-969-3040
601-355-4707—Fax

James A. Stewart III, President

1305.

Unity Life Insurance Company
415 N Farish St
Jackson Mississippi 39202
601-948-3888 or 601-948-7224

Clarie Collins Harvey, Board Chairman

1306.

United Mutual Life Insurance Company
310 Lenox Ave
New York New York 10027
212-369-4200

Arthur R. Worrel, Executive Vice President

1307.

Golden Circle Life Insurance Company
Mutual Plaza
Durham North Carolina 27701-3616
919-682-9201
919-683-1694—Fax

Cynthia Rawls Bond, President

1308.

North Carolina Mutual Life Insurance Company
114–116 Parrish St (National Historic Site)
Durham North Carolina 27701
919-682-9201

Bert Collins, CPA, President & CEO
Durham was once the home of the wealthiest black businessmen in America. Among them was John Merrick, founder of this company, once the largest black-owned business in the country, and today still a formidable financial institution.

1309.

Universal Life Insurance Company
480 Linden Ave
Memphis Tennessee 38126
901-525-3641
901-528-8266—Fax

Gerald T. Howell, President/CEO

❂ LEGAL SERVICES ❂

1310.

Southern Poverty Law Center
400 Washington Ave
Montgomery Alabama 36104
205-264-0286

Joseph J. Levin, President

Seeks to protect and advance the legal and civil rights of poor people, regardless of race, through education, litigation, and subsequent court decisions. Strives to defeat injustices that keep poor people poor, including denial of representation in government, deprivation of municipal services, and discriminatory abuse of civil rights. Does not accept fees from clients.

1311.

Western Center on Law and Poverty
1709 W 8th St
Los Angeles California 90017
213-483-1491

Legal services resources for the war on poverty in Southern California.

1312.

Lawyer's Committee for Civil Rights under the Law
1400 I St, NW, Suite 400
Washington DC 20005
202-371-1212

1313.

Thomas F. Jones and Associates
The Candler Building
Atlanta Georgia 30303
404-659-6550
404-659-6373—Fax

Attorneys specializing in many areas of law.

1314.

Black Entertainment & Sports Lawyers Association
1 Elizabeth Ct
Oak Park Illinois 60302-2009
708-386-8338

1315.

NAACP Legal Defense and Education Fund Inc.
99 Hudson St, 16th Floor
New York New York 10021
212-310-9000

Julius L. Chambers, Director-Counsel

❂ MEN'S ORGANIZATIONS ❂

1316.

Black Man's Development Center
1703 W 4th St
Wilmington Delaware 19805-3547
302-429-0206

Community service organization specializing in providing housing for low- and no-income individuals. Exclusively charitable, nonprofit educational program.

1317.

Black Men Inc.
97 Broad St, SW
Atlanta Georgia 30303-3413
404-653-0994

1318.

One Hundred Black Men of America
127 Peachtree St, NE
Atlanta Georgia 30309
404-525-7111
404-523-3953—Fax

Philanthropic, nonprofit organization serving underprivileged African-American males and females scholastically and economically.

1319.

Black Men Inc.
2715 5th St
Detroit Michigan 48201-2515
313-964-4264

1320.

Black Men Inc.
105 E 22nd St
New York New York 10010
212-777-7070

This organization works to improve the life of blacks and other minorities in this country. Its efforts include achieving better housing, edu-

cation, and employment, and gaining power in the professions and government.

1321.

One Hundred Black Men
105 E 22nd St
New York New York 10010
212-777-7070

1322.

African American Men of Westchester
65 Lake St
White Plains New York 10604-2401
914-949-9463

1323.

Black Male Coalition of Greater Cincinnati
2904 Woodburn Ave
Cincinnati Ohio 45206-1414
513-751-2624

1324.

African American Fathers Association
17000 El Camino Real
Houston Texas 77058-2636
713-480-7159

❁ MUSEUMS, ART & GALLERIES ❁

1325.

Freedom Quilting Bee
Route 1, Box 43-A
Alberta Alabama 36720
205-573-2225

Inspired by the civil rights movement, this all-black women's cooperative is nationally recognized for the quality of their quilts, the designs of which are drawn from a 140-year-old tradition.
1966

1326.

African American–Caribbean Cultural Center
BankAtlantic Building
Fort Lauderdale Florida 33316
305-467-4056

Temporary exhibits of arts, crafts, and history of the diaspora.

1327.

Hammonds House
503 Peeples St, SW
Atlanta Georgia 30310
404-752-8730

Collections of paintings by prominent African-American artists, African sculpture, Haitian paintings, and contemporary works of local black and white artists.

1328.

Afro-American Historical Society of the Niagara Frontier
Erie County Public Library, Lafayette Sq
Buffalo New York 14203
716-856-7525

1329.

Karamu House
2355 E 89th St
Cleveland Ohio 44106-9990
216-795-7070

Taking its name from the Kiswahili word for "place of joyful gathering," this community center dates back over 75 years and fosters multicultural perspectives in the arts.
1915

1330.

Afro-American Historical and Cultural Museum
Seventh and Arch Sts
Philadelphia Pennsylvania 19107
215-574-0380

Traces the importance of black America's presence in the arts and life of the nation. Art galleries, performance spaces, multimedia presentations, changing exhibitions, permanent exhibitions, and a 22-site African-American heritage tour of Philadelphia.

1331.

African American Gallery The
43 John St
Charleston South Carolina 29403-6432
803-722-8224

Charleston's premier showcase for African
and African-American art, including a special
exhibit on South Carolina's Gullah culture.

1332.

Anne Spencer House and Garden
1313 Pierce St
Lynchburg Virginia 24501
804-846-0517

Preserved home of the Harlem Renaissance
literary figure, associated with James Weldon
Johnson, Langston Hughes, Claude McKay,
Paul Robeson, Marian Anderson, W.E.B. Du
Bois, and Mary McLeod Bethune.

1333.

West Virginia State Museum
State Capitol Complex
Charleston West Virginia 25305
304-358-0220

In the capitol of the state that came into being
by refusing to follow the rest of Virginia's lead
in supporting slavery and seceding from the
Union, this museum has exhibits on slavery,
John Brown's raid at Harpers Ferry, and the
role of African-American soldiers in the Civil
War. Nearby is a memorial to Booker T.
Washington.

1334.

Fine Arts Museum of the South
Ann and Virginia Sts
Mobile Alabama 36689
205-434-7307

Surveys 2,000 years of cultural history, including a prominent showing of arts and crafts
from Africa.

1335.

African Arts & Crafts Boutique T-Tops
1710 S Cushman St
Fairbanks Alaska 99701-6606
907-452-7051

1336.

African Arts Ltd.
245 S Plumer Ave
Tucson Arizona 85719-6303
520-791-2021

1337.

Isaac Hathaway Fine Arts Center
University of Arkansas at Pine Bluff
Pine Bluff Arkansas 71601
501-543-08236

Located in a predominantly black university,
this center has a display of "interpretive panels" to chronicle the experiences of black
Arkansans.

1338.

African Connexion
468 Main
Ferndale California 95536
707-786-9211

African arts and artifacts.

1339.

African American Artists Gallery
428 E Manchester Blvd
Inglewood California 90301-1320
310-412-1773

1340.

African Arts Nbari
P.O. Box 834
Los Altos California 94023-0834
415-948-7126

1341.

African Art Design
310 E 12th
Los Angeles California 90000
213-747-5638

1342.

African Connection Arts & Crafts
7204 Melrose Ave
Los Angeles California 90046-7656
213-965-8628

1343.

Black Gallery
107 Santa Barbara Plaza
Los Angeles California 90008
213-294-9024

1344.

Museum of African American Art
4005 Crenshaw Blvd
Los Angeles California 90008
213-294-7071

The art of the diaspora in the United States, the Caribbean, and Latin America is featured here, especially the works of Palmer Hayden.

1345.

Black Art Production Co.
1732 103d Ave
Oakland California 94601
510-568-1135

1346.

Ebony Museum of Art
30 Alice St
Oakland California 94607
510-839-9000

An eclectic museum that has collections on African artifacts, paraphernalia from the days of slavery, African-American representations in popular culture, history of the local black community, and an exhibit on African-American foods. Changing exhibits on contemporary African-American art.

1347.

Oakland Art Museum
100 Oak St
Oakland California 94607
510-238-3005

Explores the rich history of African Americans in California, from the settlement days to the civil rights movement to the contemporary gains of African Americans in politics. Also includes paintings of prominent African American artists, most notably Raymond Saunders and Robert Colescott.

1348.

African American Art Gallery
4208 N Freeway Blvd, #4
Sacramento California 95834
916-568-1238

1349.

Black Art Gallery
2251 Florin Rd
Sacramento California 95822-4483
916-395-1690

1350.

African Accents Wholesale Art & Accessories
San Diego California 92126
619-566-6649

1351.

African Art
San Francisco California 94103
415-255-8806

1352.

African Arts & Crafts Center
411 Divisadero St
San Francisco California 94117-2210
415-252-0119

1353.

African-American Historical & Cultural Society
Fort Mason Center, Building C-165
San Francisco California 94123
415-441-0640 or 415-292-6172

Julian Haile, Director
Interested in the role of the African American in art and history. Houses a museum and gallery.

1354.

African American Art
1275 Piedmont Rd
San Jose California 95132-2831
408-272-3885

1355.

African Arts Etc.
1344 3rd St Promenade
Santa Monica California 90401
310-393-3212

1356.

African & Contemporary Art
Santa Rosa California 95407
707-876-3484

1357.

African Gallery
2233 Grand Canal Blvd
Stockton California 95207-6657
209-951-0291

1358.

Housatonic Museum of Art
510 Barnum Ave
Bridgeport Connecticut 06608
203-579-6727

An eclectic collection of some 400 objects from West Africa, including weapons, gold weights and scales, statues, fertility objects, and puppets.

1359.

African Arts & Crafts Shop
499 Farmington Ave
Hartford Connecticut 06105-3105
203-231-9447

1360.

Wadsworth Atheneum
600 Main St
Hartford Connecticut 06103
203-278-2670

6,000 objects are displayed in this museum that explores three centuries of African-American history and the 20th-century activities within the diaspora.

1361.

James Weldon Johnson Memorial Collection of Negro Arts & Letters
Beinecke Library
Yale University
New Haven Connecticut 06511
203-432-2977

Exhibits on black themes (open to the public) and papers of the prominent civil rights activist, author, and diplomat can be found here, as well as original manuscripts of Harlem Renaissance figures and correspondences between African Americans in the abolitionist and civil rights movements, spirituals, and blues. The research center where these documents are housed, however, is open only to scholars.

1362.

Slater Memorial Museum & Art Gallery
108 Crescent St
Norwich Connecticut 06360
203-887-2506

West African cultural artifacts are displayed prominently in this museum's African collection.

1363.

African Safari Art Gallery
7610 Georgia Ave NW
Washington DC 20011
202-722-1619

1364.

Art in the Dark Galerie 500
Software Service Division
Washington DC 20003
800-666-4476

Produces a multicultural screensaver software program.

1365.

Black Fashion Museum
2007 Vermont Ave, NW
Washington DC 20001-4029
202-667-0744

1366.

Howard University Gallery of Art
2455 6th St, NW
Washington DC 20059
202-806-7070

1367.

National Museum of African Art
950 Independence Ave, SW
Washington DC 20560
202-357-4860

The high art of Africa is thoroughly surveyed in this museum, which includes personal objects, pottery, masks, carved figures, baskets, cloth, and other cultural objects.

1368.

National Museum of American Art
Eighth and G Sts, NW
Washington DC 20001
202-357-3176

Included in this museum are works by more than 100 black artists.

1369.

National Museum Of Art
Smithsonian Institution, National Mall
950 Independence Ave
Washington DC 20002
202-357-2700

Sylvia H. Williams, Director
Collections include film footage on African art and culture, wood, metal, ceramic, ivory, and fiber objects of African art.

1370.

Phillips Collection
1612 21st St, NW
Washington DC 20009
202-387-2151

Over half of Jacob Lawrence's "Migration of the Negro" can be viewed here.

1371.

Museum of Arts & Sciences
1040 Museum Blvd
Daytona Beach Florida 32114
904-255-0285

Permanent exhibition of 160 works of African art from 30 cultures, plus long-term loan of 135 others.

1372.

African American–Caribbean Cultural Center
BankAtlantic Building
Fort Lauderdale Florida 33316
305-467-4056

Temporary exhibits of arts, crafts, and history of the diaspora.

1373.

Museum of Art
1 E Las Olas Blvd
Fort Lauderdale Florida 33301
305-525-5500

Extensive holdings of African art.

1374.

Black Cultural Arts Coalition
141 NE 3rd Ave
Miami Florida 33010
305-379-6025

1375.

Black Heritage Museum
Box 570327
Miami Florida 33257
305-252-3535

Collections of masks, carvings, and other objects from various African tribes, as well as art from Haiti (including works by Pierre Toseth, Florestant, and Berjo).

1376.

Afrikan Culture Gallery
4065 L. B. Mcleod Rd
Orlando Florida 32811-5663
407-245-1171

1377.

Museum of African American Art
1308 N Marion St
Tampa Florida 33602
813-272-2466

More than 100 paintings and 30 sculptures from 81 artists—including Hale Woodruff, Romare Bearden, and Laura Wheeler—compose this collection of African-American art, culture, and history from the late 1800s to the present.

1378.

Albany Museum of Art
311 Meadowlark Dr
Albany Georgia 31707
912-439-8400

Permanent collections of more than 1,500 pieces of art from West Africa, Ethiopia, and East Africa.

1379.

APEX Museum
135 Auburn Ave, NE
Atlanta Georgia 30312
404-521-2739

Museum that celebrates the local African-American heritage with audio-visual presentations, displays, and art exhibits.

1380.

Trevor Arnett Library
Clark Atlanta University
Atlanta Georgia 30314
404-880-8000

Features papers and works of prominent African-American literary figures as well as the works of leading modern black artists.

1381.

Harriet Tubman Historical & Cultural Museum
340 Walnut St
Macon Georgia 31208
912-743-8544

Tribute to the woman who championed the Underground Railroad. Also has permanent and traveling exhibitions of African and African-American art.

1382.

African Fine Arts
601 Sun Valley Rd
Ketchum Idaho 83340
208-726-3144

1383.

African American Arts Alliance of Chicago
1805 E 71st
Chicago Illinois 60637
312-288-5100

1384.

African American Images Inc.
1909 W 95th St
Chicago Illinois 60643-1105
312-445-0322

1385.

South Side Community Art Center
3831 S Michigan Ave
Chicago Illinois 60653
312-373-1026

Sponsors exhibits or workshops to aid black artists and writers and also provide exposure to cultural artifacts for school children.

1386.

Black Entertainment & Sports Lawyers Association
1 Elizabeth Ct
Oak Park Illinois 60302-2009
708-386-8338

1387.

African Art & More
6101 N Keystone Ave
Indianapolis Indiana 46220-2431
317-466-0036

1388.

Indianapolis Museum of Art
1200 W 38th St
Indianapolis Indiana 46208
317-923-1331

Over 14,000 objects from Africa, spanning some 10,000 square feet, comprise the "Africa Collection" of this large museum.

1389.

Davenport Museum of Art
1737 W 12th St
Davenport Iowa 52804
319-326-7804

The museum's specialty is the work of Haitian and Haitian-American artists.

1390.

Des Moines Art Center
4700 Grand Ave
Des Moines Iowa 50312
515-277-4405

A superb African collection is the highlight of this museum, which contains artifacts and ethnographic objects rarely found in museums with notable collections of African art.

1391.

University of Iowa Museum of Art
150 N Riverside Dr
Iowa City Iowa 52242
319-335-1727

One of the most comprehensive, balanced, and outstanding collections of sub-Saharan art in the nation, with particular emphasis on East African and Zairean art, which often goes unexplored at other museums.

1392.

J. B. Speed Art Museum
2035 S 3rd St
Louisville Kentucky 40208
502-636-2893

Permanent exhibition of African art from the 1600s to the early 1900s.

1393.

African American Art Gallery The
1796 Rosiere St
New Orleans Louisiana 70119-2024
504-245-4036

1394.

African Arts and Wears
5700 Read Blvd
New Orleans Louisiana 70127-2665
504-246-3936

1395.

Amistad Research Center
6823 St. Charles Ave
New Orleans Louisiana 70118
504-865-5535

The world's largest repository of primary source material on African-American history, as well as paintings of prominent African-American artists.
1966

1396.

African Imports & New England Arts
1 Union St
Portland Maine 04101-4048
207-772-9505

1397.

African Tribal Art
Portland Maine
OSKICASE3@aol.com

Offers the most outstanding museum-quality tribal objects, masks from different ethnic groups, statues, ceremonial vessels, wedding baskets, ceremonial stools, bronze baskets, wooden bowls, Benin bronze, oil paintings from Ghana, Senegal, Nigeria, and Cameroun, antique jewelry, handmade rugs from North Africa, figurative tables, calabash bowls with lid, healing vessels, and much more.

1398.

Baltimore Museum of Art
Art Museum Dr
Baltimore Maryland 21218
410-396-6310

1300 art objects from all regions of Africa, spanning the 12th through 20th centuries, make this museum an extraordinary place to visit.

1399.

Black-American Museum
1769 Carswell St
Baltimore Maryland 21218
410-243-9600

A museum primarily showcasing local African-American art; some artifacts from Africa are also present.

1400.

Great Blacks in Wax Museum
1601 E North Ave
Baltimore Maryland 21213
410-563-3404

Important political, social, and cultural figures in African-American history are immortalized in this wax museum

1401.

James E. Lewis Museum of Art The
Morgan State University
Coldspring Lane & Hillen Rd
Baltimore Maryland 21239
301-444-3030

1402.

Maryland Museum of African Art
P.O. Box 1105
Columbia Maryland 21044
410-730-7105 or 301-596-0051

More than 200 cultural artifacts from Africa are displayed here, including an enormous (10′ × 6½′) ceremonial mask of the Chewa people.

1403.

Museum of Fine Arts
Huntington Ave and The Fenway
Boston Massachusetts 02115
617-267-9300

African sculpture and the contributions of African Americans to New England's history are prominently featured.

1404.

Museum of the National Center of Afro-American Artists
300 Walnut Ave
Boston Massachusetts 02119
617-442-8614

Explores the cultural and visual arts heritage of Africa and the diaspora, including more than 4,000 works by African and Caribbean artists. Changing exhibitions, various media.

1405.

African Traditional Art
1132 Massachusetts Ave
Cambridge Massachusetts 02138-5204
617-661-8282

1406.

African Heritage Gallery
930 Main St
Worcester Massachusetts 01610-1432
508-752-1199

1407.

Afro American Museum of Detroit
301 Frederick Douglass
Detroit Michigan 48202
313-833-9800

1408.

Detroit Institute of Arts
5200 Woodward Ave
Detroit Michigan 48202
313-567-1170

Several collections, highlighting the histories
and accomplishments of the people of ancient
Egypt, North Africa, and sub-Saharan Africa.

1409.

Institute of African-American Arts
2641 W Grand Blvd
Detroit Michigan 48208
313-872-0332

Tributes to recently deceased local artists and
performance space for up-and-coming artists
in the heart of Motown.

1410.

Your Heritage House
110 E Ferry St
Detroit Michigan 48202
313-871-1667

A fine arts museum for young people.

1411.

Black Arts & Cultural Center
225 Parsons St
Kalamazoo Michigan 49007-3569
616-349-1035

1412.

**Smith Robertson Museum, School &
Cultural Center**
528 Bloom St
Jackson Mississippi 39207
601-960-1457

No longer a school, but still serves as place
where the history and culture of African
Americans in Mississippi is preserved.

1413.

Museums of the University of Mississippi
5th St and University Ave
Oxford Mississippi 38677
601-232-7073

This museum is devoted to folk art of the
South, much of it African American in origin. It
also has a substantial collection of African art.

1414.

Black Americana Museum
1238 S 13th St
Omaha Nebraska 68108-3502
402-341-6908

1415.

African American Cultural Arts
1048 W Owens Ave
Las Vegas Nevada 89106-2520
702-646-1520

1416.

Hood Museum of Art
Dartmouth College
Hanover New Hampshire 03755
603-646-2808

Especially strong in its collection of paraphernalia from men's secret societies in Africa.

1417.

Newark Museum
43–49 Washington St
Newark New Jersey 07102
201-596-6550

The museum's African collection spans the entire continent, and differs from most in that it prominently displays the artifacts and history of people from North Africa.

1418.

African Arts Museum
23 Bliss Ave
Tenafly New Jersey 07670
201-567-0450

New Jersey's only museum devoted to the art of Africa.

1419.

Brooklyn Museum
200 Eastern Parkway
Brooklyn New York 11238
718-638-5000

Six centuries and 3,000 cultural artifacts from Africa are prominently displayed.

1420.

Museum of African & African American Art & Antiquities
1097 Ellicott St
Buffalo New York 14209-1935
716-882-7676

1421.

African Artisans Company
169 Baldwin Rd
Hempstead New York 11550-6818
516-481-5642
516-481-5642—Fax

1422.

African Gallery at the Courtyard
223 Katonah Ave
Katonah New York 10536-2139
914-232-9511

1423.

African American Culture & Arts Network
501 W 145th St
New York New York 10031-5101
212-749-4408

1424.

African American Wax Museum of Harlem
316 W 115th St
New York New York 10026-2308
212-678-7818 or 800-848-7982

Raven Chanticleer, Founder and Director
Heroes and sheroes from Dr. King to Malcolm X. Historical life-size wax figures. 1989

1425.

African Art Source
127 W 26th St
New York New York 10001-6808
212-645-6526

1426.

African Hemingway Gallery
1050 Second Ave
New York New York 10022-4063
212-838-3650
212-838-3650—Fax

Brian Gais Ford, Owner
African arts and artifacts.

1427.

African Trader Art Gallery
318 W 78th St
New York New York 10024-6536
212-724-3114

1428.

Afro Arts Cultural Center
2192 Adam Clayton Powell Jr. Blvd
New York New York 10027
212-996-3333

Ethiopian religious artifacts, contemporary African painters, jazz, opera, and classical music all find a home here.

1429.

Black Fashion Museum
155–57 W 126 St
New York New York 10027
212-666-1320

The contributions of African Americans to fashion are celebrated here, from Elizabeth Keckley to contemporary designers.

1430.

Genesis 1
509 Cathedral Parkway
New York New York 10025
212-666-7222

A museum that celebrates international black culture.

1431.

Grinnell Fine Art Collections
800 Riverside Dr, Suite 5E
New York New York 10032
212-927-7941

Ademola Olugebefola, Codirector

1432.

Metropolitan Museum of Art
1000 Fifth Ave
New York New York 10028
212-535-7710

This enormous museum houses 19th- and
20th-century African-American painters, as
well as over 500 Central and West African
artifacts. Most impressive, however, is the
enormous collection of African musical instruments.

1433.

Museum for African Art
593 Broadway
New York New York 10012-3211
212-966-1313
212-966-1432—Fax

Grace Stanislaus, Executive Director
One of only two museums devoted exclusively
to historical and contemporary African art in
the United States. Broad scope, educational,
high aesthetic quality. Also sponsors Discovering Africa travel program.
1992

1434.

Museum of Modern Art
11 W 53 St
New York New York 10019
212-708-9480

30 of the 60 panels of Jacob Lawrence's "The
Migration of the Negro" are on display.

1435.

Studio Museum of Harlem
144 W 125 St
New York New York 10027
212-865-2420

America's most renowned institution for the
display of works by artists of color. Also has a
concert hall, lecture hall, and assembly hall to
complement its art collections.

1436.

Frederic Remington Art Museum
303 Washington
Ogdenburg New York 13669
315-393-2425

Frederic Remington, a soldier with the 10th
Cavalry in Arizona and a "buffalo soldier"—
one of the black cavalrymen who played a
crucial role in the settling of the West—
documented the works of buffalo soldiers
through paintings, sketches, and personal
papers. One of the few remaining records of
this period of history, his work is now preserved in the museum named in his honor, in
which buffalo soldiers prominently figure.

1437.

African Gallery at the Depot
8 Depot Plaza
Scarsdale New York 10583-3708
914-725-2727

1438.

Universal Books & Religious Articles
51 Court St
White Plains New York 10601
914-681-0484

Carrie Coard, President

1439.

Afro-American Cultural Center
401 N Myers St
Charlotte North Carolina 28202
714-374-1565

Has exhibits on arts and crafts from Africa, as well as cultural contributions of African Americans and black history and culture in the early 20th century.

1440.

North Carolina Central University Gallery
1801 Fayetteville St
Durham North Carolina 27707
919-683-6211

1441.

African American Art
202 Four Seasons Town Centre
Greensboro North Carolina 27400
910-292-3209

1442.

African American Atelier Inc.
200 N Davie St
Greensboro North Carolina 27401-2813
910-333-6885

1443.

Delta Art Center
1511 E 3rd St
Winston-Salem North Carolina 27101
919-722-2625

Run by the city's oldest nonprofit African American cultural organization, this center hosts exhibits and programs that highlight the contributions of African Americans to the arts and humanities.

1444.

African-American Assiento Memorial Museum
8716 Harkness Rd
Cleveland Ohio 44106-4504
216-229-9999

1445.

African-American Museum
1765 Crawford Rd
Cleveland Ohio 44106-2011
216-791-1700

1446.

National Afro-American Museum & Cultural Center
1350 Brush Row Rd
Wilberforce Ohio 45384
513-376-4944

Contains a museum, art gallery, library, and archives. Programs include an oral and visual history project, joint degree offerings in archival and administration and museology, and exhibit loans. Publishes a quarterly journal.

1447.

Ntu Art Association
2100 NE 52nd
Oklahoma City Oklahoma 7311
405-427-5461

1448.

Sanamu African Gallery
Kirkpatrick Museum Complex
Oklahoma City Oklahoma 73105
405-427-7529

Explores cultures of sub-Saharan Africa through traditional arts and crafts.

1449.

Children's Museum
3037 SW Second Ave
Portland Oregon 97201
503-823-2227

A permanent collections of some 31 objects from Zulu life is complemented by "Omokunle Village," a mock Yoruba village complete with marketplace, chief's house, schoolhouse, and a central village tree.

1450.

Portland Museum of Art
1219 SW Park at Jefferson Ave
Portland Oregon 97223
503-226-2811

Has one of the most comprehensive collections of Tikar, Bamum, Manbila, and other Cameroonian artifacts and items.

1451.

African Cultural Arts Forum
237 S 60th St
Philadelphia Pennsylvania 19139-3843
215-476-0680

This group promotes the efforts of black artists and seeks to publicize their activities to help them obtain due recognition.

1452.

Afro-American Historical & Cultural Museum
Seventh and Arch Sts
Philadelphia Pennsylvania 19107
215-574-0380

Traces the importance of black America's presence in the arts and life of the nation. Art galleries, performance spaces, multimedia presentations, changing exhibitions, permanent exhibitions, and a 22-site African-American heritage tour of Philadelphia.

1453.

Association of Black Storytellers
P.O. Box 27456
Philadelphia Pennsylvania 19118
215-898-5118

Linda Goss, President
Seeks to establish a forum to promote the black oral tradition and to attract an audience.

1454.

Minority Arts Resource Council
1421 W Girard Ave
Philadelphia Pennsylvania 19130-1630
215-236-2688

Provides a network for black and Hispanic artists and sponsors performances and exhibitions in the Philadelphia area.

1455.

African Heritage Classroom
University of Pittsburgh
Pittsburgh Pennsylvania 15260
412-624-6150

A re-creation of the central courtyard of an Ashanti royal residence to reveal Africa's cultural foundations and family life. Artifacts from numerous other African peoples.

1456.

African-American Gallery
43 John St
Charleston South Carolina 29403
803-722-8224

Charleston's premier showcase for African and African-American art.

1457.

South Carolina State Museum
301 Gervais St
Columbia South Carolina 29202-3107
803-737-4921

Has a permanent exhibit on slave life and the material culture of African Americans.

1458.

I. J. Stanback Museum
South Carolina State College
Orangeburg South Carolina 29117
803-536-7174

1459.

African American Art Gallery
114 Carr St
Knoxville Tennessee 37919-5117
615-584-1320

1460.

Sun Studio
706 Union Ave
Memphis Tennessee 38103
901-521-0664

A museum and working studio at once, this birthplace of rock 'n' roll launched the careers of B. B. King, Muddy Waters, Howlin' Wolf, and Elvis Presley, among others.

1461.

Aaron Douglas Gallery
Fisk University Library
Nashville Tennessee 37208
615-329-8720

Named for the famed illustrator and painter of the Harlem Renaissance and the founding chairman of Fisk University's Art Department, this museum displays the works of prominent African-American artists and a collection of African art.

1462.

Carl Van Vechten Gallery
Fisk University
Nashville Tennessee 37208
615-329-8720

Sculpture from West Africa is housed next to works by Cézanne, O'Keefe, Renoir, Rivera, Picasso, and others.

1463.

Black Arts Alliance
1157 Navasota St
Austin Texas 78702
512-477-9660

Ethnic dance, music and theater productions, films and videos, paintings, and sculpture exhibitions celebrate the richness of black culture.

1464.

Museum of African-American Life & Culture
1620 First Ave
Dallas Texas 75226
214-565-9026

Dr. Harry Robinson Jr., Director
Artifacts and folk art from Africa and the diaspora, supplemented by occasional lectures, exhibits, and festivals that celebrate the black heritage.

1465.

African Artifacts Imports
5501 Davis Blvd
Fort Worth Texas 76180-6443
817-581-6358

1466.

African Art Connection
3400 Montrose Blvd
Houston Texas 77006-4330
213-529-8266

1467.

Museum of Fine Arts
1001 Bissonet St
Houston Texas 77002
817-332-7064

Paintings, photographs, sculpture and folk art from Africa and the diaspora are prominently displayed, as are the many prominent African-American artists in its permanent collection. Temporary exhibits celebrate the works of emerging African-American artists.

1468.

African Art–Gallerie Lataj
1203 King St
Alexandria Virginia 22314-2926
703-549-0508

1469.

Valentine Museum
Wickham-Valentine House
Richmond Virginia 23219
804-649-0711 or 804-225-8730

Urban history museum with holdings of paintings, prints, manuscripts, textiles, costumes, photographs, furniture, and industrial artifacts.

1470.

Virginia Museum of Fine Arts
2800 Grove Ave
Richmond Virginia 23221
804-367-0844

Among its collections are impressive holdings
of West African art and sculpture.

1471.

**Harrison Museum of African-American
Culture**
523 Harrison Ave, NW
Roanoke Virginia 24016
703-345-4818

Small museum that documents the history of
the local black community and serves as a
forum for the exhibition of art and the performing arts.

1472.

African-American Art Gallery
3528 W Villard Ave
Milwaukee Wisconsin 53209-4712
414-536-6440

1473.

Minority Graphics Arts Organization
2209 N Martin Luther King Dr
Milwaukee Wisconsin 53212
414-263-3610

✪ MUSEUMS, HISTORIC
SITES & RESEARCH CENTERS ✪

1474.

Afro-Amer History
ftp://ftp.msstate.edu/pub/docs/history/USA/
Afro-Amer

An ftp resource for African-American history.

1475.

Birmingham Civil Rights Institute
Sixth Ave and 16th St N
Birmingham Alabama 35203
205-328-9696

Collections and exhibits on segregation, black
culture, and the civil rights movement.

1476.

Alabama Department of Archives & History
1 Dexter Dr
Montgomery Alabama 36104
205-262-0013

This complex houses eight museums, which trace the genealogy of the Diaspora. Has displays on prominent African Americans, especially those who were associated with Alabama.

1477.

Civil Rights Memorial
c/o Southern Poverty Law Center
Montgomery Alabama 36104
205-264-0286

Tribute to the lives of those killed in the civil rights struggle.

1478.

Old Depot Museum
Foot of Water Ave
Selma Alabama 36701
205-875-9918

Historical documentation of the people and events of Selma, and the formative years of Selma's self-sufficient black community.

1479.

Tuskegee Institute National Historic Site
Carver Museum
Tuskegee Alabama 36087
205-727-6390

Tributes to the accomplishments of Booker T. Washington and George Washington Carver, including a recording of Washington reading from his Atlanta Compromise address. Also houses a research center.

1480.

Fort Huachuca Museum
Fort Huachuca Military Base
Fort Huachuca Arizona 85613
602-533-5736

The largest African-American U.S. military base during World War II, housing both the 92nd and the 93rd Divisions as well as units of the black Women's Army Corps (WACS). It has also served as the regimental headquarters of the buffalo soldiers of the 10th Cavalry and the 24th Infantry.

1481.

Scott Joplin Commemorative Marker
831 Laurel St
Texarkana Arkansas 75502
501-772-9551

Tribute to the "Father of Ragtime Music."

1482.

Ethnic Minorities Memorabilia Association Museum
Franklin St
Washington Arkansas 71868
501-983-2891

Museum devoted to documenting regional black history and culture.

1483.

California Afro-American Museum
600 State Dr, Exposition Park
Los Angeles California 90037
213-744-7432
213-744-2050—Fax

Rick Moss, Director
Exhibitions include items relating to Afro-American heritage.

1484.

Northern California Center for Afro-American History & Life
5606 San Pablo Ave
Oakland California 94612
510-658-3158

Impressive and in-depth collections of black history in California. Archive is full of photos, manuscripts, records of black organizations, and oral histories.

1485.

African-American Historical & Cultural Society
Fort Mason Center, Building C-165
San Francisco California 94123
415-441-0640 or 415-292-6172

Julian Haile, Director
Interested in the role of the African American in art and history. Houses a museum and gallery.

1486.

San Francisco African-American Historical & Cultural Society
Buchanan St at Marina Blvd
San Francisco California 94123
415-441-0640

Memorabilia of Mary Ellen Pleasant, prominent 19th-century abolitionist, compliment the paintings of Sargent Johnson and West African wooden and soapstone carvings and baskets in the main holdings of this museum. Facilities also include a listening room, research library, and gift shop. Affiliated with the Center for African & African-American Art and Performing Arts Workshops and Theater Productions of Wajumbe Dancers.

1487.

Black American West Museum
3091 California St
Denver Colorado 80205
303-292-2566

Housed in the former home of Dr. Justina Ford, a pioneering black gynecologist, obstetrician, and pediatrician, is an impressive collections of pictures and artifacts documenting the African-American presence in the West, including information on black cowboys, homesteaders, and soldiers and all-black towns.

1488.

Harriet Beecher Stowe House
73 Forest St
Hartford Connecticut 06105
203-522-9258

Restored house of the author of the highly influential novel *Uncle Tom's Cabin,* which revealed the horrors of slavery and helped to precipitate the start of the Civil War.

1489.

Connecticut Afro-American Historical Society
444 Orchard St
New Haven Connecticut 06511
203-776-4907

Khalid Lum, President
Museum and research center devoted primarily to the history and contributions of African Americans in New England.

1490.

Afro-American Historical & Genealogical Society
P.O. Box 73806
Washington DC 20056

Sylvia Cooke Martin, President
Encourages scholarly research in Afro-American history and genealogy as it relates to American history and culture. Collects, maintains, and preserves relevant material, which the society makes available for research and publication.

1491.

Anacostia Museum
1901 Fort Place, SE
Washington DC 20020
202-287-3369

This branch of the Smithsonian Institution specializes in black history and urban issues of the upper South: the Carolinas, Virginia, Maryland, and Washington, D.C.

1492.

Association for the Study of African American Life & History Inc.
407 14th St, NW
Washington DC 20005-3704
202-667-2822
202-387-9802—Fax

One of the oldest black-oriented organizations. It was organized to provide more historical truth about African heritage of black people and their role in the development of the United States. It has 2,500 members, is a multiracial organization, and publishes a journal. The association sponsors an annual conference and African-American History Week.

1493.

Bethune Museum & Archives
1318 Vermont Ave, NW
Washington DC 20005
202-332-1233 or 202-332-9201

The world's largest repository for information on black women and their organizations. Former home of the highly influential black woman activist. Has two permanent exhibits: one about the public career of Mary McLeod Bethune, the other about the history and accomplishments of African-American women who have worked for social change.

1494.

Emancipation Proclamation
Library of Congress
Washington DC 20540
202-707-5000

An original draft of the presidential order that
ended slavery. On permanent exhibit.
1862

1495.

Evans-Tibbs Collection
1910 Vermont Ave, NW
Washington DC 20001
202-234-8164

Former house of the talented soprano and
founder of the Negro National Opera company; today her home is on the National
Historic Register and houses a world-famous
collection of African-American art, containing
works by Henry O. Tanner, Romare Bearden,
Richmond Barthé, Charles Alston, Jacob
Lawrence, and Elizabeth Catlett.

1496.

Frederick Douglass House
1411 West St, SE
Washington DC 20020
202-426-5960

The restored home of the famed statesman
and champion of the African-American cause.

1497.

Moorland-Spingarn Research Center
Howard University
Washington DC 20059
202-636-6108

Thomas C. Battle, Director
Black history museum. Exhibits African artifacts and historic documents pertaining to the
black experience in America.

1498.

National Museum of Natural History
Tenth St and Constitution Ave, NW
Washington DC 20004
202-357-2700

Anthropological exploration of life in Africa,
including music and rural life, are showcased
in the African Hall of this museum.

1499.

**Zora Neale Hurston Memorial Park &
Marker**
11 People St
Eatonville Florida 32751
407-647-3307

Located in America's first all-black town.
Birthplace of Zora Neale Hurston. Every
January a festival is held in her honor.

1500.

**African American–Caribbean Cultural
Center**
BankAtlantic Building
Fort Lauderdale Florida 33316
305-467-4056

Temporary exhibits of arts, crafts, and history
of the diaspora.

1501.

Black Archives History & Research Foundation
Joseph Caleb Community Center
Miami Florida 33142
305-638-6064 or 305-638-6375

This complex houses an archives, research foundation, documents, manuscripts, photographs, field trips, and works of art; all explore the mixture of southern black, Bahamian, and Caribbean cultures in southern Florida.

1502.

Black Archives, Research Center & Museum
Carnegie Library
Tallahassee Florida 32307
904-599-3020

Cultural and historical memorabilia from throughout the history of African Americans, including leg irons worn by a slave, correspondence of Mary McLeod Bethune and Dr. Martin Luther King, Jr., and Whites Only signs.

1503.

Center for African American Culture
210 S Woodward, B-105
Tallahassee Florida 32303
904-644-3252

Dr. Ashenafi Kebede, Director
As an academic unit, lectures, workshops, and artistic performances are sponsored that provide a learning experience for minority and nonminority students. As a cultural unit, quality programs are presented that exhibit the contributions of black people to the FSU as well as the local, state, and worldwide communities.

1504.

Birth Home of Martin Luther King, Jr.
501 Auburn Ave, NE
Atlanta Georgia 30312
404-331-3920

Birthplace of the renowned civil rights leader.

1505.

Herndon Home The
587 University Place, NW
Atlanta Georgia 30314
404-581-9813

Former residence of Alonzo Herndon, a Georgia-born slave who founded the Atlanta Life Insurance Company. Now a museum with a permanent exhibit of original family furnishings, decorative artwork, Venetian and Roman glass, antique silver, and historic photographs.

1506.

Martin Luther King Jr. Center for Non-Violent Social Change
449 Auburn Ave, NE
Atlanta Georgia 30312
404-524-1956 or 404-331-3919

Memorial to and documentation of King's life, including his personal papers, manuscripts, documents, oral histories, and records of the Southern Christian Leadership Conference. King's burial spot is nearby.

1507.

Martin Luther King Jr. National Historic Site
526 Auburn Ave, NE
Atlanta Georgia 30312
404-331-3919

Maintained by the National Park Service, this place houses King's birthplace, a research center, and the Ebenezer Baptist Church.

1508.

Trevor Arnett Library
Clark Atlanta University
Atlanta Georgia 30314
404-880-8000

Features papers and works of prominent African-American literary figures as well as the works of leading modern black artists.

1509.

Ma Rainey House
805 Fifth Ave
Columbus Georgia 31901
706-571-4700

The preserved house of the "Mother of Blues."

1510.

Harriet Tubman Historical & Cultural Museum
340 Walnut St
Macon Georgia 31208
912-743-8544

Tribute to the woman who championed the Underground Railroad. Also has permanent and traveling exhibitions of African and African-American art.

1511.

African American National Memorial Foundation
2241 S Indiana Ave
Chicago Illinois 60616-1329
312-842-9473

1512.

Black History Tours
1721 W 85th St
Chicago Illinois 60620-4738
312-233-8907

1513.

Chicago Historical Society
Clark St at North Ave
Chicago Illinois 60610
312-642-4600

"A House Divided: America in the Age of Lincoln" examines a tumultuous time in American history of critical significance to African Americans. Also chronicles important black figures in Chicago's history.

1514.

DuSable Historical Marker
Pioneer Court
Chicago Illinois 60611

Commemorates the accomplishments of Jean Baptiste Pointe DuSable, a black man and first settler and founder of what would eventually become the city of Chicago.

1515.

DuSable Museum of African-American History
740 E 56th St
Chicago Illinois 60637
312-947-0600

A museum devoted to the history of African Americans in the Midwest, and named after the famous fur trader who founded and settled Chicago. The nation's oldest institution dedicated to the preservation of African-American culture and history. Contains over 10,000 pieces and includes paintings, sculptures, print works, and historical memorabilia.

1516.

Field Museum of Natural History
Roosevelt Rd at Lake Shore Dr
Chicago Illinois 60605
312-922-9410

The "Africa" exhibit employs over 15,000 square feet to explore contemporary urban life, art, animals, environments, and commerce in Africa and in the diaspora.

1517.

Vivian Harsh Collection of Afro-American History & Literature
9525 S Halsted St
Chicago Illinois 60628
312-747-6910

Named for the first black librarian of Chicago, who started the collection. Now contains over 70,000 volumes, a periodicals collection, and important original papers from such figures as Richard Wright and Langston Hughes.

1518.

Africana Conference Paper Index (AFRC)
Northwestern University Library
Evanston Illinois 60208-2300
708-491-7684
708-491-8301—Fax
708-491-3070—dialup
library.ucc.nwu.edu (IP 129.105.54.2)

Online index to individual papers presented at Africana conference proceedings.

1519.

Melville J. Herskovits Library of Africana Studies
Northwestern University Library
Evanston Illinois 60208-2300
708-491-7684
708-491-8301—Fax

David L. Easterbrook, Curator
The largest separate Africana collection in the world, with collections including over 245,000 volumes, 2,500 current serials, and 300 current African newspapers, as well as comprehensive collections of sheet maps and atlases and many research materials in microform.

1520.

African American Hall of Fame Museum
309 S Dusable St
Peoria Illinois 61605-1843
309-673-2206

Honors the achievements and contributions of notable African Americans in history.

1521.

Freetown Village Museum
860 W 10th St
Indianapolis Indiana 46204
317-232-8721 or 317-631-1870

Living history museum that brings back to life the free blacks of Indianapolis in the aftermath of the Civil War.

1522.

Black Culture Center
315 University St
Lafayette Indiana 47906-2897
317-494-3092

1523.

Buxton Heritage Museum
1226 Second Ave
Des Moines Iowa 50314
515-276-2252 or 414-260-0581

Museum that commemorates this black industrial coal-mining town in the middle of America's heartland.

1524.

Carver Museum
Warren County Fairgrounds
Indianola Iowa 50125
515-961-6031

Housed in the shack in which George Washington Carver, the famous black entrepreneur, intellectual, and agronomer, spent much of his time. Memorabilia about his life, especially his academic career at nearby Simpson College, is prominently displayed.

1525.

Sumner Elementary School
330 SW Western Ave
Topeka Kansas 66606
913-357-5328

The battle for equal education for African Americans began here. This school's dubious honor in the monumental Supreme Court case *Brown vs. Board of Education of Topeka* is now commemorated with a marker mounted on the exterior wall at the right of the front entrance. Formally registered as a National Historic Site.

1526.

First National Black Historical Society of Kansas
P.O. Box 2695
Wichita Kansas 67201-2695
316-262-7651

1527.

Black History Gallery
602 Hawkins Dr
Elizabethtown Kentucky 42701-1040
502-765-2486

1528.

Louisville Free Public Library, Western Branch
604 S 10th St
Louisville Kentucky 46203
502-584-5526

First public library established for and staffed by African Americans. Houses an extensive collection of African-American historical and cultural information.
1905

1529.

Whitney M. Young Jr. House and Historical Marker
U.S. 60 W
Simpsonville Kentucky 40067
502-585-4733

Honors the author, former advisor to three presidents, and executive director of the National Urban League.

1530.

Amistad Research Center
6823 St. Charles Ave
New Orleans Louisiana 70118
504-865-5535

The world's largest repository of primary source material on African-American history, as well as paintings of prominent African-American artists.
1966

1531.

Cabildo
Chartres and St. Peter Sts
New Orleans Louisiana 70130
504-568-6968

Operated by the Louisiana State Museum, this museum focuses on an African-American perspective on the state's history.
1994

1532.

Conti Museum of Wax
917 Conti St
New Orleans Louisiana 70112
504-525-2605

Important African-American figures of 18th- and 19th-century New Orleans are commemorated through wax figures.

1533.

Banneker-Douglass Museum
84 Franklin St
Annapolis Maryland 21401
410-974-2893

Maryland's preeminent black heritage museum, named after Benjamin Banneker and Frederick Douglass, two important figures in African-American history.

1534.

Maryland Commission on Afro-American History & Culture
84 Franklin St, Suite 101
Annapolis Maryland 21401
301-269-2893

Serves as a historical body and also works with other state and governmental agencies, civil and professional organizations, and the black community. Seeks to preserve the heritage of black America and to encourage greater appreciation of that role.

1535.

Cab Calloway Jazz Institute Museum
Coppin State College
Baltimore Maryland 21216
410-383-5926

Traces the life of the legendary performer through a series of photographs, posters, memorabilia, and film stills.

1536.

**Eubie Blake National Museum &
Cultural Center**
409 Charles St
Baltimore Maryland 21201
410-396-6442

Named for the famed songwriter and composer of jazz and blues, this museum explores
Blake's life as well as the history of American
musical theater through pictorial essays and
video and audio presentations.

1537.

Great Blacks in Wax Museum
1601 E North Ave
Baltimore Maryland 21213
410-563-3404

Important political, social, and cultural figures
in African-American history are immortalized
in this wax museum.

1538.

**Maryland Historical Society Museum &
Library**
201 W Monument St
Baltimore Maryland 21202
410-685-3750

Maryland's African-American past is explored,
directly or indirectly, at this museum.

1539.

**NAACP Henry Lee Moon Library &
National Civil Rights Archives**
4805 Mt. Hope Dr
Baltimore Maryland 21215-3297
410-358-8900

Archives and library documenting the history
of civil rights and of the organization, located
in its national headquarters.

1540.

Soper Library
Morgan State University
Baltimore Maryland 21239
410-444-3333

The Beulah Davis Collections Room contains
manuscripts, pamphlets, books, abolitionist
newspapers, and the papers of Booker T.
Washington's private secretary, Dr. Emmett J.
Scott.

1541.

Harriet Tubman Historical Sites
c/o Harriet Tubman Coalition
Cambridge Maryland 21613
410-228-0401

Places that played a significant role in the life
of the woman largely responsible for the
Underground Railroad, including a historical
marker, a church, and a wharf.

1542.

**Howard County Center of African-
American Culture**
1 Commerce Center
Columbia Maryland 21044
410-715-1921, 410-997-3685, or 410-730-
6446

The local black heritage is explored through
the donations of prominent black families in
the area.

1543.

Sojourner Truth Collection
Oxon Hill Library
Oxon Hill Maryland 20745
301-839-2400

Named for the famous orator and champion of the rights of women and blacks, this library houses a collection of over 3,300 cataloged items, many of which are rare or out-of-print manuscripts, books, periodicals, posters, pictures, and pamphlets.

1544.

Harriet Tubman Museum The
566 Columbus Ave
Boston Massachusetts 02118-1195
617-536-8610

1545.

Museum of Afro-American History
46 Loy St
Boston Massachusetts 02114
617-445-7400

1546.

Old South Meetinghouse
310 Washington St
Boston Massachusetts 02108
617-482-6439

The childhood home of Phillis Wheatley, the slave, who barely a decade out of Africa had already mastered the English language to the point that her poetry was published—becoming one of the first women, black or white, to ever be published.

1547.

Houghton Library
Harvard University
Cambridge Massachusetts 02138
617-495-2441

Houses some of Phillis Wheatley's original manuscripts, correspondences, and a folio copy of Milton's *Paradise Lost*.

1548.

Sojourner Truth Memorial
Oak Hill Cemetery
Battle Creek Michigan 49017
616-964-7321

A monument to the tireless abolitionist, suffragist, and advocate of justice.

1549.

Underground Railroad Monument
1 Michigan Ave E
Battle Creek Michigan 49017
616-968-1611

A monument to the heroes of the movement through which thousands of slaves won their freedom.

1550.

Graystone International Jazz Museum & Jazz Hall of Fame
1521 Broadway
Detroit Michigan 48226
313-963-3813

Commemorates and preserves memorabilia related to America's most distinctive contribution to world culture.

1551.

Michigan Ethnic Heritage Studies Center
60 Farnsworth
Detroit Michigan 48202
313-832-7400

1552.

Museum of African-American History
301 Frederick Douglass St
Detroit Michigan 48202
313-833-9800

Spans the entire history of African Americans, from the beginning of slavery to contemporary statements about African Americans today. Sponsors the annual Africa World Festival.

1553.

National Museum of Tuskegee Airmen
6325 W Jefferson
Detroit Michigan 48209
313-843-8849

A museum devoted to preserving the history of the famous black fighter pilots and bombers, all of whom played a heroic role in World War II, as well as signaling the beginning of a desegregated armed forces.

1554.

Malcolm X Homesite Historical Marker
4705 S Logan St
Lansing Michigan 48910

A tribute to the leading black political figure/activist who spent most of his childhood inflected with racist violence in this town.

1555.

Dred Scott Memorial
Historic Fort Snelling State Park & History Center
St. Paul Minnesota 55111
612-726-1171

A tribute to and living history enactments of the life of Dred Scott, whose return to his master, ordered by the Supreme Court, was one of the precipitating moments of the Civil War.

1556.

Roy Wilkins Bust & Auditorium
St. Paul Civic Center
St. Paul Minnesota 55102
612-224-7361

The renowned civil rights activist and former leader of the NAACP is honored by the town in which he grew up.

1557.

Mississippi State Historical Museum
Old State Capitol Building
Jackson Mississippi 39201
601-359-6920

The South's first comprehensive, permanent exhibit on the civil rights movement.

1558.

Delta Blues Museum
Carnegie Public Library
Clarksdale Mississippi 38614
601-624-4461

Located in the birthplace of blues, this museum explores the connections between blues and American culture, including video-tapes, recordings, photographs, memorabilia, performances, and a blues archive.

1559.

Rooster Blues Records
232 Sunflower Ave
Clarksdale Mississippi 38614
601-627-2209

Offers a blues tour, guide to local blues clubs, and access to important buildings in the history of blues.

1560.

Booker-Thomas Museum
Hwy 12 (Tchula Rd)
Lexington Mississippi 39207
601-834-2672

Presents a rare portrait of African-American life in rural Mississippi during the early 20th century.

1561.

Wechsler School
1415 30th Ave
Meridican Mississippi 39301
601-485-8882 or 601-483-3130

First school in Mississippi for blacks that was financed by state bonds.
1894

1562.

Natchez Museum of Afro-American History & Culture
307A Marker St
Natchez Mississippi 39120
601-445-0728 or 601-442-6822

Documents the history of African Americans in southwest Mississippi, supplemented by over 500 artifacts.

1563.

Blues Archives
University of Mississippi
Oxford Mississippi 38677
601-232-7753

On the campus of Ole Miss, this archives contains collections devoted to B. B. King, Ma Rainey, Percy Mayfield, and others.

1564.

Black Archives of Mid-America
Fire Station 11
Kansas City Missouri 64108
815-483-1300

Serving as a community and intellectual center, this archive is well known for its oral histories, exhibits, workshops, storytelling, artifacts, and documents, particularly those dealing with often unappreciated contributions of Kansas City to the development of jazz.

1565.

Sedalia Ragtime Archives
State Fair Community College
Sedalia Missouri 65301
816-826-7100

Original memorabilia of Scott Joplin, the
"father of ragtime," are the highlights.
Organizes an annual June Ragtime Festival.

1566.

Great Plains Black Museum
2213 Lake St
Omaha Nebraska 68110
402-345-2212

1567.

**African American Museum & Research
Center**
705 W Van Buren Ave
Las Vegas Nevada 89106-3042
702-647-2242

1568.

**Afro-American Historical & Cultural
Society Museum**
1841 Kennedy Blvd
Jersey City New Jersey 07305
201-547-5262
201-547-5392—Fax

Exploration of the lives of prominent African
Americans.

1569.

NAACP Historical & Cultural Project
441 Bergen Ave
Jersey City New Jersey 07304
201-547-6562

1570.

Newark Museum
43–49 Washington St
Newark New Jersey 07102
201-596-6550

The museum's African collection spans the
entire continent, and differs from most in that
it prominently displays the artifacts and history of people from North Africa.

1571.

**Paul Robeson Center of Rutgers
University at Newark**
175 University Ave
Newark New Jersey 07102
201-648-5568

Explores the turbulent life of the actor, singer,
and activist, who graduated from Rutgers as a
Phi Beta Kappa valedictorian.

1572.

**New York African-American Research
Institute**
State University of New York
Albany New York 12246
418-433-5798

1573.

Harriet Tubman House
180 South St
Auburn New York 13901
315-252-2081

The preserved home of the tireless woman who conducted the Underground Railroad.

1574.

Africana Research Museum
345 Franklin St
Buffalo New York 14202-1702
716-854-8330

1575.

Afro-American Historical Society of the Niagara Frontier
Erie County Public Library, Lafayette Sq
Buffalo New York 14203
716-856-7525

1576.

African American Museum
110 N Franklin St
Hempstead New York 11550
516-485-0470

The history of African Americans on Long Island.

1577.

Black History Exhibit Center
106 N Main St
Hempstead New York 11550
526-538-2274

1578.

Peg-Leg Bates Country Club
Route 2, Box 703
Kerhonkson New York 12446
914-626-3781

The owner of this place is the one-legged tap dancer who won television fame with his appearances on the *Ed Sullivan Show.* The dining room has seen performances by Cab Calloway, Sarah Vaughn, Lena Horne, Harry Belafonte, and others.

1579.

African Burial Ground Project
290 Broadway (burial site)
New York New York 10048
212-432-5707
323-432-5920—Fax

Dr. Sherrill Wilson, Director of Office of Public Education; Steve Harper, Office Manager
Estimated 10,000 to 20,000 enslaved and free blacks were buried here during the colonial period. Community outrage in 1991 prevented its being paved over. Plans are now in the works to build a museum exploring the lives of Africans who were brought here in the late 1700s. Three hundred and ninety burials were actually excavated, and are being studied at Howard University.
1993

1580.

Audubon Ballroom & Malcolm X Memorial
165th St and Broadway
New York New York 10032

For decades a vibrant community center, the Audubon Ballroom was the place where Malcolm X was assassinated. Recently converted into a biotechnology research center by Columbia University. A memorial commemorates the leadership of Malcolm X.
1994

1581.

Museum of the City of New York
Fifth Ave at 103rd St
New York New York 10029
212-534-1672

Permanent exhibits explore three hundred years of black history in New York City.

1582.

Schomburg Center for Research in Black Culture
New York Public Library
New York New York 10037
212-491-2200
212-491-6760—Fax

The premiere research center for black studies, with over 5,000 volumes, 3,000 manuscripts, 2,000 etchings, several thousand pamphlets, and 250,000 pictures spanning the time between 8th-century Africa to the Harlem Renaissance and beyond. Named after Arthur A. Schomburg, the self-taught historian, bibliophile, art collector, and political activist whose collections formed the core of the research center.
1926

1583.

Frederick Douglass Grave
Mount Hope Cemetery
Rochester New York 14620
716-473-2755

The grave site of the 19th century's most influential African-American abolitionist.

1584.

Somerset Place
P.O. Box 215
Creswell North Carolina 27928
919-797-4560

Once the home of 21 slave families, this preserved plantation now has guided tours and a small museum, and is the site of an annual reunion of the descendants of slaves who once worked there.

1585.

Hayti Heritage Center
804 Old Fayetteville St
Durham North Carolina 27702
919-687-0288

Houses the William Tucker African American Archive (a collection devoted to the famous author and illustrator of children's books) as well as an art gallery and dance studio.

1586.

North Carolina Mutual Life Insurance Company
Mutual Plaza
Durham North Carolina 27701-3616
919-682-9201
919-683-1694—Fax

Bert Collins, CPA, President/CEO

1587.

Martin Luther King Museum of Black Culture
511 N Henry St
Eden North Carolina 27288

1588.

Black Cultural Center
The University of Akron
Akron Ohio 44325
216-972-7030

1589.

Sojourner Truth Monument
37 N High St
Akron Ohio 44308

A monument at the site of this famous suffragist and abolitionist's impromptu "Ain't I a Woman?" address.

1590.

Consortium Black History Museum
1515 Linn St
Cincinnati Ohio 45214
513-381-0645

1591.

African American Museum
1765 Crawford Rd
Cleveland Ohio 44106
216-791-1700

Explores the contributions of Africans and African Americans throughout Western history.

1592.

African-American Archives
The Western Reserve Historical Society
Cleveland Ohio 44106-1788
216-721-5722

1593.

Afro-American Cultural & Historical Society
1765 Crawford Rd
Cleveland Ohio 44106
216-791-1700

The society seeks to increase the recognition of the role played by blacks in the development of the United States. It is concerned with school textbooks and memorials for outstanding black leaders. It operates a speaker's bureau and hopes to develop a museum.

1594.

Harriet Tubman Museum
9250 Miles Park
Cleveland Ohio 44128
216-341-1202

A museum dedicated to preserving relics from the era of slavery, abolition, and reconstruction.

1595.

Paul Laurence Dunbar House
219 N Summit Ave
Dayton Ohio 45407
513-224-7061

The preserved home of the preeminent African-American writer and poet, including his personal belongings, such as a ceremonial sword presented to him by President Theodore Roosevelt and original manuscripts of his poems.

1596.

Black Heritage Library
837 Liberty St
Findlay Ohio 45840-3027
419-423-3315

1597.

Boley Historic District
c/o Boley Chamber of Commerce
Boley Oklahoma 74829
918-667-3477

An all-black town that drew its settlers from the descendants of slaves held by the Creek Indians. All of its public and prominent officials were black. Now a National Historic Landmark, it serves to give a glimpse of the African-American presence in the American West, as well as the site of an annual Black Rodeo held on Memorial Day weekend.

1598.

Greenwood Cultural Center
322 N Greenwood
Tulsa Oklahoma 74120
918-585-2548

Documents the history of Tulsa's black community, including the devastating race riots of 1921 and the efforts of the community to rebuild in the riots' aftermath.

1599.

All-Wars Memorial to Black Soldiers
42nd St and Parkside Ave
Philadelphia Pennsylvania 19121
215-685-0001

Memorial to black American veterans who served in the U.S. Armed Forces.

1600.

John W. Coltrane Home & Historical Marker
1511 N 33rd St
Philadelphia Pennsylvania 19121
215-763-1118

Historical marker marks the impact of the famed saxophonist on the music world, as well as a museum devoted to Philadelphia's African-American musical heritage.

1601.

African Heritage Classroom
University of Pittsburgh
Pittsburgh Pennsylvania 15260
412-624-6150

A recreation of the central courtyard of an Ashanti royal residence to reveal Africa's cultural foundations and family life. Artifacts from numerous other African peoples.

1602.

LeMoyne House
49 E Maiden St
Washington Pennsylvania 15301
412-225-6740

The house of Dr. Francis J. LeMoyne, an early abolitionist and activist within the Underground Railroad. His home now serves as a museum of 19th-century American history.

1603.

Rhode Island Black Heritage Society
One Hilton St
Providence Rhode Island 02905
401-751-3490

A society devoted to promoting, interpreting, and preserving Rhode Island's African-American past.

1604.

Rhode Island Black Heritage Society
46 Aborn St
Providence Rhode Island 02903
401-751-3490

Creates an environment and understanding about the contributions of African Americans and the importance of the African-American culture to the development of American culture. Dedicated to discovering, preserving, interpreting, and exhibiting black history and culture and to educating the public at large. 1974

1605.

Avery Research Center for African American History and Culture
125 Bull St
Charleston South Carolina 29424
803-792-5742 or 803-727-2009

Depository for African-American and Gullah history and culture of South Carolina.

1606.

Mann Simon's Cottage
1403 Richland St
Orangeburg South Carolina 29201
803-252-1450

1607.

Old Slave Mart Museum The
P.O. Box 446
Sullivan's Island South Carolina 29482
803-883-3797

1608.

Adams Memorial Museum
54 Sherman
Deadwood South Dakota 57732
605-578-1714

Documents the local African-American history, including black cowboys, miners, and residents, especially the infamous "Nat Love."

1609.

Shrine to Music Museum
414 E Clark St
Vermillion South Dakota 57069
605-677-5306

The continuum of African musical tradition is traced throughout the diaspora, including musical instruments from Egypt and sub-Saharan Africa, slave stringed instruments, and the emergence of jazz and ragtime.

1610.

Chattanooga African American Museum
730 Martin Luther King Blvd
Chattanooga Tennessee 37403
615-267-1076

The famed singer Bessie Smith's piano and other memorabilia form the centerpiece of this museum, which also documents the history of the local African-American community.

1611.

Alex Haley House Museum
200 S Church St
Henning Tennessee 38041
901-738-2240

Museum devoted to the life of the highly influential author of *Roots* and *The Autobiography of Malcolm X.*

1612.

Beck Cultural Exchange Center
1927 Dandridge Ave
Knoxville Tennessee 37915
615-524-8461

Documents Eastern Tennessee's regional history and commemorates the life of the first African American employed by the U.S. Post Office, who later went on to become a wealthy real estate entrepreneur and philanthropist.

1613.

Beale St Historic District
Beale St Management
Memphis Tennessee 38103
901-526-0110

A prominent residence for many educated African Americans after the Civil War, this city was the place where black music began moving into the mainstream with the birth of rock 'n' roll: Elvis Presley, Jerry Lee Lewis, Carl Perkins, and Johnny Cash all began their careers here. Several generations of black entertainers have called Memphis home, beginning with W. C. Handy and the birth of the blues.

1614.

Center for Southern Folklore
152 Beale St
Memphis Tennessee 38101
901-525-3655

Chronicles the heritage of the South through exhibits, photographs, tours, festivals, and films, with African-American contributions prominently displayed.

1615.

Ida B. Wells Plaque
First Baptist Church
Memphis Tennessee 38103
901-527-4832

Braving death threats, this courageous woman published *Free Speech*, a newspaper that scathingly denounced lynchings. This plaque commemorates her accomplishments.

1616.

National Civil Rights Museum
450 Mulberry St
Memphis Tennessee 38103
901-521-9699

Extensively chronicles important events and accomplishments during the civil rights movement. Erected at the motel where Dr. King was assassinated; today the rooms where he was shot are preserved as they were on the day of his death.

1617.

George Washington Carver Museum
1165 Angelina St
Austin Texas 78702
512-472-4809

Willie C. Madison, Superintendent/CEO
Once the home of Austin's first "colored" library, this building now houses a tribute to the famed "peanut doctor" and documents the local black heritage. Changing exhibitions, special programs, and classes explore the African-American experience.

1618.

Black Heritage Gallery
5408 Almeda St
Houston Texas 77004-7442
713-529-7900

1619.

Taylor-Stevenson Ranch
11822 Almeda St
Houston Texas 79045
713-433-4441

One of the first and few remaining black family-owned working cattle ranches in America.

1620.

Institute of Texas Cultures
801 S Bowie
San Antonio Texas 78294
210-226-7651

Celebrates the heritages of ethnic minorities in Texas through permanent and traveling exhibits, artifacts, photographs, and demographic and statistical data.

1621.

University of Utah Library
400 South and University Sts
Salt Lake City Utah 84102
801-581-8864 or 801-581-8863

Oral histories, photographs, microfilm of the black newspaper *Broad Axe,* and documentation of the relationship between African Americans and the Mormon church are significant in the library's holdings.

1622.

Alexandria Black History Resource Center
638 Alfred St
Alexandria Virginia 22314
703-838-4356

Housed in the African-American community's first public library, this institution chronicles the contributions of African Americans to the city's history through paintings, photographs, books, and other memorabilia.

1623.

Black History Resource Center
638 N Alfred St
Alexandria Virginia 22314-1823
703-838-4356

1624.

**Fredericksburg Area Museum &
Cultural Center**
904 Princess Anne St
Fredericksburg Virginia 22401
703-371-3037

Local African-American history, and the impact of African culture on Anglo culture, are explored here.

1625.

Slave Block
Charles and Williams Sts
Fredericksburg Virginia 22401

An original platform on which slaves where inspected and auctioned.

1626.

**Booker T. Washington National
Monument**
Route 3, Box 310
Hardy Virginia 24101

Birthplace and childhood home of the famous intellectual, college president, and statesman; run by the National Park Service.

1627.

Lynchburg Museum
901 Court St
Lynchburg Virginia 24505
804-846-1459

Highlights the 20th-century African-American social and business presence.

1628.

**Newsome House Museum & Cultural
Center**
2803 Oak St
Newport News Virginia 23607
804-247-2380

This son of former slaves rose up to become the editor of the *Newport News Star* and was licensed to practice law before the Virginia Supreme Court. His restored home now offers programs and exhibits on African-American history and culture.

1629.

War Memorial Museum of Virginia
9285 Warwick Blvd
Newport News Virginia 23607
804-247-8523

In the "Black Soldier" gallery, an exhibit explores the roles and contributions of black soldiers in the armed forces, as well as chronicling the injustices done against them, including their exclusion from the historical record.

1630.

Black Civil War Veterans' Memorial
Elmwood Cemetery
Norfolk Virginia 23510
804-441-2576

The South's only memorial honoring black veterans of the Civil War. Gravestones of African-American sailors and soldiers who died in the Civil War and Spanish-American War can also be found here.

1631.

Black History Museum & Cultural Center of Virginia
00 Clay St
Richmond Virginia 23219
804-780-9093

A central repository for the memoirs, documents, oral histories, artifacts, and memorabilia of central Virginia's African-American community. Two small exhibits explore the African-American presence in Jackson Ward and the struggle for voting rights.

1632.

Jackson Ward
Bordered by 4th, Marshall, and Smith Sts and I-95
Richmond Virginia

Important center of activity for urban black America at the turn of the century and home of the "Wall Street of Black America." Now on the Register of National Historic Places.

1633.

Maggie Walker House
110 Leigh St
Richmond Virginia 22323
804-780-1380

The daughter of former slaves, this woman was a significant force in Richmond's black community, the NAACP, the National Association of Colored Women, and the Virginia Industrial School for Girls. Her house has been designated a National Historic Site.

1634.

Museum of the Confederacy
1201 E Clay St
Richmond Virginia 23210
804-649-1861

Although still in large part dominated by the leadership of the Confederacy, this museum now has exhibits and outreach programs that explore African-American life in the South, paying particular attention to the games, stories, music, dance, food, and drama of life as a slave.

1635.

Virginia E. Randolph Cottage Museum
2200 Mountain Rd
Richmond Virginia 23060
804-261-5029 or 804-262-3363

Home of the woman who played a key role in fostering black vocational training in Virginia, especially for women.

1636.

Harrison Museum of African-American Culture
523 Harrison Ave, NW
Roanoke Virginia 24016
703-345-4818

Small museum that documents the history of the local black community and serves as a forum for the exhibition of art and the performing arts.

1637.

Jimi Hendrix Grave
Greenwood Memorial Park Funeral Home
350 Monroe Ave, NE
Renton Washington 98056
206-255-1511

The grave of the greatest rock guitarist of all time.

1638.

Camp Washington-Carver Museum
HC 35, Box 5
Clifftop West Virginia 25831
304-438-3005

At the site of the nation's first State Negro 4-H Camp (now on the National Register of Historic Places), this organization is now primarily devoted to exploring black culture through arts camps for youth, photographs, and artifacts.

1639.

Harpers Ferry National Historic Park
P.O. Box 65
Harpers Ferry West Virginia 25425
304-535-6298

This living history museum encompasses an entire town, and explores the impact of the industrial revolution, John Brown's raid, African-American history, and the Civil War.

1640.

Kimball War Memorial
E Main St
Kimball West Virginia 24853
304-448-2118

One of the country's few tributes to the black soldiers that served in WWI, this memorial was created by the hard work of black coal miners in the area.

1641.

State Historical Society of Wisconsin
816 State St
Madison Wisconsin 53703
608-264-6588 or 608-264-6535

The library's civil rights collection includes the archives of CORE (Congress of Racial Equality), papers from the Angela Davis trial, the FBI file on Dr. Martin Luther King, Jr., and documents of SNCC (Student Nonviolent Coordinating Committee) and the Mississippi Freedom Democratic Party. Its museum recently opened exhibits that explore African-American history in Wisconsin.

1642.

America's Black Holocaust Museum
2233 N 4th St
Milwaukee Wisconsin 53203
414-264-2500

James Cameron, Founder & Tour Guide Explores the "genocide and injustices experienced by African Americans."

❀ MUSIC ❀

1643.

W. C. Handy Birthplace, Museum & Library
620 W College St
Florence Alabama 35630
205-760-6434

Tribute to the legendary blues musician. It also houses a resource center for black history and culture, and is the site of an annual music festival.

1644.

African Percussion
Calabasas California 91302
818-591-3111

1645.

Evans-Tibbs Collection
1910 Vermont Ave, NW
Washington DC 20001
202-234-8164

Former house of the talented soprano and founder of the Negro National Opera company. Today her home is on the National Historic Register and houses a world-famous collection of African-American art, containing works by Henry O. Tanner, Romare Bearden, Richmond Barthé, Charles Alston, Jacob Lawrence, and Elizabeth Catlett.

1646.

Ma Rainey House
805 Fifth Ave
Columbus Georgia 31901
706-571-4700

The preserved house of the "Mother of Blues."

1647.

Gospel Music Foundation
10053 South Halsted Street
Chicago Illinois 60628
312-239-5570
312-239-9674—Fax

Dr. Princella Hudson-Gilliam, Executive Director
Foundation offers programs and activities to educate young people in gospel music.

1648.

New Orleans Jazz & Heritage Festival
1205 N Rampart St
New Orleans Louisiana 70153
800-535-8747 or 504-522-4786
or 504-561-8747

Splendid regional food, African-American arts and crafts, and almost every variety of jazz around.

1649.

Cab Calloway Jazz Institute Museum
Coppin State College
Baltimore Maryland 21216
410-383-5926

Traces the life of the legendary performer through a series of photographs, posters, memorabilia, and film stills.

1650.

Eubie Blake National Museum & Cultural Center
409 Charles St
Baltimore Maryland 21201
410-396-6442

Named for the famed songwriter and composer of jazz and blues, this museum explores Blake's life as well as the history of American musical theater through pictorial essays and video and audio presentations.

1651.

Jazz Times
7961 Eastern Ave, Suite 303
Silver Spring Maryland 20910
301-588-4114

Glenn Sabin, Publisher

1652.

Gospel Music Workshop of America Inc.
P.O. Box 4632
Detroit Michigan 48234
313-989-2340

Edward D. Smith, Executive Secretary

1653.

Graystone International Jazz Museum & Jazz Hall of Fame
1521 Broadway
Detroit Michigan 48226
313-963-3813

Commemorates and preserves memorabilia related to America's most distinctive contribution to world culture.

1654.

Motown Museum
2648 W Grand Blvd
Detroit Michigan 48202
313-875-2264

A tribute to the sound and musicians of the legendary music label.

1655.

Delta Blues Museum
Carnegie Public Library
Clarksdale Mississippi 38614
601-624-4461

Located in the birthplace of blues, this museum explores the connections between blues and American culture, including videotapes, recordings, photographs, memorabilia, performances, and a blues archive.

1656.

Rooster Blues Records
232 Sunflower Ave
Clarksdale Mississippi 38614
601-627-2209

Offers a blues tour, guide to local blues clubs, and access to important buildings in the history of blues.

1657.

Blues Archives
University of Mississippi
Oxford Mississippi 38677
601-232-7753

On the campus of Ole Miss, this archives contains collections devoted to B. B. King, Ma Rainey, Percy Mayfield, and others.

1658.

African International Records
289 Buffalo Ave
Brooklyn New York 11213-4105
718-771-6268

1659.

African Record Centre Ltd.
1194 Nostrand Ave
Brooklyn New York 11225-5912
718-493-4500

1660.

African Flavor Master Music
226-10 Merrick Blvd
Jamaica New York 11413-2101
718-723-4956

1661.

African American Musicians
125 E 126th St
New York New York 10035-1624
212-348-4944

1662.

African Roots Sound
West Babylon New York 11704-1312
516-491-4545

Concert sound company.

1663.

Chattanooga African American Museum
730 Martin Luther King Blvd
Chattanooga Tennessee 37403
615-267-1076

The famed singer Bessie Smith's piano and other memorabilia form the centerpiece of this museum, which also documents the history of the local African-American community.

1664.

Memphis Music & Blues Museum
97 S 2nd St
Memphis Tennessee 38103
901-525-4007

Vintage posters, advertisements, rare recordings, photographs, instruments, film footage of Bessie Smith, Furry Lewis, Sleepy John Estes, and others, and a re-creation of Pee Wee's Saloon can all be found here.

❋ NEWSPAPERS & MAGAZINES ❋

1665.

Birmingham Times
115 Third Ave W
Birmingham Alabama 32504
205-251-5158

James E. Lewis, Publisher-Editor
Weekly black community newspaper.
1964

1666.

Birmingham World
407 15th St N
Birmingham Alabama 35203
205-251-6523
205-252-2518—Fax

Joe N. Dixon, Publisher-Editor
Weekly black community newspaper.
1930

1667.

Greene County Democrat
P.O. Box 598
Eta Alabama 35462
205-372-3344
205-372-2243—Fax

Carol P. Zippert, Copublisher
Weekly black community newspaper.

1668.

Shoals News Leader
P.O. Box 427
Florence Alabama 35630
205-766-5542

William R. Liner, Publisher-Editor
Weekly black community newspaper.

1669.

Speakin' Out News
2006 Roole Dr, Suite A, P.O. Box 2826
Huntsville Alabama 35804
205-852-9449
205-852-9484—Fax

William D. Smothers, Publisher-Editor
Weekly black community newspaper.

1670.

Inner City News
P.O. Box 1545
Mobile Alabama 36633
205-452-9330 or 205-933-9331
or 205-452-9329

Charles W. Porter, Publisher-Editor
Weekly African-American community-oriented
newspaper.

1671.

Mobile Beacon
2311 Costarides St
Mobile Alabama 36617
334-479-0629

Cleretta Blackmon, Publisher-Editor
Weekly black community newspaper.

1672.

New Times
156 S Broad St
Mobile Alabama 36602
205-432-0356

Vivian D. Figures, Managing Editor
Biweekly black community newspaper.

1673.

Montgomery-Tuskegee Times
3900 Birmingham Hwy
Montgomery Alabama 36108
205-264-7149

Rev. Alvin Dixon, Editor

1674.

Arizona Informant
1746 E Madison St, #2
Phoenix Arizona 85034
602-257-9300

Cloves Campbell Sr., Publisher
Weekly black community newspaper.

1675.

Black Commerce Directory
Phoenix Arizona 85012
602-230-8161

1676.

Bakersfield News Observer
P.O. Box 3624
Bakersfield California 93385
805-324-9466
805-324-9472—Fax

Joseph L. Coley, President-Publisher

1677.

California Voice
2956 Sacramento St, Suite C
Berkeley California 94703
510-644-2446
415-839-3474—Fax

Dr. Ruth C. Love, Publisher-Editor
Weekly black community newspaper.

1678.

Black Progress Review
3010 Wilshire Blvd
Beverly Hills California 90210
310-285-0112

Publication for minority recruitment at corporations and school districts.

1679.

Compton Bulletin
P.O. Box 4248
Compton California 90224
213-774-0018

O. Ray Watkins, President-Publisher
Black community newspaper.

1680.

California Advocate
P.O. Box 11826
Fresno California 93775
209-268-0941

Mark Kimber, Publisher

1681.

Compton Metropolitan Gazette
First-Line Publishers
Granada Hills California 91344
818-782-8695
818-782-2924—Fax

Hillary Hamm, Publisher
Weekly black community newspaper serving
Compton and Carson.

1682.

Minority Employment Journal
110 S La Brea Ave
Inglewood California 90301-1768
310-330-3670

1683.

African Connection Newspaper
5429 Crenshaw Blvd
Los Angeles California 90043-2407
213-292-6397

1684.

African Times Newspapers The
6363 Wilshire Blvd
Los Angeles California 90048-5701
213-951-0717

1685.

CAAS Publications
Center for Afro-American Studies
Publications
Los Angeles California 90024-1545
310-825-3528

Toyomi Ingus, Managing Editor

1686.

Compton/Carson Wave
Central News–Wave Publications
Los Angeles California 90043
212-290-3000
212-291-0219—Fax

C. Z. Wilson, Publisher
Weekly black community newspaper.

1687.

Herald Dispatch
3860 Crenshaw Blvd, #110
Los Angeles California 90008
213-291-9486
213-291-2123—Fax

John H. Holoman, President
Weekly black community newspaper.

1688.

Los Angeles Sentinel
1112 E 43rd St
Los Angeles California 90011
213-299-3800
213-232-8035—Fax

Kenneth R. Thomas, Esq., Publisher-CEO
Weekly black community newspaper.

1689.

One Million Black Men Magazine
201 N Figueroa St
Los Angeles California 90012
213-975-1553
Covers lifestyles and attitudes of today's black men.

1690.

Players Magazine
8060 Melrose Ave
Los Angeles California 90046
213-653-8060

Joe Nazel, Editor
Monthly entertainment magazine for the 18- to 40-year-old black male.

1691.

African Forum The
Oakland California 94601
510-535-2292

A magazine for African issues.

1692.

Black Business Listings
Oakland California 94601
510-839-0690

1693.

Black Scholar Magazine
P.O. Box 2869
Oakland California 94609
510-547-6633

Robert Crisman, Publisher

1694.

El Mundo
630 20th St
Oakland California 94612
510-763-1120
510-763-9670—Fax

Thomas Berkeley, Publisher
Weekly newspapers with general news, sports, and entertainment (Spanish and English).

1695.

Minority Business & Professional Directory
Oakland California 94601
510-874-7740

1696.

Oakland Post Newspaper Group
630 20th St
Oakland California 94612
510-763-1120
415-763-9670—Fax

Thomas Berkeley, Publisher
Black community newspaper published two times per week.

1697.

Observer Newspaper
3540 4th Ave
Sacramento California 95817
916-452-4781

Dr. William H. Lee, Publisher

1698.

Precinct Reporter
1677 W Baseline St
San Bernardino California 92411
909-889-1706
714-889-1706—Fax

A. Brian Townsend, Publisher
Weekly black community newspaper.

1699.

San Bernardino American News
1583 W Baseline St
San Bernardino California 92411-0010
714-889-7677
714-889-2882—Fax

Willie Mae Martin, Publisher/Owner
Weekly black community newspaper.

1700.

San Diego Voice & Viewpoint
1729 Euclid Ave
San Diego California 92105
619-266-2233
619-266-0533—Fax

John E. Warren, Publisher
Weekly black American newspaper.

1701.

Minority Law Journal
1 Market Plaza
San Francisco California 94105-1313
415-896-1310

1702.

San Francisco New Bayview
1624 Oakdale Ave (at 3rd St)
P.O. Box 24477
San Francisco California 94124-0477
415-282-7894
415-282-4822—Fax

Muhammad Al-Kareem, Publisher
Weekly black community newspaper.

1703.

San Francisco Sun-Reporter
1366 Turk St
San Francisco California 94115
415-931-5778
415-931 0214—Fax

Dr. Carlton B. Goodlett, Publisher
Weekly black community newspaper.

1704.

Image Magazine
11012 Ventura Blvd
Studio City California 91604
310-338-6610
310-338-6616—Fax
Magazine focused on empowering men of
color. Published bimonthly.

1705.

LA Metropolitan Gazette
First Line Publishers Inc.
14621 Titus St
Van Nuys California 91402
818-782-8695 (Advertising) or 818-782-8696
(Editorial)
818-782-2924—Fax

Beverly J. Hamm, Administrator; Hillard Hamm, Founder; Hillary R. Hamm, President

1706.

Long Beach Express
First Line Publishers Inc., LA Metro Group
14621 Titus St
Van Nuys California 91402
818-782-8695 (Advertising) or 818-782-8696 (Editorial)
818-782-2924—Fax

Beverly J. Hamm, Administrator; Hillard Hamm, Founder; Hillary R. Hamm, President

1707.

Palmdale-Lancaster Sun Journal
First Line Publishers Inc., LA Metro Group
14621 Titus St
Van Nuys California 91402
818-782-8695 (Advertising) or 818-782-8696 (Editorial)
818-782-2924—Fax

Beverly J. Hamm, Administrator; Hillard Hamm, Founder; Hillary R. Hamm, President

1708.

Pasadena Gazette
First Line Publishers Inc., LA Metro Group
14621 Titus St
Van Nuys California 91402
818-782-8695 (Advertising) or 818-782-8696 (Editorial)
818-782-2924—Fax

Beverly J. Hamm, Administrator; Hillard Hamm, Founder; Hillary R. Hamm, President
Weekly black community newspaper serving Pasadena, Altadena, Monrovia, and Duarte.

1709.

San Fernando Valley Gazette Express
First Line Publishers Inc., LA Metro Group
14621 Titus St
Van Nuys California 91402
818-782-8695 (Advertising) or 818-782-8696 (Editorial)
818-782-2924—Fax

Beverly J. Hamm, Administrator; Hillard Hamm, Founder; Hillary R. Hamm, President

1710.

Africa Today
c/o Graduate School of International Studies, University of Colorado
Denver Colorado 80208
303-753-3678

Edward H. Hawley, Executive Director

1711.

Denver Weekly News
P.O. Box 732
Denver Colorado 80201
303-839-5800
303-839-5891—Fax

F. Cosmo Harris, Publisher-Editor
Weekly black community newspaper serving Denver and surrounding areas.

1712.

Hartford Inquirer
P.O. Box 1260
Hartford Connecticut 06143
203-522-1462
203-522-3014—Fax

William R. Hales, Publisher
Black community newspaper.

1713.

Hartford Star
P.O. Box 606
Hartford Connecticut 06101

Henry Morris, Publisher-Editor

1714.

African Link Magazine
788 Long Hill Ave
Shelton Connecticut 06484-5409
203-925-1632

1715.

African American Journal of Dentistry
731 Kennedy St, NW
Washington DC 20011-3031
202-882-9689

1716.

African News Service
134 North Carolina Ave, SE
Washington DC 20003
202-546-3675

1717.

American Visions
1156 15th St, NW
Washington DC 20005
202-496-9593
202-496-9851—Fax

Gary Puckrein, Publisher
A magazine for African-American culture, published six times per year.

1718.

Black Congressional Monitor
P.O. Box 75035
Washington DC 20013
202-488-8879
202-554-3116—Fax

Publishes a nutritional legislation and funding report.

1719.

Black Film Review
2025 I St, NW
Washington DC 20006-1902
202-466-2753

1720.

Capitol Spotlight
2112 New Hampshire Ave, NW
Washington DC 20009
202-628-0700

Ricardo Watts, Editor; Bette Brooks, Acting Publisher
Weekly black community newspaper.

1721.

Emerge Magazine
One BET Plaza
Washington DC 20018-1211
800-888-0488

"Black America's Newsmagazine." Published monthly.

1722.

Washington Afro-American
1612 14th St, NW
Washington DC 20009
202-332-0080
202-939-7461—Fax

Frances L. Murphy, Publisher
Weekly newspaper serving the black community.

1723.

Washington Informer
3117 Martin Luther King Jr. Ave, SE
Washington DC 20032
202-561-4100
202-5743785—Fax

Dr. Calvin Rolark, Publisher
Weekly newspaper serving Washington's metropolitan area black community.

1724.

Washington New Observer
811 Florida Ave, NW
Washington DC 20001
202-232-3060

Robert B. Newton, Publisher/Editor
Weekly black community newspaper.

1725.

Wilmington Defender
1702 Locust St
Wilmington Delaware 19802
302-656-3252

Leroy E. Brown Sr., Publisher
Weekly black community newspaper.

1726.

Daytona Times
P.O. Box 1110, 429 S Campbell St
Daytona Beach Florida 32015
904-253-0321
904-2547510—Fax

Charles W. Cherry II, Managing Editor
Weekly black community newspaper.

1727.

Black College Today
6721 NW 44th Ct
Fort Lauderdale Florida 33319-4030
305-749-4560

1728.

Westside Gazette
701 NW 18th Ave, Building D
Fort Lauderdale Florida 33311-7879
305-523-5115
305-522-2553—Fax

Bobby Henry Jr., Publisher
Black community newspaper published twice a week.

1729.

Community Voice
3046 Lafayette St
Fort Myers Florida 33916
813-337-4444
813-334-8289—Fax

Charles B. Weaver, Publisher-Editor

1730.

African USA Magazine
Hollywood Florida 33021
305-966-0000

1731.

Black Pages USA
9951 Atlantic Blvd
Jacksonville Florida 32225-6585
904-727-7451

1732.

Florida Star News
5196-C Norwood Ave
Jacksonville Florida 32208
904-766-8834

Mary W. Simpson, Publisher

1733.

Jacksonville Free Press
Afro American Building, P.O. Box 43580
Jacksonville Florida 32203
904-634-1993 or 384-0235

Rita Perry, Publisher/Editor

1734.

Black Business Pages Magazine
12902 SW 133rd Ct
Miami Florida 33186-5806
305-234-8689

1735.

Black Miami Weekly
6025 NW 6th Ct
Miami Florida 33127
305-754-8800

Joel B. Dyer, Publisher/Editor

1736.

Black Nation Magazine
16375 NE 18th Ave
Miami Florida 33162-4700
305-956-9753

1737.

Miami Times
900 NW 54th St
Miami Florida 33127
305-757-1147
813-756-0771—Fax

Garth C. Reeves, Publisher
Weekly black community newspaper.

1738.

Orlando Times
4403 Vineland Rd, Suite B-5
Orlando Florida 32811-7362
407-841-3710
407-849-0434—Fax

Calvin Collins Jr., M.D., Publisher/Editor
Weekly black community newspaper.

1739.

New American Press
521 W Cervantes St
Pensacola Florida 32501
904-432-8410

Walter Leroy, Publisher

1740.

Pensacola Voice
213 E Yonge St
Pensacola Florida 32503
904-434-6963
904-469-8745—Fax

Les Humphrey, Publisher-Editor
Weekly black community newspaper.

1741.

Broward Times The
2001 W Sample Rd, #410
Pompano Beach Florida 33064
305-351-9070
305-968-3316—Fax

Keith A. Clayborne, Publisher

1742.

Bulletin
P.O. Box 2560
Sarasota Florida 34230-2560
813-953-3990 or 813-953-4299
813-753-9843—Fax

Fred L. Bacon, Publisher
Weekly black community newspaper.

1743.

Weekly Challenger
2500 9th St
St. Petersburg Florida 33705
813-896-2922

Cleveland Johnson, Publisher/Editor
Weekly black community newspaper.

1744.

Capital Outlook
1501 E Park Ave
Tallahassee Florida 32301
904-681-1852

Roosevelt Wilson, Publisher
Weekly black community newspaper.

1745.

Dollar Stretcher
P.O. Box 8205
Tampa Florida 33674
813-247-4313

Nathaniel G. Hannah, Publisher/President

1746.

Florida Sentinel Bulletin
2207 21st Ave
Tampa Florida 33605
813-248-1921

C. Bly Andrews Jr., Publisher/President
Black community newspaper published twice
per week.

1747.

Florida Photo News The
P.O. Box 1583-46
West Palm Beach Florida 33402
305-833-4511

Yasmin Williams-Cooper, Publisher/Editor

1748.

Palm Beach Gazette
P.O. Box 18469
West Palm Beach Florida 33416-8469
407-844-5501
407-844-5551—Fax

Gwen Ivory, President

1749.

Albany Southwest Georgian
P.O. Box 1943
Albany Georgia 31702
912-436-2156

A. C. Searles, Publisher

1750.

African World News
300 Peachtree St, NE
Atlanta Georgia 30308-3210
404-577-7250

1751.

Atlanta Daily World
145 Auburn Ave, NE
Atlanta Georgia 30335-1201
404-659-1110

CA Scott, Editor/General Manager
Black community newspaper published four
times per week.

1752.

Atlanta Inquirer
947 Martin Luther King Jr. Dr, NW
Atlanta Georgia 30314
404-523-6086

John B. Smith, Publisher/CEO

1753.

Atlanta Voice
P.O. Box 92405
Atlanta Georgia 30314
404-524-6426

Janis L. Ware, Publisher
Weekly black community newspaper.

1754.

Upscale Magazine
Upscale Communications, P.O. Box 10798
Atlanta Georgia 30310
404-758-7467

Bernard Bronner, Publisher

1755.

Augusta Focus
P.O. Box 10112
Augusta Georgia 30903
404-722-7327

Charles Walker, Publisher
Weekly general newspaper.

1756.

Metro Country Courier
314 Walton Way
Augusta Georgia 30901
404-724-6556
404-724-4200—Fax

Barbara A. Gordon, Publisher
Weekly black community newspaper.

1757.

Columbus Times
2230 Buena Vista Rd
Columbus Georgia 31906
404-324-2404

Ophelia D. Mitchell, Publisher-Editor
Weekly black community newspaper.

1758.

Voice of the Black Community
625 E Wood St
Decatur Georgia 62523-1152
217-423-2231

Horace Livingston, Publisher

1759.

Fort Valley Herald
315 N Camellia Blvd
Fort Valley Georgia 31030
912-825-7000

Bob James, Publisher
Black community newspaper.

1760.

Black Pages The
590 Cotton Ave
Macon Georgia 31201-7503
912-738-0616

1761.

Macon Courier
P.O. Box 4423
Macon Georgia 31208-4423
912-742-4508 or 912-746-5605

Melvyn J. Williams, Publisher

1762.

Macon Metro Times
1691 Forsyth St
Macon Georgia 31201
912-746-2405
912-745-8511—Fax

Charles E. Richardson, Publisher

1763.

Atlanta Tribune
875 Old Roswell Rd, Suite C-100
Roswell Georgia 30076
404-587-0501
404-642-6501—Fax

Patricia Lottier, Publisher
Monthly black community newspaper.

1764.

Herald The
P.O. Box 486
Savannah Georgia 34102
912-232-4505
912-232-4079—Fax

Floyd Adams Jr., Publisher
Weekly black community newspaper.

1765.

Savannah Tribune
P.O. Box 2066
Savannah Georgia 31402
912-233-6128
912-233-6128—Fax

Shirley B. James, Publisher
Weekly black community newspaper.

1766.

African-American Outreach Newspaper
218 10th St
Cairo Illinois 62914-1924
618-734-4510

1767.

African American Chronicle The
3014 W Walnut St
Chicago Illinois 60612-1847
312-826-4292

1768.

African American Reader Newspaper The
746 E 79th St
Chicago Illinois 60619-3118
312-783-3850

1769.

Black Enterprise Magazine
625 N Michigan Ave
Chicago Illinois 60611
312-664-8667

1770.

Black Writer
Terrell Associates
Chicago Illinois 60690
312-995-5195
312-924-3818—Fax

Mable Terrell, Editor/Publisher.
Quarterly magazine offering information to African-American writers and serving as a forum for publishing works by black writers.

1771.

Blackbook International Business and Entertainment Reference Guide
National Publications Sales Agency Inc.
National Plaza 1610
Chicago Illinois 60649
312-375-6800

Donald C. Walker, Publisher/Editor

1772.

Chicago Citizen
412 E 87th St
Chicago Illinois 60619
312-487-7700
312-487-7931—Fax

William Garth, Publisher/President
Weekly black community newspaper.

1773.

Chicago Defender
2400 S Michigan Ave
Chicago Illinois 60616
312-225-2400
312-225-6954—Fax

Fred D. Sengstacke, Publisher
The most influential black newspaper in America for much of this century, and one of the driving forces behind the migration of black sharecroppers into the North.

1774.

Chicago Independent Bulletin
2037 W 95th St
Chicago Illinois 60643
312-783-1040

Hurley L. Green Sr., Publisher
Weekly black community newspaper.

1775.

Chicago New Crusader
6429 S King Dr
Chicago Illinois 60637
312-752-2500
312-752-2817—Fax

Dorothy Leavell, Publisher/Editor

1776.

Chicago Tri-City Journal
8 S Michigan Ave, #1111
Chicago Illinois 60603
312-346-8123

Ibn Sharrieff, Publisher/General Manager
Weekly black community newspaper

1777.

Citizen Newspapers
412 E 87th St
Chicago Illinois 60619
312-487-7700
312-487-7931—Fax

William Garth, Publisher/President

1778.

Dollars & Sense Magazine
National Publications Sales Agency Inc.
National Plaza
Chicago Illinois 60649
312-375-6800

Donald C. Walker, Publisher/Editor

1779.

Ebony
Johnson Publishing Company
820 S Michigan Ave
Chicago Illinois 60605
312-322-9200

John H. Johnson, Publisher

1780.

Ebony Man
Johnson Publishing Company
820 S Michigan Ave
Chicago Illinois 60605
312-322-9200

John H. Johnson, Publisher

1781.

Jet Magazine
Johnson Publishing Company
820 S Michigan Ave
Chicago Illinois 60605
312-322-9200

John H. Johnson, Publisher

1782.

Muslim Journal
910 W Van Buren St, #100
Chicago Illinois 60607
312-243-7600 or 312-243-9778

Ayesha K. Mustafaa, Editor
Weekly international Islamic newspaper.

1783.

A Positive Note
10053 South Halsted St
Chicago Illinois 60628
800-795-9379
African-American political/social/health magazine. Published bimonthly.

1784.

Signature Bride
101 W Grand Ave
Chicago Illinois 60610
312-527-6590
A bridal lifestyle magazine for African-
American women.

1785.

Chicago Standard News
615 Halsted
Chicago Heights Illinois 60411
708-755-5021
708-755-5020—Fax

Lorenzo E. Martin, Publisher
Weekly black community newspaper serving
Chicago and south suburbs.

1786.

Black Pages USA Inc.
2401 Main St
Columbia Illinois 29201-1947
803-254-6404

1787.

East St. Louis Monitor
1501 State St
East St. Louis Illinois 62205
618-271-0468

Anne E. Jordan, Publisher
Weekly black community newspaper.

1788.

Chicago Westside Journal
16618 S Hermitage
Markham Illinois 60426
708-333-2210

Don McIlvaine, Publisher/Editor

1789.

Black Pages USA Inc.
269 S Church St
Spartanburg Illinois 29306-3496
803-585-7172

1790.

Frost Illustrated
3121 S Calhoun
Fort Wayne Indiana 46807
219-745-0552

Edward Smith, Publisher
Weekly black community newspaper.

1791.

Gary Crusader
1549 Broadway
Gary Indiana 46407
219-885-4357

Dorothy Leavell, Publisher
Weekly black community newspaper.

1792.

Gary Info
1953 Broadway
Gary Indiana 46401
219-882-5591

Imogene Harris, Publisher
Weekly black newspaper with a Democratic orientation. Northwest Indiana's leading weekly.

1793.

Indiana Herald
2170 N Illinois St
Indianapolis Indiana 46202
317-923-8291
317-923-8292—Fax

Mary Tandy, Publisher
Weekly community newspaper.

1794.

Indianapolis Recorder
2901 N Tacoma Ave
Indianapolis Indiana 46218
317-924-5143
317-257-6878 or 317-924-5148—Fax

William Mays, Publisher/Editor
Weekly black community newspaper.

1795.

Black Magazine Agency
1226 E Broadway
Logansport Indiana 46947-3254
219-753-2429

1796.

Louisville Defender
1720 Dixie Hwy
Louisville Kentucky 40210
502-772-2591
502-775-8655—Fax

Clarence Leslie, Executive Vice President & General Manager; Yvonne D. Coleman, Director
Weekly community newspaper.

1797.

Alexandria News Weekly
1746 Mason St
Alexandria Louisiana 71301
318-443-7664

Leon Coleman, Publisher
Weekly general newspaper for the black community.

1798.

Baton Rouge Weekly Press
1384 Swan Ave, P.O. Box 74485
Baton Rouge Louisiana 70807
504-775-2002

Ivory Payne, Publisher

1799.

Black Pages
1553 Harding Blvd
Baton Rouge Louisiana 70807-5441
504-774-1553

1800.

Black Collegian Magazine
1240 S Broad St
New Orleans Louisiana 70125-2091
504-821-5694

Kuumba Ferrouilet, Managing Editor
Career opportunity magazine featuring job-
searching role models, interviews, entertainment, art, and African-American history, published four times per year.

1801.

Louisiana Weekly
616 Barone St
New Orleans Louisiana 70150
504-524-5563

Henry Dejoie, Publisher/Editor
Weekly black community newspaper.

1802.

New Orleans Data News Weekly
P.O. Box 51933
New Orleans Louisiana 70151
504-522-1418

Terry B. Jones, Publisher
Weekly black community newspaper.

1803.

Shreveport Sun
2224 Jewella Ave
Shreveport Louisiana 71139
318-631-6222

Sonya Landry, Publisher/Editor
Weekly black community newspaper.

1804.

African American News World
3002 Druid Park Dr
Baltimore Maryland 21215-7814
410-554-8200
410-554-8213—Fax

1805.

Afro-American Newspapers
2519 N Charles St
Baltimore Maryland 21218-4634
410-554-8282

1806.

Baltimore Afro-American
2519 N Charles St
Baltimore Maryland 21218
410-554-8200
410-554-8218—Fax

John J. Oliver Jr., Publisher
Weekly black community newspaper.

1807.

Baltimore Times
12 E 25th St
Baltimore Maryland 21218
410-366-3900

Joy Bramble, Publisher

1808.

Black Professional
Career Communications Group
729 E Pratt St
Baltimore Maryland 21202
410-244-7101
410-752-1837—Fax

Tyrone D. Taborn, President/CEO

1809.

Professional Magazine
Career Communications Group Inc.
729 E Pratt St
Baltimore Maryland 21202
410-224-7101

Keith T. Clinkscales, Publisher

1810.

Urban Profile Magazine
Career Communications Group Inc.
729 E Pratt St
Baltimore Maryland 21202
410-224-7101

Keith T. Clinkscales, Publisher
Monthly magazine covering African-Amerian
student interests.

1811.

US Black Engineer
Career Communications Group
729 E Pratt St, Suite 504
Baltimore Maryland 21202
410-244-7101
410-752-1837—Fax

Tyrone D. Taborn, Publisher
Magazine for black engineers, published five
times per year.

1812.

Jazz Times
7961 Eastern Ave, Suite 303
Silver Spring Maryland 20910
301-588-4114

Glenn Sabin, Publisher

1813.

Bay State Banner
925 Washington St
Dorchester Massachusetts 02124
617-288-4900

M. B. Miller, Publisher
Weekly newspaper serving the black community.

1814.

African American Journal
384 Penobscot Bldg
Detroit Michigan 48200
313-222-7600

1815.

Black Yellow Pages
11000 W McNichols Rd
Detroit Michigan 48221-2357
313-342-1717

1816.

Michigan Chronicle
479 Ledyard St
Detroit Michigan 48201
313-963-5522
313-963-8788—Fax

Sam Logan, Vice President/General Manager
Weekly black community newspaper.

1817.

Ecorse Telegram
4122 10th St
Ecorse Michigan 48229
313-928-2955

J. C. Wall, Publisher/Editor
Weekly black community newspaper.

1818.

Afro-American Gazette
Grand Rapids Michigan 49507
616-243-0577

1819.

Grand Rapids Times
2016 Eastern, SE
Grand Rapids Michigan 49507
616-245-8737

Yergan Pulliam, Copublisher
Weekly newspaper targeted for black population in Grand Rapids, Muskegon, Battle Creek and Kalamazoo.

1820.

Michigan Citizen
211 Glendale, Suite 216
Highland Park Michigan 48203
313-869-0033
313-869-0430—Fax

Charles E. Kelly, Publisher
Weekly newspaper serving African-American communities in Michigan.

1821.

Minneapolis Spokesman
3744 4th Ave S
Minneapolis Minnesota 55409
612-827-4021
612-827-0577—Fax

Launa Q. Newman, President/Copublisher
Weekly black community newspaper.

1822.

Insight News
422 University Ave
St Paul Minnesota 55103
612-227-1245

Al McFarlane, Publisher/Editor

1823.

Blazer The
P.O. Box 806
Jackson Mississippi 49204

Ben Wade, Publisher/Editor

1824.

Jackson Advocate
P.O. Box 3708
Jackson Mississippi 39207
601-948-4122
601-948-4125—Fax

Charles Tisdale, Publisher/Editor
Weekly black community newspaper.

1825.

Mississippi Memo Digest
2511 5th St
Meridian Mississippi 39301
601-693-2372

Robert E. Williams, Publisher/Editor

1826.

Call The
17-15 E 18 St
Kansas City Missouri 64141
816-842-3804

Lucille H. Bluford, Publisher
Weekly black community newspaper.

1827.

Kansas City Globe
615 E 29th St
Kansas City Missouri 64109
816-531-5253
816-531-5256—Fax

Marion Jordon, Publisher/Editor
Weekly black community newspaper.

1828.

African American Information Network
9653 Dielman Rock Island Ind Dr
St. Louis Missouri 63132
314-997-5577

1829.

St. Louis American
4144 Lindell Blvd, Suite B5
St. Louis Missouri 63108
314-533-8000
314-533-0038—Fax

Dr. Donald M. Suggs, Publisher
Weekly black community newspaper.

1830.

St. Louis Argus
4595 Martin Luther King Dr
St. Louis Missouri 63113
314-531-1323

Dr. Eugene Mitchell, Publisher
Weekly black community newspaper.

1831.

St. Louis Crusader
4371 Finney St
St. Louis Missouri 63113
314-531-5860

William P. Russell, Chairman/President
Weekly black community newspaper.

1832.

St. Louis Metro Sentinel
2900 N Market
St. Louis Missouri 63106
314-531-2101
314-531-4442—Fax

Jane E. Woods, President/Publisher

1833.

Omaha Star
2216 N 24th St
Omaha Nebraska 68110
402-346-4041

Marguerita L. Washington, Publisher

1834.

Black Business Directory of Las Vegas
Las Vegas Nevada 88901
702-646-4223

1835.

Las Vegas Sentinel-Voice
1201 S Eastern Ave
Las Vegas Nevada 89104
702-383-4030

Lee Brown, Publisher/Editor
Weekly black community newspaper.

1836.

Minority Achievement Journal
2618 State St
Las Vegas Nevada 89109-1603
702-893-0026

1837.

Minority Entrepreneur Magazine
626 Central Ave
East Orange New Jersey 07018-1403
201-672-3494

1838.

Greater News of Northern New Jersey
1188 Raymond Blvd
Newark New Jersey 07102
201-643-3364

Dr. Betty Mansfield, Managing Editor

1839.

Today's Black Woman Magazine
210 Rte 4 East
Paramus New Jersey 07652
201-843-4004

Fashion and beauty magazine. Published bimonthly.

1840.

Minority Business Journal of New Jersey
144 North Ave
Plainfield New Jersey 07060-1223
908-754-3400

1841.

Connection The
P.O. Box 2122, 362 Cedar Lane
Teaneck New Jersey 07666
201-801-0771
201-692-1655—Fax

Ralph Johnson, Publisher/Editor

1842.

Africa World Press
P.O. Box 1892
Trenton New Jersey 08607
609-771-1666
609-771-1616—Fax

Kassahun Checole, Publisher; Pamela A. Sims, Office Manager

1843.

Afro-American Times
P.O. Box 4295
Brooklyn New York 11247
718-636-9500
718-857-9115—Fax

Keri Watkins, Publisher
Weekly black community newspaper.

1844.

City Sun The
P.O. Box 560
Brooklyn New York 11202
718-624-5959
718-596-7429—Fax

Andrew Cooper, Publisher
Weekly newspaper with a black orientation.

1845.

Crisis Magazine The
260 5th Ave, 6th Floor
Brooklyn New York 10001
212-481-4100

Fred Beauford, Editor

1846.

New York Daily Challenge
1360 Fulton St
Brooklyn New York 11216
718-636-9500
718-857-9115—Fax

Thomas H. Watkins Jr., Publisher
Daily black community newspaper.

1847.

Al-Nisa Challenger
1303 Fillmore Ave
Buffalo New York 14211
716-897-0442
716-897-3307—Fax

Barbara Banks, Publisher/Editor

1848.

Buffalo Criterion
623–625 Williams St
Buffalo New York 14203
716-882-9570

Frank E. Merriweather, Publisher/Editor
Weekly black community newspaper.

1849.

New York Voice
61-17 190th St
Fresh Meadows New York 11365
718-264-1500
718-264-7708—Fax

Kenneth Drew, Chairman/Founder

1850.

African Profiles International Magazine
P.O. Box 2530
New York New York 10108-2530
212-714-3579

1851.

African Voice of Peace
42 Broadway
New York New York 10004-1617

1852.

Amalgamated Publishers Inc.
45 W 45th St
New York New York 10036
(212) 869-5220

Garth Reeves, CEO
A national newspaper advertising rep company representing 153 of the country's leading and oldest African-American newspapers. API has a total weekly circulation of over 3 million, with a reach of over 8 million people in 67 top markets across the United States.

1853.

Black Elegance Magazine
475 Park Ave S
New York New York 10016
800-877-5549

Lifestyles' magazine for today's black women. Published nine times a year.

1854.

Black Enterprise Magazine
130 5th Ave
New York New York 10011
212-242-8000

Earl G. Graves Sr., Publisher
Business publication specifically geared toward black American entrepreneurs, corporate executives, and professionals.

1855.

Essence Magazine
1500 Broadway
New York New York 10036
212-642-0600
212-921-5173—Fax

Ed Lewis, Publisher

1856.

Minority News Service
166 Madison Ave
New York New York 10016-5432
212-686-6850

1857.

National Black Monitor Magazine
231 W 29th St, Suite 1205
New York New York 10001
212-222-3556 or 212-967-4000

Jean Jason, Editor

1858.

New York Amsterdam News
2340 Frederick Douglass Blvd
New York New York 10027
212-932-7400

Wilbert Tatum, Publisher
Weekly black community newspaper.

1859.

New York Beacon/Weekend Big Red
15 E 40th St, Suite 402
New York New York 10016
212-213-8585

Walter Smith, Publisher

1860.

New York Caribbean News
28 W 39th St
New York New York 10018
212-944-1991

Karl B. Rodney, Copublisher

1861.

The Source Magazine
594 Broadway
New York New York 10012
212-274-0464

Magazine of hip-hop music, culture, and politics. Published monthly.

1862.

Hudson Valley Black Press
P.O. Box 2160
Newburgh New York 12550
914-562-1313

Chuck Stewart, Publisher/Editor
Weekly black community newspaper.

1863.

Minority Business Times Inc.
40 Underhill Blvd
Syosset New York 11791-3421
516-921-9264

1864.

Impartial Citizen
P.O. Box 98
Syracuse New York 13205
315-638-7868
315-638-0778—Fax

Dr. Robert Starling Pritchard II, Publisher
Newspaper for multiethnic communities,
published twice per month.

1865.

Westchester County Press
1 Prospect Ave
White Plains New York 10607
914-684-0006

M. Paul Redd, Publisher
Weekly newspaper directed to the total community, with special emphasis on the positive issues about the black community.

1866.

Black Conscience Syndication
21 Bedford St
Wyandanch New York 11798
516-491-7774

Clyde Davis, President
Buys 1,000 features annually. Uses material
for magazines, newspapers, radio, and television.

1867.

Charlotte Post
P.O. Box 30144
Charlotte North Carolina 28230
704-376-0469
704-342-2160—Fax

Gerald O. Johnson, Publisher
Weekly black community newspaper.

1868.

Africa News
P.O. Box 3851
Durham North Carolina 27702
919-286-0747
919-286-2614—Fax

Bertie Howard, Executive Director
News agency that supplies information about
Africa for broadcast and print media.
1973

1869.

Carolina Times
923 Old Fayetteville St
Durham North Carolina 27701
919-682-2913

Vivian A. Edmonds, Publisher/Editor
Weekly black community newspaper.

1870.

Carolina Peacemaker
P.O. Box 20853
Greensboro North Carolina 27420
910-274-6210
919-275-6854—Fax

John M. Kilimanjaro, Publisher/Editor
Weekly black community newspaper.

1871.

Public Post
P.O. Box 1093
Raeford North Carolina 28376
910-875-5845

Roosevelt McPherson, General Manager

1872.

Carolinian The
649 Maywood Ave
Raleigh North Carolina 276013
919-834-5558

Prentiss Monroe, Publisher/Editor
Black community newspaper published twice
per week.

1873.

Wilmington Journal
412 S 7th St
Wilmington North Carolina 28401
910-762-5502

T. C. Jervay, Publisher/Editor
Weekly black community newspaper.

1874.

Black College Sports Review
Winston-Salem Chronicle
Winston-Salem North Carolina 27102
919-723-9026
919-723-9173—Fax

Ernest H. Pitt, Publisher
Magazine covering black college sports.

1875.

Winston-Salem Chronicle
617 N Liberty, P.O. Box 3154
Winston-Salem North Carolina 27102
919-722-8624
919-723-9173—Fax

Ernest H. Pitt, Publisher
Weekly black community newspaper.

1876.

Reporter The
P.O. Box 2042
Akron Ohio 44309
216-773-4196

William R. Ellis Jr., City Editor

1877.

Cincinnati Herald
863 Lincoln Ave
Cincinnati Ohio 45206
513-221-5440
513-221-2959—Fax

Marjorie B. Parham, Publisher/Editor
Weekly black community newspaper.

1878.

Black Pages Cleveland
3030 Euclid Ave
Cleveland Ohio 44115-2518
216-391-7735

1879.

Call & Post The
1949 E 105th St, P.O. Box 6237
Cleveland Ohio 44101
216-791-7600
216-791-6568—Fax

John H. Bustamante, Chairman/Publisher
Weekly black community newspaper.

1880.

Columbus Call & Post
109 Hamilton Ave
Columbus Ohio 43203
614-224-8123
614-224-8517—Fax

Amos Lynch, General Manager

1881.

Toledo Journal
3021 Douglas Rd
Toledo Ohio 43606
419-472-4521
419-472-1604—Fax

Sandra R. Stewart, Publisher
Weekly African-American newspaper.

1882.

Black Chronicle The
P.O. Box 17498
Okalahoma City Oklahoma 73136
405-424-4695
405-424-6708—Fax

Russell M. Perry, Publisher/Editor
Weekly black community newspaper.

1883.

Black Economic Times The
1300 NE 4th St
Oklahoma City Oklahoma 73117-2409
405-236-2050

1884.

Oklahoma Ebony Tribune
800 NE 36th St
Oklahoma City Oklahoma 73105
405-525-9885

Lecia D. Swain, Publisher

1885.

Oklahoma Eagle
P.O. Box 3267
Tulsa Oklahoma 74101
918-582-7124
918-582-8905—Fax

James O. Goodwin, Publisher

1886.

Portland Observer
P.O. Box 3137
Portland Oregon 97208
503-288-0033
503-288-0015—Fax

Joyce Washington, Publisher/Editor
Weekly black community newspaper.

1887.

Portland Skanner
P.O. Box 5455
Portland Oregon 97228
503-287-3562
503-284-5677—Fax

Bernard V. Foster, Publisher/Editor
Weekly black community newspaper.

1888.

Renaissance Magazine
P.O. Box 842
Ardmore Pennsylvania 19003
215-473-7060

Suzanne Vargus Holloman, Publisher

1889.

Health Quest Magazine
200 Highpoint Dr
Chalfont Pennsylvania 18914
215-822-7935

Health magazine for black men and women.
Published six times a year.

1890.

Heart and Soul Magazine
Rodale Press
Emmaus Pennsylvania 18098
610-967-5171

Health and fitness magazine for African-
American women. Published six times a year.

1891.

Philadelphia New Observer
1930 Chestnut St, #S 900
Philadelphia Pennsylvania 19103
215-665-8400
215-665-8914—Fax

J. Hugo Warren, Publisher
Weekly newspaper with features for black and
Hispanic audience.

1892.

Philadelphia Tribune
522 S 16th St
Philadelphia Pennsylvania 19146
215-893-4050
215-735-3612—Fax

Robert W. Bogle, President
Newspaper with an independent orientation
published three times per week.

1893.

Homewood Brushton Informer
805 N Homewood
Pittsburgh Pennsylvania 15208
412-243-4114
412-243-4114—Fax

Matt Hawkins, Editor

1894.

Minority Business Journal
511 Junilla St
Pittsburgh Pennsylvania 15219-4837
412-682-4386

1895.

New Pittsburgh Courier
315 E Carson St
Pittsburgh Pennsylvania 15219
412-481-8302
412-481-1360—Fax

Rod Doss, Vice President/General Manager
Black community newspaper published two
times per week.

1896.

Pittsburgh Renaissance News
1516 Fifth Ave
Pittsburgh Pennsylvania 15219
412-391-8208
412-391-8006—Fax

Connie Portiss, President

1897.

Charleston Chronicle
534 King St
Charleston South Carolina 29403
803-723-2785
803-577-6099—Fax

J. John French, Publisher/Editor
Weekly black community newspaper.

1898.

Black News
1310 Harden St
Columbia South Carolina 29204-1820
803-799-5252

Weekly black community newspaper.

1899.

Black Pages USA Inc.
2401 Main St
Columbia South Carolina 29201-1947
803-254-6404

1900.

South Carolina Black Media Group Inc.
P.O. Box 1128
Columbia South Carolina 29211
803-799-5252
803-799-7709—Fax

Isaac Washington, Publisher & President

1901.

Pee Dee Times
1457 W Evans St
Florence South Carolina 29501
803-667-1018
803-662-9880—Fax

Larry D. Smith, Publisher

1902.

Black Pages USA
2320 E North St
Greenville South Carolina 29607-1247
803-271-0441

1903.

View South News
P.O. Box 1849
Orangeburg South Carolina 29116
803-531-1662

Cecil J. Williams, Publisher/Editor
Weekly black community newspaper.

1904.

Black Pages USA Inc.
269 S Church St
Spartanburg South Carolina 29306-3496
803-585-7172

1905.

Black Business Directory
1177 Madison Ave
Memphis Tennessee 38104-2227
901-272-1077

1906.

Black Pages
1177 Madison Ave
Memphis Tennessee 38104-2227
901-272-1077

1907.

Memphis Silver Star News
3144 Park Ave
Memphis Tennessee 38111
901-452-8828
901-452-8828—Fax

J. Delnoah Williams, Publisher
Weekly black community newspaper.

1908.

Tri-State Defender
124 E Calhoun Ave
Memphis Tennessee 38103
901-523-1818
901-523-1820—Fax

John H. Sengstacke, Publisher
Weekly black community newspaper.

1909.

Black Yellow Pages Inc.
1106 28th Ave N
Nashville Tennessee 37208-2812
615-321-0807

1910.

Nashville Pride
1215 9th Ave N, #200
Nashville Tennessee 37208-2552
615-255-9800
615-320-7410—Fax

Larry Davis, Publisher

1911.

Capital City Argus
P.O. Box 140471
Austin Texas 78714
512-451-6600

Charles Miles, Publisher/Editor

1912.

Nokoa—The Observer
P.O. Box 1131
Austin Texas 78767
512-499-8713 or 512-499-8715

Akwasi Evans, Publisher/Editor

1913.

Research in African Literatures
University of Texas Press, P.O. Box 7819
Austin Texas 78712
512-471-8716

Bernth Lindfors, Editor

1914.

Villager The
1223A Rosewood Ave
Austin Texas 78702-2022
512-476-0082

T. I. Wyatt, Publisher
Weekly community service newspaper for the
black community.

1915.

Black Economic Times The
1402 Corinth St
Dallas Texas 75215-2181
214-421-7063

1916.

Black Tennis Magazine
P.O. Box 210767
Dallas Texas 75211
214-670-7618
214-330-1318—Fax

Marcus A. Freeman, Jr., Editor/Publisher
Monthly sports magazine featuring black tennis players, clubs, and parks.

1917.

Dallas Examiner
424 Center St, P.O. Box 3720
Dallas Texas 75208
214-948-9175
214-948-9176—Fax

Molly Bell, Copublisher
Weekly black community newspaper.

1918.

Dallas Post Tribune
2726 South Beckley, P.O. Box 24727
Dallas Texas 75224
214-946-7678
214-946-6823—Fax

T. R. Lee Jr., Publisher
Weekly black community newspaper.

1919.

Dallas Weekly
3101 Martin Luther King Jr. Blvd
Dallas Texas 75215
214-428-8958

Yolanda Adams, Editor
Weekly black community newspaper.

1920.

Out Texas Magazine
P.O. Box 4463
Dallas Texas 75208-9902
214-943-7374

General E. Berry Jr., Publisher

1921.

Mahogany
1520 Royster Rd, Suite 1000
Fort Worth Texas 76134-3604
817-551-5551

Isaac DuBose Jr., Publisher

1922.

Texas Times
P.O. Box 1341
Fort Worth Texas 76101
817-926-4666
817-932-9209—Fax

Woodle Weber, Publisher

1923.

Black Entrepreneur Directory
2600 S Loop W
Houston Texas 77054-2653
713-661-2852

1924.

Houston Defender
2626 S Loop W, Suite 250
Houston Texas 77054
713-663-7716
713-668-0952—Fax

Sonny Messiah-Jizes, Publisher
Weekly black community newspaper.

1925.

Houston Forward Times
P.O. Box 2962
Houston Texas 77252
713-526-4727

Lenora Carter, Publisher
Weekly black community newspaper.

1926.

Houston Newspages
4997 Martin Luther King Jr. Blvd
Houston Texas 77021-2909
713-645-6386

Francis Page Sr., Publisher

1927.

Houston Sun
2322 Blodgett, P.O. Box 600603
Houston Texas 77219-0603
713-524-4474
713-524-0089—Fax

Dorris Ellis, Copublisher
Weekly black community newspaper.

1928.

Southwest Digest
902 E 28th St
Lubbock Texas 79404
806-762-3612

Eddie P. Richardson, Managing Editor

1929.

San Antonio Register
P.O. Box 1598
San Antonio Texas 78296
512-222-1721

Edwin Glosson, Publisher

1930.

Waco Messenger
504 Clifton St
Waco Texas 76703
817-799-6911

M. P. Harvey, Editor/Owner

1931.

Black Conservative Journal
1401 Wilson Blvd
Arlington Virginia 22209-2306
703-284-3613

1932.

Journal & Guide
P.O. Box 209, 3535 "F" Tidewater Dr
Norfolk Virginia 23509
804-543-6531
804-625-3142—Fax

Brenda Andrews, Publisher
Weekly black community newspaper.

1933.

Richmond Afro-American & Richmond Planet
301 E Clay St
Richmond Virginia 23219
804-649-8478
804-649-8477—Fax

Frances M. Draper, Publisher
Weekly black community newspaper.

1934.

Voice Newspaper Inc.
214 E Clay St, #202
Richmond Virginia 23219
804-644-9060
804-644-5617—Fax

Jack Green, Publisher

1935.

Roanoke Tribune
2318 Melrose Ave, P.O. Box 6021
Roanoke Virginia 24017
703-343-0326

C. A. Whitworth, Publisher

1936.

African Wildlife News Service
4739 Foxtrail Dr, NE
Olympia Washington 98516-2125
360-459-8862

1937.

Western Journal for Black Studies
Washington State University
Pullman Washington 99163
509-335-8681

Talmadge Anderson, Editor

1938.

Seattle Medium
2600 S Jackson St
Seattle Washington 98144
206-323-3070
206-322-6518—Fax

Christopher H. Bennett, Publisher
Weekly black community newspaper.

1939.

Kitsap County Dispatch
1108 S 11th St
Tacoma Washington 98405
206-272-7587
206-272-4418—Fax

Virginia Taylor, Publisher

1940.

Northwest Dispatch
1108 S 11th St
Tacoma Washington 98405
206-272-7587
206-272-4418—Fax

Virginia Taylor, Publisher

1941.

Tacoma True Citizen
1206 S 11th St
Tacoma Washington 98405
206-627-1103

Connie Cameron, Publisher
Weekly black community newspaper.

1942.

Thurston County Dispatch
1108 S 11th St
Tacoma Washington 98405
206-272-7587
206-272-4418—Fax

Virginia Taylor, Publisher

1943.

Beacon Digest
900 Maccorkle Ave, SW
South Charleston West Virginia 25303
304-342-4600
304-342-4671—Fax

Stephen R. Starks, Publisher

1944.

Milwaukee Community Journal
3612 Martin Luther King Jr. Dr
Milwaukee Wisconsin 53212
414-265-5300
414-265-1536—Fax

Patricia O. Thomas, Publisher-President
Black community newspaper published twice
per week.

1945.

Milwaukee Courier
2431 W Hopkins St
Milwaukee Wisconsin 53206
414-449-4860
414-449-4872—Fax

Carole Geary, Publisher
Weekly black community newspaper.

1946.

Milwaukee Star
3815 N Teutonia Ave
Milwaukee Wisconsin 53206
414-449-4870
414-449-4872—Fax

Carole Geary, Publisher
Weekly black community newspaper.

1947.

Milwaukee Times
2216 N Dr. Martin Luther King Dr
P.O. Box 16489
Milwaukee Wisconsin 53216-0489
414-444-8611

Nathan Conyers, Publisher
Weekly black community newspaper.

1948.

Pride Magazine
370 Coldharbour Lane
London England SW98PL
0171-737-5559
0171-274-8994—Fax

Magazine for black women.

❂ PERFORMING ARTS ❂

1949.

Black Theater Troupe Inc.
333 E Portland St
Phoenix Arizona 85004-1841
602-258-8128

1950.

Black Actors Network
1680 Vine St
Los Angeles California 90028-8855
213-962-4408

1951.

"The Vision"/Marla Gibbs Crossroads Arts Academy & Theater
4310 Degnan Blvd
Los Angeles California 90008
213-295-9685

Marla Gibbs, Founder/President; Remon Rami, General Manager

1952.

African American Drama Company
195 Ney St
San Francisco California 94112-1642
415-333-2232

1953.

African American Performing Arts
1332 Morris Rd, SE
Washington DC 20020-5216
202-610-1571

1954.

African Continuum Theater Coalition
410 8th St, NW
Washington DC 20004-2103
202-783-6547

1955.

African Heritage Dance Center
4018 Minnesota Ave, NE
Washington DC 20002
202-399-5252

Provides instruction, specialized training, and sponsors exhibits as a part of a program of supporting African arts. It is concerned with art, music, graphics, jewelry, and other media. Works with professional artists from African countries who are visiting the United States. Also offers dance classes.

1956.

Black Ensemble Theater
4520 N Beacon St
Chicago Illinois 60640-5519
312-769-4451

1957.

Afrikan-American Studio Theater Co.
3944 Chalmers St
Detroit Michigan 48215-2300
313-885-5222

1958.

Negro Ensemble Company Inc.
Development Office
New York New York 10019-7413
212-582-5860

A black theater group made up of professional actors and actresses. Produces new plays on the black experience and sponsors many activities, such as workshops for playwrights, to encourage new ideas for its plays.

1959.

Afro-American Childrens Theater Inc.
345 N College St
Charlotte North Carolina 28202-2113
704-372-7410

1960.

African Drumming and Dance Camp/African Cultural Camp '95
Camp Sealth
Vashon Island Washington
206-722-6602

Seven days and six nights of hands-on participation in playing traditional drums and percussion, song and dance folkloric presentations. Songs, plays, games, and social greetings.

1961.

African American Children's Theater
2821 N 4th St
Milwaukee Wisconsin 53212-2361
414-263-2233

❂ PROFESSIONAL ORGANIZATIONS ❂

1962.

International Association of Black Business Educators
915 S Jackson
Montgomery Alabama 36195
205-293-4124

Dr. Percy I. Vaughn Jr., President
Consisting of all deans and directors of business units on the campuses of historically African-American colleges and universities in the United States, IABBE's mission is to promote and enable development of business-related academic programs and educational activities designed to enhance participation of minorities in business throughout the nation and the world.

1963.

Alliance of Black Entertainment Technicians
1869 Buckingham Rd
Los Angeles California 90019
213-933-0746
213-934-7643—Fax

1964.

Black Creative Professionals Association
P.O. Box 34272
Los Angeles California 90034
213-964-3550

1965.

National Association of Black Reading & Language Instructors
P.O. Box 51566
Palo Alto California 94303
510-997-3768

1966.

National Association of Bench & Bar Spouses
42 La Salle Ave
Piedmont California 94611
510-652-3256

Harriet A. Pitcher, President
Spouses of attorneys united to conduct civil, cultural, and social activities in order to enhance the prestige of the legal profession and to encourage fellowship among attorneys' spouses. Sponsors conferences on the family and child advocacy programs.

1967.

African American Writers Guild
4108 Arkansas Ave, NW
Washington DC 20011
202-722-2760

1968.

African-American Women's Clergy Association
P.O. Box 1493
Washington DC 20013
202-797-7460

The Rev. Imagene Bigham Stewart, National Chairwoman
The association's 26 local affiliates operate the only African-American shelter for homeless families and satellite centers for battered men and battered women in the nation's capital. 1969

1969.

American Association of Blacks in Energy
801 Penn Ave, SE, #250
Washington DC 20003
202-547-9378

An organization of blacks in energy-related professions, including engineers, scientists, consultants, academicians, and entrepreneurs. Seeks to increase the awareness of the minority community in energy issues by serving as an information source for policy makers, recommending blacks and other minorities to appropriate officials and executives, and encouraging students to pursue professional careers in the energy industry.

1970.

Association of Black American Ambassadors
440 R St
Washington DC 20001

1971.

Association of Black Psychologists
P.O. Box 55999
Washington DC 20040
202-722-0808

Dennis E. Chestnut, Ph.D., President
Purposes are to enhance the psychological well-being of black people in America, to define mental health in consonance with newly established psychological concepts and stan-

dards, and to develop policies for local, state, and national decision-making bodies that have an impact on the health of the black community.

1972.

Association of Black Sociologists
Department of Sociology & Anthropology
Washington DC 20059
202-806-6853

Prof. Aldon Morris, President
Promotes the professional interest of black sociologists, increases the number of professionally trained sociologists, helps stimulate and improve the quality of research and the teaching of sociology, provides perspectives regarding black experiences as well as expertise for understanding and dealing with problems confronting black people.

1973.

Capital Press Club
P.O. Box 19403
Washington DC 20036
301-922-3863

Lon G. Walls, President
The nation's oldest predominantly African-American press organization, with a present membership of over 200. Members come from varied communications backgrounds, including public relations, print and broadcast journalism, and communications law.

1974.

Coalition of Black Trade Unionists
P.O. Box 73120
Washington DC 20056
202-429-1203

William Lucy, President
Members of 76 labor unions united to maximize the strength and influence of black and minority workers in organized labor. Activities include voter registration and education, economic development, and improvement of employment opportunities for minority and poor workers.

1975.

Conference of Minority Public Administrators
1120 G St, NW
Washington DC 20005
202-398-7878

1976.

National Alliance of Black School Educators
2816 Georgia Ave, NW
Washington DC 20001
202-483-1549

Theodore Kimbrough, President; William Saunders, Executive Director
Through its 60 local and state chapters, the alliance speaks on behalf of 4,000 teachers, administrators, policy makers, and support workers to articulate educational policy and cultivate African-American leadership. The organization also formulates strategies for broadening educational horizons for African Americans.

1977.

National Alliance of Postal & Federal Employees
1628 11th St, NW
Washington DC 20001
202-939-6325

Robert L. White, President
Works to eliminate employment discrimination in the federal government.

1978.

National Alliance of Third World Journalists
P.O. Box 43208
Washington DC 20010
(202) 462-8197

Lelia McDowell-Head & Gwen McKinney, National Co-Coordinators
An organization of African-American, Hispanic, Asian, and other minority journalists in the United States dedicated to improving the quality and quantity of news coverage of the Third World by the Western press. NATWJ sponsors forums, seminars, and fact-finding press tours focusing on international affairs and the struggles of minorities in the United States.

1979.

National Association of Black Consulting Engineers
6406 Georgia Ave, NW
Washington DC 20012
202-291-3550

John W. Levermore, President
Purpose is to gain recognition and increase professional opportunities for black consult-

ing engineers. Lobbies the federal government and encourages black students to pursue careers in engineering consulting.

1980.

National Association of Black Women Attorneys
3711 Macomb St, NW, Suite #4
Washington DC 20016
202-966-9693
202-244-6648—Fax

Mabel D. Haden, Esq., President; Sandra H. Robinson and Robin Alexander, Executive Assistants
Purposing to advance jurisprudence and the administration of justice by increasing opportunities for women and aiding in the protection of civil and human rights for all individuals, the association functions as a source of professional information for African-American women in law and law-related fields.
1972

1981.

National Association of Black-Owned Broadcasters
1730 M St, NE, #412
Washington DC 20036
202-463-8970

Pierre Sutton, Chairman
Trade association designed to improve the business climate for African-American radio and television station owners in the private and public sectors and to increase the number and effectiveness of African-American station owners throughout the country.

1982.

National Association of Blacks in Criminal Justice
1225 11th St, NW
Washington DC 20035
301-681-2365

James B. Eaglin, Chairman
Criminal justice professionals concerned with the impact of criminal justice policies and practices on the minority community. Advocates with local, state, and federal criminal justice agencies for the improvement of minority hiring and promotional practices.

1983.

National Association of Health Services Executives
50 F St, NW, #1040
Washington DC 20001
202-628-3953

1984.

National Association of Minority Contractors
1333 F St, NW, Suite 500
Washington DC 20004
202-347-8259
202-628-1876—Fax

James Harrell, President; Samuel A. Carradine Jr., Executive Director
NAMC is a nonprofit membership advocacy and educational organization representing African-American, Puerto Rican, Mexican-American, Native American, and Asian-American construction contractors from 48 states, the District of Columbia, and the Virgin Islands.
1969

1985.

National Association of Minority Political Women USA
6120 Oregon Ave, NW
Washington DC 20015
202-686-1216

1986.

National Association of Negro Business & Professional Women's Clubs
1806 New Hampshire Ave, NW
Washington DC 20009
202-483-4206

1987.

National Bar Association
1225 11th St, NW
Washington DC 20001
202-842-3900
202-289-6170—Fax

Paulette Brown, President
Representing 15,000 lawyers, judges, and faculty, administrators and students, NBA strives "to advance the science of jurisprudence, uphold the honor of the legal profession, promote social intercourse among members of the bar and to protect the civil and political rights of all citizens of the United States." NBA is the oldest and largest organization of African-American attorneys throughout the United States.
1925

1988.

National Black Media Coalition
38 New York Ave, NE
Washington DC 20002
202-387-8155

Pluria Marshall, Chairman
A public interest organization whose main interest is to maximize media access for African Americans and other minorities in the communications industry through minority ownership, employment, and programming. The coalition has affiliates in several states and publishes a monthly newsletter called *Media Lane.*

1989.

National Black Nurses' Association Inc.
1012 10th St, NW
Washington DC 20001
202-393-6870
202-347-3808—Fax

Linda Burnes Bolton, Ph.D., President
The association's philosophy is "to investigate, define and determine what the health care needs of African Americans are and to implement changes to make available to African-Americans and other minorities health care commensurate to that of the larger society."
1971

1990.

National Black Police Association Inc.
3251 Mt. Pleasant St, NW
Washington DC 20010
202-986-2070

Leslie Seymore, Chairman; Ronald Hampton, Executive Director

A nonprofit organization that was founded as a national voice for African-American police officers, NBPA's goals are to fight racism and job discrimination and to encourage minorities to join the police force. The organization currently has in the works programs such as minority recruitment seminars and crime prevention projects.
1972

1991.

National Business League
1511 K St, NW, Suite 432
Washington DC 20005
202-737-4430

Benjamin S. Ruffin, Chairman; Sherman N. Copelin, President; Franklin O'Neal, Senior Vice President
Organizational vehicle for minority business-people. Promotes the economic development of minorities, encourages minority ownership and management of small businesses, and supports full minority participation within the free enterprise system. Maintains file of minority vendors and corporate procurement and purchasing agents.

1992.

National Forum for Black Public Administrators
777 N Capitol St, NE, #807
Washington DC 20002
202-408-9300

1993.

National Medical Association
1012 10th St, NW
Washington DC 20001
202-347-1895

Richard O. Butcher, President
Professional society of black physicians. Plans to establish a library and physician placement service.

1994.

National Organization for Professional Advancement of Black Chemists & Chemical Engineers
525 Howard St
Washington DC 20059
202-269-4129

Clarence Tucker, Board Chairman
Black professionals in science and chemistry. Seeks to aid black scientists and chemists in reaching their full professional potential, encourages black students to pursue scientific studies and careers, and promotes participation of blacks in scientific research.

1995.

National Organization of Black County Officials
440 1st St, NW, #500
Washington DC 20001
202-347-6953

Crandall O. Jones, Project Manager
Black county officials organized to provide program planning and management assistance to selected counties in the United States. Acts as a technical information exchange to develop resolutions to problems on the local and national levels. Promotes the sharing of knowledge and methods of improving resource utilization and government operations.

1996.

National Organization of Black Law Enforcement Executives
908 Pennsylvania Ave, SE
Washington DC 20003
202-546-8811

Dr. Elsie Scott, Executive Director
Law enforcement executives above the rank of lieutenant, police educators, and academy directors. Goals are to provide a platform to express the concerns and opinions of minority law enforcement executives, to facilitate exchange of programmatic information, to increase minority participation at all levels of law enforcement, to eliminate racism within criminal justice, and to reduce urban crime and violence.

1997.

Organization of Black Designers
300 M St, SW, Suite N-110
Washington DC 20024-4019
202-659-3918
202-488-3838—Fax
OBDesign@aol.com

David Rice, President & Founder; Shauna Stallworth, Executive Director
Non-profit national professional organization dedicated to promoting the visibility, education, empowerment and interaction of its membership and the understanding the value that diverse design perspectives contribute to world culture and commerce.

1998.

Women Ministers of Greater Washington
624 17th St, NE
Washington DC 20002
212-683-5656

Rev. Mozelle J. Fuller, President

1999.

Black Models Network
3850 NE Miami Ct
Miami Florida 33137-3636
305-571-9224

2000.

National Conference of Black Political Scientists
Albany State College
Department of History & Political Science
Albany Georgia 31705
912-430-4873

Joseph P. Siler, President; Dr. Lois Hollis, Executive Director
The conference was formed to address some of the concerns of African-American professional political scientists, such as the role of African Americans in the political arena, the role of the United States in oppressing African states and the role of African Americans in elections.
1969

2001.

Minority Health Professions Foundation
20 Executive Park Dr, NE
Atlanta Georgia 30329-2206
404-634-1993

2002.

National Association of Market Developers
1422 W Peachtree St, NW, #500
Atlanta Georgia 30309
404-892-0244

Bunnie Jackson Ransom, Executive Director
Professionals engaged in marketing, sales, sales promotion, advertising, or public relations who are concerned with the delivery of goods and services to the minority consumer market.

2003.

National Organization of Minority Architects
120 Ralph McGill Blvd, NE
Atlanta Georgia 30308

Seeks to increase the number and influence of minority architects by encouraging minority youth and by taking an active role in the education of new architects. Works in cooperation with other associations, professionals, and architectural firms to promote the professional advancement of members.

2004.

Black Professional Secretaries
3113 Roswell Rd
Marietta Georgia 30062-5500
770-578-5005

2005.

Afro-American Police League
P.O. Box 41922
Chicago Illinois 60649
312-753-9454

Edgar Gosa, Executive Officer
An organization of police officers that seeks to improve the relationship between the black community and police departments, improve the relationship between black and white police officers, educate the public about police departments, and aid police departments in planning successful law enforcement programs in the black community.

2006.

National Black MBA Association
180 N Michigan Ave
Chicago Illinois 60601
312-236-2622

Darryl L. Reed, President
A nonprofit organization of minority MBAs in both the private and public sectors nationwide, membership is comprised primarily of MBA graduates and those students pursuing the advanced degree. Currently 70 percent of the approximately 2,000 members in 24 chapters across the United States are graduates from the top 10 business schools in the nation.

2007.

National Black Public Relations Society
30 W Washington, Room 503
Chicago Illinois 60602
312-782-7703

Robbie Smith, President
Professionals who are employed by advertising agencies, radio and television stations, businesses, or nonprofit organizations. Provides a forum for discussion of topics related to public relations, and holds professional development workshops.

2008.

National Insurance Association
P.O. Box 53230
Chicago Illinois 60653-0230
312-924-3308

John W. Mardis, President; Josephine King, Chairman
A trade association founded to encourage, foster, and stimulate the business of insurance, doing business through 500 offices in 35 states, Washington, D.C., and the Virgin Islands.
1921

2009.

National Newspaper Publishers Association
2400 S Michigan Ave
Chicago Illinois 60616

National professional society comprised of publishers of Negro newspapers. Initiates action programs, disseminates information, supports other phases of civil rights movement.

2010.

National Optometric Association
2838 S Indiana Ave
Chicago Illinois 60616
312-326-2929

Dr. Norma J. Levingston, President
Optometrists dedicated to increasing minority optometric manpower. Conducts research programs and national recruiting program.

2011.

Black Entertainment & Sports Lawyers Association

1 Elizabeth Ct
Oak Park Illinois 60302-2009
708-386-8338

Kendall Minter, Executive Director
Black attorneys specializing in entertainment and sports law. Purpose is to provide more efficient and effective legal representation to African-American entertainers and athletes.

2012.

National Association of Black Sales Professionals

P.O. Box 5303
River Forest Illinois 60305
708-445-1010
708-848-6008—Fax

Juan F. Menefee, President
NABSP provides a national network and forum for the minority sales professional. Its activities include an annual conference, various seminars, mentor programs with select corporate sponsors, an awards forum to spotlight distinguished accomplishments by black sales professionals, and scholarship programs for students who are promising prospective sales professionals.

2013.

National Association of African American Entrepreneurs

P.O. Box 1191
Indianapolis Indiana 46206
317-466-9556

Linda Clemons, Chief Executive Officer

To encourage the economic growth and development of minority business enterprise, the organization provides support in the areas of business planning, marketing, and technical & financial assistance. It also provides matchmakers with major corporations, major networking events on the local, state, and national level, discounts on travel, express mail service, retail products, etc. Membership is open to individuals, small businesses, organizations, and supporting corporations.

2014.

Black Organization of Police

2051 Senate St
New Orleans Louisiana 70122-3157
504-286-2051

2015.

Women Entrepreneurs for Economic Development

817 N Claiborne Ave
New Orleans Louisiana 70116
504-827-1066

Linda De Cuir, President

2016.

National Association of Black Book Publishers

P.O. Box 22080
Baltimore Maryland 21203
410-358-1098

Trade organization for those interested in advancing the cause of black publishing through networking. Ensures that black publishing remains a viable part of the publishing industry. Fosters exchange of information between members.

2017.

National Coalition of Black Meeting Planners

10320 Little Patuxent Pkwy, Suite 1106
Columbia Maryland 21044
202-628-3952
301-588-0011—Fax

Howard F. Mills, Chairman; Oliver B. Childs, President
The National Coalition of Black Meeting Planners (NCBMP) is a nonprofit corporation dedicated to the improvement of minority meetings and the professional development of minority meeting planners.

2018.

National Association of Black Accountants

7249-A Hanover Parkway
Greenbelt Maryland 20770
301-474-NABA
301-474-3114—Fax

Lawrence T. Matthews, Ph.D., CPA, National President
The goals of the association, which was organized by nine African-American accountants and currently boasts over 3,000 members in 120 professional and student chapters, are to promote the professional development of its members, to encourage and help minorities in their efforts to enter the accounting profession, and to aid in improving the quality of education available to minority accounting students.
1969

2019.

National Association of Urban Bankers

1010 Wayne Ave, Suite 1210
Silver Spring Maryland 20910-5600
301-589-2141

Paul R. Wiggens, President; Lloyd Griffin, Vice President; Richard Holmes, Treasurer
An organization for minority professionals in the financial services industry. Offers support to minorities in banking and sponsors programs to further careers for minority bankers.

2020.

Association of Black Admissions & Financial Aid Officers of Ivy League & Sister Schools

P.O. Box 1402
Cambridge Massachusetts 02138
401-863-2378

Present and former admissions and financial aid officers at Brown, Columbia, Cornell, Dartmouth, Harvard/Radcliffe, MIT, University of Pennsylvania, Princeton, Yale, Barnard, Bryn Mawr, Mount Holyoke, Smith, and Wellesley. Seeks to improve recruitment, admittance, and financial services to support the growth and maintenance of minority student populations at these institutions.

2021.

National Association of Black Social Workers

15231 W McNichols Ave
Detroit Michigan 48235
313-836-0210

2022.

National Association of Black Women Entrepreneurs
20111 James Couzens Fwy
Detroit Michigan 48235-1844
313-341-7400

Marilyn French-Hubbard, Founder
Black women who own and operate their own businesses or interested in starting one. Acts as a national support system for black businesswomen. Purpose is to enhance business, professional, and technical development.

2023.

International Black Women's Congress
1081 Bergen St
Newark New Jersey 07112
201-926-0570

Dr. La Francis Roders-Rose, President
Objective is to unite members for mutual support and socioeconomic development through establishing networks, assisting women in starting their own businesses, providing information on investments, assisting members in developing resumes, and other business needs.

2024.

National Political Congress of Black Women
P.O. Box 411
Rancocas New Jersey 08073
609-871-1500

2025.

National Association of Black Hospitality Professionals
P.O. Box 5443
Warren New Jersey 07060
908-354-5117

Mikoel Turner, President
Purposes are to provide a forum for the sharing of ideas and job opportunity information, to improve the image of blacks in the hospitality industry, and to encourage students to pursue careers in the hospitality industry.

2026.

Organization of Black Airline Pilots
P.O. Box 86
Flushing New York 11371
201-568-8145

Eddie R. Hadden, General Manager
Cockpit crew members of commercial air carriers and corporate pilots. Seeks to enhance minority participation in the aerospace industry, maintains liaison with airline presidents and minority and pilot associations, and conducts lobbying efforts, including congressional examinations into airline recruitment practices.

2027.

Africa Travel Association
347 Fifth Ave
New York New York 10016
212-447-1926

Organization of travel-industry professionals. Promotes travel to Africa.

2028.

African Heritage Studies Association
P.O. Box 1733
New York New York 10037
212-795-2096
212-795-6674—Fax

Dr. John Henrik Clarke, Founder & President
Organization of scholar-activists (Ph.D.s and
professors) throughout the world who specialize in Africans in the continent and the diaspora. Conferences, seminars, colloquia.

2029.

Black Retail Action Group
P.O. Box 1192, Rockefeller Center Station
New York New York 10185
212-308-6017

J. J. Thomas, President; Nan Puryear, Vice
President; Marlene Freeman, Vice President

2030.

**International Multiracial Shared
Cultural Organization (IMSCO)**
4 Park Ave
New York New York 10016-5339
212-532-5449
212-532-4680—Fax

Frank Weston, Chairman
Member of UN economic council to develop
network of international and national African
and African-American businesses.

2031.

**Minority International Traders
Association**
204 W 20th St
New York New York 10011-3502

2032.

Minority Management Association
1095 Ave of the Americas
New York New York 10036-6797
212-302-4636

2033.

National Afro-American Labor Council
13 Astor Place
New York New York 10003
212-673-5120

National association of trade union members
working to eliminate discrimination in employment and in unions.

2034.

**National Alliance of Black Salesmen &
Saleswomen**
P.O. Box 2814
New York New York 10027

2035.

National Association of Media Women
157 West 126th St
New York New York 10027
212-666-1320 or 212-675-0975

Rev. Rhea E. Callaway, Founder
Women professionally engaged in mass communications. Purposes are to exchange ideas,

sponsor studies, research, and seminars, and create opportunities for women in communications

2036.

Afro American Patrolman's League
1001 Indiana Ave
Toledo Ohio 43607-4004
419-255-2275

2037.

National Association of Management Consultants
1800 Chester Ave, Suite 200
Cleveland Ohio 44114
216-241-0101

Hosiah Huggins Jr., National President; Ingrid Smith, Executive Director
A nonprofit organization for independent (full-time) minority management consultants, The primary objective is to increase the opportunities for minority participation in the consulting industry through communications, collaboration, and professional development. The organization serves as a liaison for the minority professional to ensure the highest professional standards of its members.

2038.

African American Museums Association
P.O. Box 548
Wilberforce Ohio 45384
513-376-4611

Ronald LaMarr Sharps, Executive Director
An association of museums, museum professionals, and scholars concerned with preserving, restoring, collecting, and exhibiting African-American history and culture. Provides technical information to African-American museums, conducts professional training workshops, surveys, evaluations, and consultant and referral services.

2039.

Association of Black Storytellers
P.O. Box 27456
Philadelphia Pennsylvania 19118
215-898-5118

Linda Goss, President
Seeks to establish a forum to promote the black oral tradition and to attract an audience.

2040.

Minority Architect Engineers Alliance
608 N 32nd St
Philadelphia Pennsylvania 19104-2013
215-222-4290

2041.

Negro Trade Union Leadership Council
929 N Broad St
Philadelphia Pennsylvania 19123-1013
215-787-3600

2042.

Association for Multi-Cultural Counseling and Development
5999 Stevenson Ave
Alexandria Virginia 22302
703-823-9800

Professionals involved in personnel and guidance careers in educational settings, social services, and community agencies. Seeks to develop programs aimed at improving ethnic and racial empathy and understanding, foster personal growth and improve educational opportunities for minorities, and enhance members' ability to serve as behavioral change agents.

2043.

National Society of Black Engineers
1454 Duke St
Alexandria Virginia 22314
703-549-2207
listserv@suvm.syr.edu

Kevin E. Harris, National Chairman
Seeks to increase the number of minority graduates in engineering and technology.

2044.

National Association of Black Journalists
Box 17212
Dulles Airport Virginia 20041
703-648-1270

Sidmel Estes-Sumpter, President
Members of the working press who represent the nation's major newspapers, magazines, and radio and television stations, including the networks. NABJ seeks to create a favorable climate for African-American journalists. Its primary aim is to ensure that the major media expands to provide balanced coverage of the total African-American community and to hire more African-Americans.

2045.

National Association of Minority Media Executives
1401 Concord Point Lane
Reston Virginia 22091
703-709-5245

2046.

Black Public Elected & Appointed Officials
101 Municipal Building
Seattle Washington 98104

2047.

Minority Executive Directors Coalition
105 14th Ave
Seattle Washington 98122-5558
206-325-2542

❂ PUBLIC POLICY THINK TANKS ❂

2048.

Southern Poverty Law Center
400 Washington Ave
Montgomery Alabama 36104
205-264-0286

Joseph J. Levin, President
Seeks to protect and advance the legal and civil rights of poor people, regardless of race, through education, litigation, and subsequent court decisions. Strives to defeat injustices that keep poor people poor, including denial of representation in government, deprivation of municipal services, and discriminatory abuse of civil rights. Does not accept fees from clients.

2049.

Western Center on Law and Poverty
1709 W 8th St
Los Angeles California 90017
213-483-1491

Legal services resources for the war on poverty in Southern California.

2050.

Congressional Black Caucus Foundation Inc.
1004 Pennsylvania Ave, SE
Washington DC 20003
202-675-6730

Hon. Alan Wheat (D-MO), President; LeBaron Taylor, Vice President
The Congressional Black Caucus Foundation Inc. was incorporated to support and conduct nonpartisan research, technical assistance, training, education, and informational activities and programs to advance political participation by blacks and other minority group members. The foundation sponsors a graduate internship program and conducts the Congressional Black Caucus Legislative Weekend, an annual event bringing black leaders to Washington to investigate issues of mutual concern.
1976

2051.

Joint Center for Political and Economic Studies
1090 Vermont Ave, NW, Suite 1100
Washington DC 20005-4961
202-789-3500
202-789-6390—Fax

Eddie N. Williams, President
The center is a national, nonprofit, tax-exempt institution that conducts research on public policy issues of special concern to black Americans and promotes informed and effective involvement of blacks in the governmental process.
1970

2052.

National Conference of Black Political Scientists
Albany State College, Department of History
& Political Science
Albany Georgia 31705
912-430-4873

Joseph P. Siler, President; Dr. Lois Hollis,
Executive Director
The conference was formed to address some
of the concerns of African-American professional political scientists, such as the role of
African Americans in the political arena, the
role of the United States in oppressing African
states, and the role of African Americans in
elections.
1969

2053.

Center for Democratic Renewal
P.O. Box 50469
Atlanta Georgia 30302
404-221-0025

Rev. C. T. Vivian, Chairman
Organized to counteract the influence of the
KKK, this is a membership group composed
of both organizations and individuals. It provides a communications network and an information resource.

2054.

Voter Education Project Inc.
604 Beckwith St, SW
Atlanta Georgia 30314
404-522-7495

Ed C. Brown, Executive Director

VEP provides financial and technical assistance to local voter registration and education
drives in the old Confederate states of
Alabama, Arkansas, Florida, Georgia, Louisiana, Mississippi, North Carolina, South
Carolina, Tennessee, Texas, and Virginia. It
also provides policy research and technical
assistance to African-American elected officials.
1962

2055.

Jackie Robinson Foundation
80 Eighth Ave
New York New York 10011
212-675-1511

2056.

**NAACP Legal Defense and Education
Fund Inc.**
99 Hudson St, 16th Floor
New York New York 10021
212-310-9000

Julius L. Chambers, Director/Counsel

2057.

National Council on Black Aging
Box 51275
Durham North Carolina 27701
919-684-3175

Jacquelyne J. Jackson, Director
Persons interested in research and policies
affecting older blacks and other minorities,
and in the dissemination of research findings.

2058.

**United Church of Christ Commission for
Racial Justice**
700 Prospect Ave
Cleveland Ohio 44115-1100
216-241-5400

Rev. Dr. Benjamin F. Chavis Jr., Executive
Director

❂ PUBLISHING ❂

2059.

**African Americans in Alaska Resource
Guide**
Anchorage Alaska 99507
907-344-1554

2060.

**The Multicultural Publishing and
Education Council**
2280 Grass Valley Hwy, #181
Auburn California 95603
916-889-4438
916-888-0690—Fax
MPEC@aol.com

MPEC is a national networking and support
organization for independent publishers of
multicultural books and materials.

2061.

TechniPlus Publishing Company
887 S Lucerne Blvd, Suite 4
Los Angeles California 90005
213-934-3001

Aaron Jones III, Marketing/Publicist

2062.

Black Writers Guild
P.O. Box 29351
Oakland California 94604-9351
510-569-8298

2063.

African American Writers Guild
4108 Ark Ave, NW
Washington DC 20011
202-722-2760

2064.

Howard University Press
1240 Randolph St, NE
Washington DC 20008
202-806-4935

Rudolph Aggrey, Director

2065.

JMA Enterprises Inc.
218 46th St, NE
Washington DC 20019-4639
202-398-3787

Aretha S. Frizzell, President/CEO
Reading is exciting when the story is about
you. That's the message of JMA Enterprises
Inc., a create-a-book dealer. JMA uses a computer and laser printer to make personalized
children's storybooks and other items. Let's
encourage our children to read.

2066.

New Beacon Books Limited
76 Strong Green Rd
London England N4

2067.

Ashley Publishing Company Inc.
4600 W Commercial Blvd
Fort Lauderdale Florida 33319
305-739-2221

Billie Young, President

2068.

Bayside To-Go
401 Biscayne Blvd, Suite P107
Miami Florida 33132
305-374-5935

Carole Ann Taylor, Owner

2069.

Fordham Distribution
487 S U.S. Hwy One
Ormond Beach Florida 32174
904-672-6993

Daron Fordham, Publisher
This is a diversified company specializing in
information products such as software, books,
and tapes. Fordham Distribution markets
how-to books, business manuals, special interest reports, self-help publications, and more.

2070.

Mind Productions and Associates, Inc.
P.O. Box 11221
Tallahassee Florida 32302
904-222-1764
904-224-5331—Fax

An Afrocentric publishing and motivational-
training service that specializes in the educational and personal development of African
Americans.

2071.

Who's Who Publishing Company
2221 Peachtree Rd, Suite D-310
Atlanta Georgia 30309-1106

C. Sunny Martin, Publisher

2072.

Paragon
2527 Park Central Blvd
Decatur Georgia 30035
404-322-9181

Lou Walker
Motion picture production, public relations, management consulting, miscellaneous publishing.

2073.

African-American Images
1909 W 95th St
Chicago Illinois 60643
312-445-0322
312-445-9844—Fax

Dr. Jawanza Kunjufu, Chief Executive Officer; Rita Kunjufu, Executive Director
African-American Images is a full-service communications company that offers a bookstore, gift shop, video, publishing, curriculum materials, and tutorial services for children.

2074.

Afro-American Publishing Company Inc.
407 E 25th St, Suite 600
Chicago Illinois 60616
312-791-1611

Eugene Winslow, President

2075.

Path Press
53 W Jackson Blvd
Chicago Illinois 60604
312-663-0167
312-663-5318—Fax

Bennett Johnson, President; Herman Gilbert, Executive Vice President/Editorial Director

2076.

Shoptalk Publications Inc.
8825 S Greenwood
Chicago Illinois 60619
312-978-6400

Bettiann G. Gardner, Publisher; Barbara J. Giles, General Manager

2077.

Third World Press
7822 S Dobson
Chicago Illinois 60619-1999
312-651-0700
312-651-7286—Fax

Haki Madhubuti, Founder/President

2078.

Urban Research Press Inc.
840 E 87th St
Chicago Illinois 60619
312-994-7200

Dempsey J. Travis, President

2079.

Xodus Publishing Co. Inc.
P.O. Box 50177
New Orleans Louisiana 70150
504-944-5514

Teresa Crushshon, President

2080.

African American Books & Publishing
2313 W Lafayette Ave
Baltimore Maryland 21216
410-945-8429

2081.

Career Communications Group
729 E Pratt St, Suite 504
Baltimore Maryland 21202
410-244-7101
410-752-1837—Fax

Tyrone D. Taborne, President/CEO
The country's largest minority-owned media services company producing information about education and careers for black and Hispanic professionals.

2082.

Duncan & Duncan Inc.
2809 Pulaski Hwy
Edgewood Maryland 21040
410-538-5759
410-538-5584—Fax

Mike Duncan, President; Shirley Duncan, Vice President
Duncan & Duncan Inc. specializes in book publishing, book marketing, Afrocentric children's books, author management, and other specialized publishing services.

2083.

Majority Press The
P.O. Box 538
Dover Massachusetts 02030
508-655-5636

Anthony Martin, Chief Executive

2084.

Broadside Press
P.O. Box 04257
Detroit Michigan 48204
313-934-1231

Hilda Vest, Publisher; Donald Vest, Business Manager

2085.

Lotus Press
P.O. Box 21607
Detroit Michigan 48221
313-861-1280

Naomi Madgett, Executive Director

2086.

African Latino Press
1213 Kalamazoo Ave SE
Grand Rapids Michigan 49507-1922
616-241-4600

2087.

African American Reference Guide Inc.
1083 Allenwood Dr
Plainfield New Jersey 07061
908-755-0655

2088.

Horn of Africa
P.O. Box 803
Summit New Jersey 07901
202-273-1515

Osman Ali, Editor

2089.

Red Sea Press
15 Industry Court
Trenton New Jersey 08638
609-771-1666
609-771-1616—Fax

Kassahun Checole, Publisher; Pamela A. Sims, Office Manager

2090.

Kitchen Table: Women of Color Press
Livingston Ave
Albany New York 12200
518-434-2057

Barbara Smith, Publisher

2091.

Blind Beggar Press (Lamplight Editions)
P.O. Box 437
Bronx New York 10467
914-683-6792

C. D. Grant and Gary Johnston, Publishers

2092.

African American Family Press
170 W 74th St
New York New York 10023-2350
800-297-5577

2093.

Africana Publishing
160 Broadway
New York New York 10038
212-374-0100
212-374-1313—Fax

Miriam J. Holmes, Managing Director
Academic, scholarly, publishing press for books about African subjects. Publishes several journals as well for research in Africa.

2094.

Amistad Press Inc.
1271 Ave of the Americas
New York New York 10020
212-522-8566
212-522-7282—Fax

Charles F. Harris, Publisher/President
Amistad Press is an independent, African-American-controlled book publishing company with a commitment to the publication of works by and about African Americans. "At Amistad our goal is to publish books that will in some way break those subtle shackles of ignorance, distortion, and defeat that begin to feel almost comfortable when unchallenged."

2095.

World Institute of Black Communications Inc.
463 Seventh Ave
New York New York 10018

2096.

Vincom, Inc.
P.O. Box 702400
Tulsa Oklahoma 74170
918-254-1276

George Vinnett, President

2097.

Renaissance Publications
1516 Fifth Ave
Pittsburgh Pennsylvania 15219
412-391-8208
412-391-8006—Fax

Connie Portis, President
Publishers of: *Greater Pittsburgh Black
Business Directory, Pittsburgh Renaissance
News, Renaissance Too Magazine.*

2098.

African American Publications
Washington Crossing Pennsylvania 18977
215-321-7742

2099.

Juju Publishing Company
1310 Harden St
Columbia South Carolina 22902
803-799-5252

Isaac Washington, Publisher

2100.

National Baptist Publishing Board
6717 Centennial Blvd
Nashville Tennessee 37209
615-350-8000

One of the largest black-owned and operated
enterprises in America, this family-owned
business produces more than 14 million books
and periodicals every year.
1896

2101.

Black Registry Publishing Company
1223 Rosewood Ave
Austin Texas 78702
512-476-0082

T. L. Wyatt, Publisher

❂ READING AND LITERACY ❂

2102.

**National Association of Black Reading &
Language Instructors**
P.O. Box 51566
Palo Alto California 94303
510-997-3768

2103.

Anne Spencer House and Garden
1313 Pierce St
Lynchburg Virginia 24501
804-846-0517

Preserved home of the Harlem Renaissance literary figure, associated with James Weldon Johnson, Langston Hughes, Claude McKay, Paul Robeson, Marian Anderson, W.E.B. Du Bois, and Mary McLeod Bethune.

❂ RELIGIOUS HISTORIC SITES ❂

2104.

African Islamic Mission
1390 Bedford Ave
Brooklyn New York 11216-3507
718-638-4588

2105.

Sixteenth Street Baptist Church
Sixth Ave and 16th St N
Birmingham Alabama 35203
205-251-9402

This church is historically important because of the people who have spoken there: W.E.B. Du Bois, Booker T. Washington, Mary McLeod, and Dr. Martin Luther King, Jr. In 1963, a Ku Klux Klan bombing here killed four.
1873

2106.

Dexter Avenue King Memorial Baptist Church
454 Dexter Ave
Montgomery Alabama 36104
205-263-3970

Served as the home base of the Montgomery Bus Boycott, and now has memorials to prominent people and moments in the civil rights movement.
1887

2107.

St. Andrews A.M.E. Church
2131 Eighth St
Sacramento California 95818
916-448-1428

Houses the first AME congregation on the West Coast, and was the site of the first two conventions of Colored Citizens of the State of California, as well as the place where the first school of blacks, Indians, and Asians was opened.

2108.

Ebenezer Baptist Church
407 Auburn Ave, NE
Atlanta Georgia 30312
404-688-7263

Renowned church in the black community of Atlanta, it is well known for housing the congregation that had Martin Luther King, Jr. as its pastor.

2109.

New Zion Baptist Church
2319 Third St
New Orleans Louisiana 70113
504-891-4283

Founding site of the Southern Christian Leadership Conference and congregation of the Rev. A. L. Davis, noted civil rights activist and New Orlean's first black councilman.

2110.

African Baptist Church
York and Pleasant Sts
Nantucket Massachusetts 02554
617-742-1854 (Afro-American Museum in Boston)

This building was once the center of Nantucket's black community and the training grounds of Frederick Douglass's career as public orator. It is now being restored by the Afro-American Museum in Boston.

2111.

Elijah Muhammad Temple No. 1 (Masjid Wali Mohammed Mosque)
11529 Linwood Ave (Elijah Mohammed Mosque)
Detroit Michigan 48206
313-868-2131

The transformation of the Nation of Islam into a major political and religious force within the African-American community and the nation began with the establishment of this building by Elijah Muhammad.
1931

2112.

Mount Zion United Methodist Church
Route 2 (Hwy 747)
Philadelphia Mississippi 38677
601-656-8277

During the "Freedom Summer" of 1964, which was based at this church, three civil rights workers were murdered by the Ku Klux Klan with the complicity of local authorities. Today, a marker at this church commemorates their lives.

2113.

Abyssinian Baptist Church
132 W 138 St
New York New York 10030
212-862-7474

The largest and best-known African-American church in the country, which launched the career of the influential black legislator, Adam Clayton Powell, Jr.
1808

2114.

Mother A.M.E. Zion Church
140–146 West 137 St
New York New York 10030
212-234-1545

The first church built by and for African Americans in New York City.
1796

2115.

Church of the Advocate
18th and Diamond Sts
Philadelphia Pennsylvania 19121
215-236-0568

Many civil rights gatherings were held here, including the second Black Power Convention and the final Black Panther Party Congress.

2116.

Mother Bethel African Methodist Episcopal Church
419 S Sixth St
Philadelphia Pennsylvania 19147
215-925-0616

Organized by Richard Allen and named for the first bishop of the AME Church, this site also housed the first ever national convention for blacks, and today houses a small museum tracing the history of the AME Church.
1787

2117.

St. Thomas African Episcopal Church Historical Marker
St. James Place and Fifth St
Philadelphia Pennsylvania 19139
215-473-3065

A church founded by Absalom Jones in protest of the Methodist Church's segregated seating practices. The church received a state charter in 1796, becoming the first incorporated African-American institution in the United States.

2118.

Allen Chapel A.M.E. Church
508 Cedar St
Yankton South Dakota 57078
605-665-1449

The oldest church in the state, it also once served as the duty station for the buffalo soldiers of the 25th infantry.

2119.

Calvary Baptist Church
532 E 700 South St
Salt Lake City Utah 84102
801-355-1025

The oldest black Baptist church in Utah.
1892

2120.

Trinity A.M.E. Church
239 E 600 South St
Salt Lake City Utah 84102
801-531-7374

The first African-American church in Utah.
1907

2121.

First Baptist Church
236 Harrison St
Petersburg Virginia 23804
804-732-2841

The oldest Christian congregation in the United States.
1756

2122.

Gillfield Baptist Church
29 Perry St
Petersburg Virginia 23803
804-732-3565

Housed in the same church building for over 100 years, this congregation of African Americans is one of the oldest in the country.
1788

2123.

Mount Tabor Baptist Church
200 Foster St
Lewisburg West Virginia 24901
304-645-1000

This congregation, which dates back to 1796, is housed in a church with a three-level bell tower.
1796

❂ RELIGIOUS ORGANIZATIONS ❂

2124.

African Baptist World Conference
8928 S Figueroa St
Los Angeles California 90003-3228
213-750-6929

2125.

African Center for Religious Education
5225 Wilshire Blvd
Los Angeles California 90036-4301
213-932-0082

2126.

Black Christians Political Convention
P.O. Box 161659
Sacramento California 95816-1659
916-363-8583

2127.

African Methodist Episcopal Church
1134 11th St, NW
Washington DC 20001
202-371-8700

Bishop Harold B. Senatle, President of the Council of Bishops; Dr. Joseph C. McKinney, Treasurer
One of the oldest and largest congregations in America, the AME Church was founded by Richard Allen in Philadelphia. Today its 3.5 million members, representing over 8,000 congregations worldwide, 2,000 of which are in Africa, operate a Home and Foreign Missions Board for the maintenance of churches and support of schools, hospitals and other operations in eight overseas missions in Africa, the West Indies, and South and Central America.
1787

2128.

African-American Women's Clergy Association
P.O. Box 1493
Washington DC 20013
202-797-7460

The Rev. Imagene Bigham Stewart, National Chairwoman
The association's 26 local affiliates operate the only African-American shelter for homeless families and satellite centers for battered men and battered women in the nation's capital.
1969

2129.

Congress of National Black Churches Inc.
1225 I St, NW, Suite 750
Washington DC 20005-3914
202-371-1091

Bishop William H. Graves, Chairman
CNBC is a voluntary, nonprofit religious organization designed to promote Christian unity, charity, and fellowship among the member denominations. Its program thrusts are theological education, African-American church executive training, economic development, evangelism in the African-American tradition, and human development and media in the African-American church.

2130.

National Association of Black Catholic Administrators
P.O. Box 29260
Washington DC 20017
301-853-4576

Jacqueline E. Wilson, President

Members are 75 black Catholic leaders for black Catholic ministries offices who share resources to address issues and concerns facing African-American communities; to assist implementation of the National Black Catholic Congress Agenda and Plan, and of the Bishops' 1979 Pastoral Letter on Racism.
1976

2131.

National Black Sisters' Conference
1001 Lawrence St, NE, Suite 102
Washington DC 20017
202-529-9250

Sister Barbara Spears, OSP, President; Sister Gwynette Proctor, SND, Executive Director
The National Black Sisters' Conference, with approximately 700 African-American nuns in the United States, is devoted to supporting African-American religious advocacy in African-American communities, to upholding equal educational opportunities for all, and to developing African-American leadership.
1968

2132.

National Catholic Conference for Interracial Justice
3033 4th St, NE
Washington DC 20017
202-529-6480

Jerome Ernst, Executive Director
Catholic organization working for interracial justice and social concerns in America. Initiates programs within and outside the Catholic church to end discrimination in community development, education, employment, health care, and housing.

2133.

National Office for Black Catholics
3025 4th St, NE
Washington DC 20017
202-635-1778

James B. McConduit, President; Walter
Hubbard, Executive Director
A service organization, established through
the concerted efforts of priests, religious men
and women, and lay people, the National
Office for Black Catholics' primary role is to
serve as an advocate for African-American
Catholics and non-Catholics within the
Catholic church and society at large.
1970

2134.

Progressive National Baptist Convention
601 50th St, NE
Washington DC 20001
202-356-0558

Rev. Charles Adams, President

2135.

**Women Ministers of Greater
Washington**
624 17th St, NE
Washington DC 20002
202-683-5656

Rev. Mozelle J. Fuller, President

2136.

African American Evangelization Center
4305 Michigan Ave
Fort Myers Florida 33905-4501
941-337-5477

2137.

**African American Council of Christian
Clergy**
8340 NE Second Ave
Miami Florida 33010
305-757-1955

2138.

African Christian Fellowship
Atlanta Georgia 30316
404-212-8175

2139.

Black Women in Church and Society
c/o Interdenominational Church & Society
Atlanta Georgia 30314
404-527-7740

Jacquelyn Grant, Director

2140.

Interdenominational Theological Center
671 Beckwith St, SW
Atlanta Georgia 30314
404-527-7700
404-527-0901—Fax

James H. Costten, President
Dr. Edith Thomas, Registrar, 404-527-7707
Founded as a consortium of six seminaries:
Gammon Theological Seminary (United
Methodist), Charles H. Mason Theological
Seminary (Church of God in Christ),
Morehouse School of Religion (Baptist),
Phillips School of Theology (Christian
Methodist Episcopal), Johnson C. Smith
Seminary (Presbyterian Church USA) Arnold
Turner Theological Seminary (African

Methodist Episcopal). Degrees: M.Div., M.A.C.Ecl.
1958

2141.

Southern Christian Leadership Conference
334 Auburn Ave, NE
Atlanta Georgia 30312
404-522-1420

Rev. Dr. Joseph Lowery, President
Nonsectarian coordinating and service agency for local organizations seeking full citizenship rights, equality, and the integration of African-Americans in all aspects of life in the US and subscribing to the Ghandian philosophy of nonviolence. Works primarily in 16 southern and border states to improve civic, religious, economic, and cultural conditions. Fosters nonviolent resistance to all forms of racial injustice and conducts leadership training programs in voting and registration, social protest, prejudice and government policies.

2142.

Black Evangelism & Counseling Association
6635 Doublegate Ln
Rex Georgia 30273-2138
404-474-0085

2143.

Black Methodists for Church Renewal
4611 S Ellis Ave
Chicago Illinois 60653-3624
312-538-6865

Caucus of black United Methodist churches.

2144.

Nation of Islam
7351 S Stony Island Ave
Chicago Illinois 60649
312-324-6000

Minister Louis Farrakhan, National Representative of the Honorable Elijah Muhammad
The growth of this organization since its reemergence in 1977 under the leadership of Minister Farrakhan has been phenomenal, with branches now in every major city in America, as well as satellites in the Caribbean, England, Australia, and the South Pacific, and an official information center in Accra, Ghana. Following the teachings of the Honorable Elijah Muhammad, the NOI has repurchased its prized National Center in Chicago, including reopening the University of Islam. The NOI has also gained international recognition for *The Final Call,* a biweekly newspaper; the Dopebusters, a drug reform program; and the Clean 'n' Fresh personal-care products produced by the NOI.

2145.

National Black Catholic Seminarian Association
1818 W 71st St
Chicago Illinois 60636
312-994-7468

Dr. Robert Smith, President

2146.

Universal Foundation for Better Living Inc., Christ Universal Complex
11901 S Ashland
Chicago Illinois 60643
312-568-2282

The Rev. Johnnie Colemon, Founder and President
A nondenominational worldwide foundation of New Thought ministers in the Americas as well as Trinidad, and other countries worldwide.

2147.

African Christian Mission
120 Maple
Kansas Illinois 61933
217-948-5486

Ed Bule, Director
Recruits and send missionaries to countries in Africa. Nonprofit organization.

2148.

African American Catholic Council
1425 N Chautauqua St
Wichita Kansas 67214-2426
316-686-1798

Deacon Ronald R. Ealey, Episcopal Liaison
Represents the interests of African-American Catholics to the church hierarchy.

2149.

African American Catholic Ministry
1200 S Shelby St
Louisville Kentucky 40203-2627
502-636-0296

M. Annette Turner, Director
Office that works in collaboration with all offices and agencies in implementing the National Black Catholic Pastoral Plan by serving as a vehicle for spiritual, cultural, educational, and social nourishment for African-American Catholics, provides outreach to the community, and articulates the needs of African-American Catholics.

2150.

National Baptist Convention U.S.A. Inc.
356 East Blvd
Baton Rouge Louisiana 70802
504-383-5401

The Rev. Dr. T. J. Jemison, President
The National Baptist Convention U.S.A. Inc. is considered the world's largest African-American organization, with 7 million members. Nearly 200 African-American Baptists formed an organization to support missionary work in Africa. From that base, the organization expanded and became incorporated in 1915. In 1962, a million-dollar fund was established to support educational institutions, purchase books and aid churches with financial problems.
1880

2151.

Knights and Ladies of St. Peter Claver
1825 Orleans Ave
New Orleans Louisiana 70116
504-821-4225

Paul C. Condoll, Supreme Knight
The Knights of St. Peter Claver and Ladies Auxiliary, a Catholic organization now boasting over 100,000 family members nationwide, began in Mobile, Alabama, over 81 years ago when four Josephite priests and three laymen came together to officially form the Knights. In 1926, the Ladies Auxiliary was organized. The members of this noble order are involved in education liturgy, social apostolate,

parochial and diocesan activities and religious institutions. Since its organization, the Knights have been engaged in programs to help eliminate poverty, to foster human justice and freedom, and to serve God.
1909

2152.

National Baptist Convention of America Inc.
1540 Pierre Ave
Shreveport Louisiana 71103
318-742-3701

Dr. E. Edward Jones, President
The Foreign Mission Baptist Convention, the American National Baptist Convention, and the National Baptist Educational Convention united and formed the National Baptist Convention of the United States of America. A controversy arose in 1915 that divided the Convention into the National Baptist Convention U.S.A. Inc. and the National Baptist Convention of America (NBCA). In 1987 the NBCA was incorporated. Currently, it has approximately three and a half million members with mission fields in the Caribbean, the Virgin Islands, Panama, Haiti, and Ghana, West Africa.
1895

2153.

National Black Catholic Congress
320 Cathedral St
Baltimore Maryland 21202
301-547-5330

Leodia Gooch, Executive Director

2154.

African Christian Fellowship
13215 Mockingbird Ln
Bowie Maryland 20720-4739
301-805-1980

2155.

African Mission Fathers
337 Common St
Dedham Massachusetts 02026-4030
617-326-4670

Father Gillis, Superior

2156.

St. Augustine Seminary
199 Seminary Dr
Bay St. Louis Mississippi 39520
601-467-6414

America's first institute for training black Catholic seminarians.
1923

2157.

Society of African Missions
23 Bliss Ave
Tenafly New Jersey 07670
201-567-0450

Father Douglas Gilbert, Provincial
Missionary work in different parts of Africa, and operates an African arts museum.

2158.

African American Islamic Center
1218 Brook Ave
Bronx New York 10456
718-538-9191

2159.

United Black Church Appeal
860 Forest Ave
Bronx New York 10456
212-992-5315

Honorable Wendell Foster, President
Black clergy and laity united to awaken the power of the black clergy and black church to provide leadership for the liberation of the black community. Concerned with black economic development and political power, and strengthening black families and churches.

2160.

African People's Christian Organization
415 Atlantic Ave
Brooklyn New York 11217
718-596-1991

Rev. Herbert Daughtry, President
A multifaceted cultural organization: prison ministry, lecture series, radio broadcasts, research division newsletter, college counseling, adopt-a-school program.

2161.

Interreligious Foundation for Community Organization (IFCO)
402 W 145th St
New York New York 10031
212-926-5757

Rev. Lucius Walker Jr., Executive Director
The IFCO is a nonprofit, ecumenical agency that coordinates church and community action programs for social justice. IFCO seeks to forward the struggles of oppressed people for justice and self-determination by supporting their community organizing efforts, through education programs, training, problem identification, conflict resolution, fundraising, and fiscal agent service.

2162.

National Black Catholic Clergy Caucus
St. Aloysius Church
Cleveland Ohio 44108
216-451-3262

Rev. Paul Marshall, President
Founded in Detroit by a group of African-American Catholic priests to serve as a fraternity for African-American Catholic clergy, the caucus functions as a mediator between the church and the African-American community by battling institutional racism within the Catholic church while striving to bring the contributions of African Americans to fruition within the church community.
1968

2163.

African American Clergies
103 NE Morris St
Portland Oregon 97212-3018
503-282-3975

2164.

African Methodist Episcopal Zion Church

1200 Windermere Dr
Pittsburgh Pennsylvania 15218
412-242-5842

Rev. Dr. W. Robert Johnson III, General Secretary/Auditor
This organization's 1.5 million members, encompassing 2,500 churches, have founded and continue to support a number of institutions of higher learning. The AME Zion Church also maintains missions in the United States and abroad.
1796

2165.

Church of God in Christ Inc.

272 S Main St
Memphis Tennessee 38103
901-578-3811

Bishop Louis H. Ford, Presiding Bishop
Formally organized in Memphis, Tennessee, by Bishop Charles Harrison Mason, the Church expanded operations between 1910 and 1916 in four major areas: women's department, Sunday schools, young people's department, and home and foreign missions. Today the church's 3.7 million members in 38 countries believe in a basically Trinitarian doctrine teaching the infallibility of the Scriptures and the need for regeneration and subsequent baptism in the Holy Spirit.
1907

2166.

Black Church Consultants of America

510 Holly Hill Ct
Nashville Tennessee 37221-3411

2167.

Christian Methodist Episcopal Church

National Headquarters
2323 West Illinois Ave
Dallas Texas 75224
214-339-5129

Caesar D. Coleman, Senior Bishop/CEO
Founded in Jackson, Tennessee, the CME Church is coordinated through 10 districts, each headed by a bishop. The church operates its own publishing house and boasts of over 863,000 members nationwide and in Haiti, Jamaica, Ghana, and Nigeria.
1870

2168.

African American Lutheran Association

6020 Beacon Ave S
Seattle Washington 98108
206-722-5165

Rev. Victor C. Langford III, President
The African American Lutheran Association is a caucus of primarily African Americans who are also members of the Evangelical Lutheran Church in America (ELCA). It serves as a vehicle for unifying and conveying needs and concerns of African Americans in the ELCA throughout all the structures, especially through the Commission for Multicultural Ministries. It is working to develop strong partnerships between the ELCA, and

the African-American and African communities through worship, education, evangelism, stewardship, social ministry, and global awareness.

❂ RELIGIOUS PUBLICATIONS ❂

2169.

Black Church Magazine
2509 Saint Paul St
Baltimore Maryland 21218-4610

2170.

Black Church Magazine The
2321 Main St
Columbia South Carolina 29201-1955
803-254-8362

❂ SCHOLARSHIPS ❂

2171.

Omega Psi Phi Fraternity Scholarship Programs
1327 R St, NW
Washington DC 20001
202-667-7158

2172.

Phi Beta Sigma Fraternity Scholarship Programs
2714 Georgia Ave, NW
Washington DC 20011
202-726-5434

2173.

McDonald's Black Makers of Tomorrow
Paragon Public Relations
Decatur Georgia 30035

2174.

McDonald's Crew College Education Program
Paragon Public Relations
Decatur Georgia 30035

2175.

Delta Sigma Theta Sorority Scholarship Program
Marietta-Roswell Alumnae Chapter
Marietta Georgia 30007-0786
404-344-8280

2176.

Sigma Gamma Rho Sorority Scholarship Program
840 E 8th St
Chicago Illinois 60619
312-873-9000

2177.

National Achievement Scholarship Program
One American Plaza
Evanston Illinois 60201

2178.

African American Voters League
310 S Broad St
New Orleans Louisiana 70119-6416
504-822-2890

Colleen Johnson
Scholarship foundation, community service organization, and political organization. Sponsors a feed-the-needy program.

2179.

A Taste of Heritage Foundation
627 Glyrita Circle
Reistertown Maryland 21136
410-526-3655

Chef Joseph Randall, Founder
Raises scholarship funds for minority students going into the culinary profession.

2180.

African American Institute
833 United Nations Plaza
New York New York 10017-3581
212-994-9566
212-682-6174—Fax

Vivian Lowery Derryck, President
Works to further development in Africa, improve African-American understanding, and inform Americans about Africa. Offers fellowships for students.
1954

2181.

Black Analysis Inc.
549 W 123rd St
New York New York 10027
212-866-2275

A minority doctoral program for full-time students at an American university. Individuals are eligible if studying education, sociology, or psychology. Funds are available for one year.

2182.

Eleanor Roosevelt Scholarship Program
CORE Scholarship, Education & Defense Fund
New York New York 10038
212-598-4000

Awards of up to $1,500 for students who have been actively involved in the civil rights movement.

2183.

Herbert Lehman Education Fund
10 Columbus Circle, Suite 2040
New York New York 10019

Scholarship for black students at recently desegregated colleges in the Deep South.

2184.

Pan Africanist Congress of America
211 E 43rd St, Suite 703
New York New York 10017
212-986-7378

Henry Isaacs

2185.

Reformed Church of America Scholarship Programs
475 Riverside Dr, Room 1819
New York New York 10027
212-870-3071

2186.

Roy Wilkins Educational Scholarship Program
144 W 125th St
New York New York 10027
212-316-2100

2187.

Scholarship, Education and Defense Fund for Racial Equality Inc.
164 Madison Ave
New York New York 10016
212-532-8216

Develops leadership programs and community organization techniques, handles legal problems, engages in voter registration, and provides scholarship assistance with demonstrated leadership in civil rights activities.

2188.

Thurgood Marshall Scholarship Fund
100 Park Ave
New York New York 10017
212-878-2221

Scholarship money for students at historically black public colleges and universities.

2189.

United Presbyterian Church Scholarship Program
475 Riverside Dr, Room 430
New York New York 10115
212-697-4568

2190.

Martin DePorres Foundation
Minority Groups Scholarship Program
Philadelphia Pennsylvania
215-228-8330

For Philadelphia Catholics planning to attend one of the nearby Catholic colleges.

2191.

Negro Education Emergency Drive
643 Liberty Ave
Pittsburgh Pennsylvania 15123
412-566-2760

NEED is a voluntary organization that provides financial assistance for Negro students to continue their education beyond the high-school level. In addition to cash awards, other funds are procured in the form of remission of tuition, federal and state aid, and grants from other financial resources. Volunteers work directly with secondary schools and also with higher education institution to obtain supplemental financial aid. They provide a link between individual students, secondary schools, colleges, and universities.

2192.

African Christian Scholarship Foundation
2932 Foster Creighton Dr
Nashville Tennessee 37204-3719
615-244-8181

2193.

United Methodist Church Scholarship Fund
P.O. Box 871
Nashville Tennessee 37202

2194.

Alfred P. Sloan Foundation
The College Fund/UNCF
Fairfax Virginia 22031-4511
703-205-3400

Scholarships for male students who will attend one of the ten major black colleges and universities.

2195.

College Fund The/UNCF (formerly United Negro College Fund Inc.)
8260 Willow Oaks Corporate Dr
Fairfax Virginia 22031-4511
703-205-3400

William H. Gray III, President/CEO
A national fund-raising organization for private historically African-American accredited colleges, universities, and professional schools that provide quality education for 51,000 students in 41 member institutions.
1944

2196.

Martin Luther King Jr. Scholarship
The College Fund/UNCF
Fairfax Virginia 22031-4511
703-205-3400

2197.

Phi Lambda Scholarship Program
5313 Halter Lane
Norfolk Virginia 23502

❂ SENIOR CITIZENS ❂

2198.

Emergency Action Switchboard for the Elderly
810 Potomac Ave, SE
Washington DC 20003
(202) 546-4717

Eva Toney, Director

2199.

National Caucus and Center on Black Aged Inc.
1424 K St, NW, Suite 500
Washington DC 20005
202-637-8400

Samuel J. Simmons, President
A national membership organization whose mission is to improve the quality of life for older African Americans. Activities include legal and legislative advocacy, development and management of rental housing, job training and employment programs, and other services for the elderly in selected institutions.

2200.

Phillip T. Johnson Senior Citizens Center
5929 E Capitol St, SE
Washington DC 20019
202-581-8500

Mernelle Burkett, Director

2201.

National Association for the Advancement of the Black Aged
1101 Gratiot
Detroit Michigan 48027
313-521-1474

Patricia Abston, Chairperson
Advocates on behalf of elderly blacks on issues of health, economics, social values, and the law.

2202.

Associated Black Charities
105 E 22nd St
New York New York 10010
212-777-6060

Nonprofit federation of organizations in the five boroughs that offer health and human services to African Americans, including senior services and childcare.

2203.

National Council on Black Aging
Box 51275
Durham North Carolina
919-684-3175

Jacquelyne J. Jackson, Director
Persons interested in research and policies affecting older blacks and other minorities, and in the dissemination of research findings.

2204.

Saunders B. Moon Senior Citizens Center
8100 Fordson Rd
Alexandria Virginia 22306
202-360-2100

Sadie Lyons, Director

❂ SICKLE-CELL ANEMIA ❂

2205.

National Association for Sickle Cell Disease Inc.
3345 Wilshire Blvd, Suite 1106
Los Angeles California 90010-1880
213-736-5455

Kwaku Ohene-Fremprong, M.D., National President; Lynda K. Anderson, Executive Director
The only national volunteer organization working full time for comprehensive sickle cell disease programming. NASCD programs include training counselors, preparing and distributing educational materials worldwide, conducting workshops and seminars, providing technical assistance, maintaining blood banks, testing and screening, tutoring services and operating summer camps for children with sickle cell anemia. NASCD also provides vocational rehabilitation and support for research activities leading to improved treatment and eventual cure.

2206.

Sickle Cell Disease Research Foundation
4401 S Crenshaw Blvd, Suite 208
Los Angeles California 90043
213-299-3600

Mary Brown, Executive Director

2207.

Sickle Cell Anemia Disease Research Foundation (SCADRF)
1332 Haight St
San Francisco California 94117
415-626-5834

Willie W. Curry, Acting Executive Director

2208.

Howard University Center for Sickle Cell Disease
2121 Georgia Ave, NW
Washington DC 20059
202-638-3912

Roland B. Scott, Director

2209.

Sickle Cell Foundation of Georgia
2391 Benjamin E. Mays Dr, SW
Atlanta Georgia 30311-3291
404-755-1641

2210.

Midwest Association for Sickle Cell Anemia
65 E Wacker Place
Chicago Illinois 60601
312-663-5700

Howard D. Anderson, President

2211.

National Association for Sickle Cell Anemia of Baton Rouge
2301 North Blvd
Baton Rouge Louisiana 70806
504-346-8434

2212.

Northwest Louisiana Sickle Cell Anemia Foundation & Research Center
2200 Milam St
Shreveport Louisiana 71103
318-226-8975

2213.

Sickle Cell Anemia Foundation of Greater New York
127 W 127th St
New York New York 10027
212-865-1500

2214.

National Association for Sickle Cell Disease
951 S Independence Blvd
Charlotte North Carolina 28204
704-332-4184

2215.

Eastern Area Sickle Cell Association Inc.
P.O. Box 5253
Jacksonville North Carolina 28540
910-346-2510

Marcia Wright, Executive Director

2216.

Sickle Cell Awareness Group of Greater Cincinnati Inc.
3770 Reading
Cincinnati Ohio 45229
513-281-4450

John Chenault, Executive Director

2217.

Peninsula Association for Sickle Cell Anemia Inc.
1520 Aberdeen Rd, Suite 314
Hampton Virginia 23666
804-838-4721

Judy Braithwaite, Executive Director

❂ SPORTS ORGANIZATIONS ❂

2218.

African American Club
216 E 3rd St
Mount Vernon New York 10550-5113
914-665-2204

2219.

African American Athletic Association
355 Lexington Ave
New York New York 10017-6603
212-953-3100

2220.

National Brotherhood of Skiers
2575 Donegal Dr S
San Francisco California 94080
415-589-5980

2221.

National Association of Black Scuba Divers
1605 Crittenden St, NE
Washington DC 20017

2222.

Black Entertainment & Sports Lawyers Association
1 Elizabeth Ct
Oak Park Illinois 60302-2009
708-386-8338

2223.

African American Sports Group
1232 Drexel Ct NE
Grand Rapids Michigan 49505-5450
616-361-2525

2224.

Black College Sports Review
Winston-Salem Chronicle
Winston-Salem North Carolina 27102
919-723-9026
919-723-9173—Fax

Ernest H. Pitt, Publisher
Magazine covering black college sports.

❊ TENNIS ❊

2225.

American Tennis Association
P.O. Box 3277
Silver Spring Maryland 20901
301-496-6784

Margaret H. Gordon, Executive Secretary
Promotes and develops tennis among blacks
by sponsoring training programs for young
players and regional tournaments.

2226.

**Association of Minority Tennis
Professionals**
P.O. Box 8002
New York New York 10150
212-838-1009
212-752-1780—Fax

Maureen Alicia Rankine, Executive Director/
Founder

AMTP endeavors to enhance the image of
minority tennis professionals. We do so by
promoting and advertising teaching positions;
establishing programs to help minority tennis
pros, their students, and their programs;
establishing a youth training program; and
providing a friendly and supportive environment where minority teaching pros can bene-
fit from social and professional interaction as
well as enhance their playing skills through
competition.

2227.

Black Tennis Magazine
P.O. Box 210767
Dallas Texas 75211
214-670-7618
214-330-1318—Fax

Marcus A. Freeman, Jr., Editor/Publisher
Monthly sports magazine featuring black tennis players, clubs, and parks.

❊ TRAVEL ❊

2228.

African American Traveler
438 W Cypress St
Glendale California 91204-2402
818-247-3697

2229.

African Tours & Travel
2170 Avenida de la Playa
La Jolla California 92092
619-454-9551

2230.

Africa Travel Arrangements/Eckdahl-Sun
Pasadena California 91050
818-799-3027

2231.

Africa Tours
210 Post St
San Francisco California 94108-5102
415-391-5788

2232.

Africa Travel Consultants
1312 18th Ave
San Francisco California 94122-1808
415-564-8230

2233.

African Safari
1221 Divisadero St
San Francisco California 94115-3910
415-922-2899

2234.

African Express Travel & Tours
2932 Wilshire Blvd
Santa Monica California 90403-4908
310-828-4321

2235.

Denver Minority Convention Tourism Authority
1763 Vine St, City Park West
Denver Colorado 80206
301-333-8625

L. Jennie Potts, Executive Director

2236.

African Caribbean Group Travel
1547 9th St, NW
Washington DC 20001-3207
202-265-9488

2237.

Rodger's Travel Services
50 SW Beal Parkway
Fort Walton Beach Florida 32548
800-853-1128
904-243-2693—Fax

Black owned and operated, RTS is a full-service travel agency specializing in airline reservations, ticketing, corporate, leisure, cruise, and group travel, and car rentals and hotel accommodations.

2238.

African American Heritage Tours
240 W Randolph St
Chicago Illinois 60606-1812
312-443-9575
312-443-9575—Fax

Gregory Sims
Offers group tours related to African-American history in Chicago and nationwide.

2239.

Afrikan Diaspora Tours & Trail
1809 E 71st
Chicago Illinois 60637
312-288-2388

2240.

Black History Tours
1721 W 85th St
Chicago Illinois 60620-4738
312-233-8907

2241.

African American Tourism Council Inc.
Indianapolis Indiana 46268
317-876-0853

2242.

Greater New Orleans Black Tourism Network Inc.
Louisiana Superdome, 1520 Sugar Bowl Dr
New Orleans Louisiana 70112
504-523-565

Caleth Powell, Executive Director

2243.

African American Travel
7676 New Hampshire Ave
Hyattsville Maryland 20783
301-431-1162

2244.

African Fantasy Travel Agent
161 Massachusetts Ave
Boston Massachusetts 02115-3050
617-859-1877

2245.

African Division of Alken Group Tours
1661 Nostrand Ave
Brooklyn New York 11226-5524
718-856-9100

2246.

African American Tours
8029 Walnut Creek Ln
Charlotte North Carolina 28227-0334
704-537-9441

2247.

African Travel Association
3912 Prospect Ave E
Cleveland Ohio 44115-2710
216-431-6756

2248.

African Travel Bureau
338 New Byhalia Rd
Collierville Tennessee 38017-3706
901-853-6200

2249.

African Travel Bureau
610 228th Ave NE
Redmond Washington 98052
206-868-4300

2250.

African American Tourism Coalition
2431 W Hopkins St
Milwaukee Wisconsin 53206-1251
414-449-4874

❁ VETERANS' ORGANIZATIONS ❁

2251.

Black Vietnam Veterans of America
3306 E 30th
Indianapolis Indiana 46218
317-542-9665

2252.

Tuskegee Airmen Inc.
65 Cadillac Sq, #3200
Detroit Michigan 20036
313-965-8858

This is an organization of persons affiliated with the black air force of WWII. These groups trained at Tuskegee. Annual reunions are held.

2253.

Black Veterans
686 Fulton St
Brooklyn New York 11217
718-935-1116

Job Mashariki, President

Black veterans of the military services. Goals are: to aid black veterans in obtaining information concerning their rights, ways to upgrade a less-than-honorable discharge, and VA benefits due them and their families. Seeks to prohibit discrimination against black veterans. Services include counseling and community workshops on veteran issues and programs for veterans in local prisons. Assist veterans who have suffered ill effects of Agent Orange.

2254.

National Association for Black Veterans
3929 N Humboldt
Milwaukee Wisconsin 53211
414-332-3931

Thomas H. Wynn, Executive Officer
An organization for black and other minority veterans, primarily those who fought in Vietnam. Represents the interests of minority veterans before the VA. Offers programs to assist veterans who received less-than-honorable discharge and incarcerated veterans. Counseling, job creation, geriatric, and homelessness services.

❂ WOMEN'S ORGANIZATIONS ❂

2255.

Black Women's Task Force
Phoenix Arizona 85045
602-258-7731

2256.

Black Women's Forum
3870 Crenshaw Blvd, Suite 210
Los Angeles California 90008
213-292-3009
213-292-2605—Fax

2257.

Black Women's Network
P.O. Box 56106
Los Angeles California 90056-0106
213-292-6547 Ext. 0106
213-964-4003—Fax

Bayyinah Ali, President
An organization of more than 175 women that
provides professional entrepreneurial and
career women interested in upward mobility
with resources and opportunities for networking. It sponsors seminars, workshops, and networking sessions of special interest to women
in the organization and community.

2258.

**Black Women Organize for Educational
Development**
518 17th
Oakland California 94601
510-763-9501

2259.

Black Women's Resource Center
518 17th St, Suite 202
Oakland California 94601
510-763-9501

Focus on special needs of African-American
women and youth. Information, referrals, job
counseling, stress support, network, and
opportunities. Open to all who need assistance.
Monday–Friday 10–4

2260.

African American Women on Tour
P.O. Box 152537
San Diego California 92195-2537
619-560-2770
619-560-9190—Fax

"The Nation's Foremost Black Women's
Empowerment Conference."

2261.

African-American Women's Clergy Association
P.O. Box 1493
Washington DC 20013
202-797-7460

The Rev. Imagene Bigham Stewart, National Chairwoman
The association's 26 local affiliates operate the only African-American shelter for homeless families and satellite centers for battered men and battered women in the nation's capital.
1969

2262.

Black Women's Agenda Inc.
3501 14th St, NW
Washington DC 20010-1305
202-387-4166

2263.

National Association of Colored Women's Clubs Inc.
5808 16th St, NW
Washington DC 20011
202-726-2044

Dr. Savanah Jones, President
An organization with more than 30,000 members dedicated to "raising to the highest plane the home life, moral standards and civic life of the African-American race." Founded in Washington, D.C., by the National Federation of Afro-American Women, the Women's Era Club of Boston, and the Colored Women's League of Washington, D.C., the association has become a significant voice in national affairs and has remained in the mainstream of national life for many years.
1896

2264.

National Council of Negro Women Inc.
1211 Connecticut Ave, NW, Room 702
Washington DC 20036
202-659-0006

Dorothy I. Height, National President
American educator Mary McLeod Bethune founded the council to help African-American women become more self-sufficient. The council operates through 214 local sections and 28 affiliates administering such projects as a campaign against hunger and malnutrition, child care and child development programs, youth counseling, teen pregnancy prevention, community leadership training for youth and women, and self-help programs in Africa.
1935

2265.

Black Women in Church & Society
c/o Interdenominational Church & Society
Atlanta Georgia 30314
404-527-7740

Jacquelyn Grant, Director

2266.

National Black Women's Consciousness-Raising Association
1906 N Charles St
Baltimore Maryland 21218
301-685-8392

2267.

Black Womens Health Council Inc.
311 68th Pl
Capital Heights Maryland 20743-2108
301-808-0786

2268.

National Coalition of 100 Black Women
300 Park Ave, 17th Floor
New York New York 10022
212-838-0150

❀ WRITING, POETRY & LITERATURE ❀

2269.

Black Writers Guild
P.O. Box 29351
Oakland California 94604-9351
510-569-8298

2270.

African American Writers Guild
4108 Arkansas Ave, NW
Washington DC 20011
202-722-2760

2271.

Black Writer
Terrell Associates
Chicago Illinois 60690
312-995-5195
312-924-3818—Fax

Mable Terrell, Editor and Publisher
Quarterly magazine offering information to
African-American writers and serving as a
forum for publishing works by black writers.

2272.

African Heritage Literature Society
7676 New Hampshire Ave
Hyattsville Maryland 20780
301-445-7616

2273.

Alex Haley House Museum
200 S Church St
Henning Tennessee 38041
901-738-2240

Museum devoted to the life of the highly
influential author of *Roots* and *The Autobiography of Malcolm X.*

2274.

Anne Spencer House & Garden
1313 Pierce St
Lynchburg Virginia 24501
804-846-0517

Preserved home of the Harlem Renaissance
literary figure, associated with James Weldon
Johnson, Langston Hughes, Claude McKay,
Paul Robeson, Marian Anderson, W.E.B. Du
Bois, and Mary McLeod Bethune.

❂ SUBJECT INDEX ❂

❂ NAMES INDEX ❂

Name	Entry Number	Name	Entry Number
Mississippi Industrial College	552	Museum for African Art	1433
Mississippi Legislative Black Caucus	1249	Museum of African & African American	
Mississippi Memo Digest	1825	Art & Antiquities	1420
Mississippi Minority Supplier		Museum of African American Art	1344
Development Council	238	Museum of African American Art	1377
Mississippi State Historical Museum	1557	Museum of African-American History	727
Mississippi Valley State	554	Museum of African-American History	1552
Missouri Legislative Black Caucus	1250	Museum of African-American Life	
Mitchell-Street Associates	310	& Culture	1464
Mobile Beacon	1671	Museum of African-American Life	
Mobile Black Chamber of Commerce	345	and Culture	770
Modern Free and Accepted Masons		Museum of Afro-American History	1545
of the World Inc.	436	Museum of Art	1373
MOLIS: Minority On-Line Information		Museum of Arts & Sciences	1371
Service	665	Museum of Fine Arts	1403
Montgomery West	304	Museum of Fine Arts	1467
Montgomery-Tuskegee Times	1673	Museum of Modern Art	1434
Moon Senior Citizens Center,		Museum of the City of New York	1581
Saunders B.	2204	Museum of the Confederacy	1634
Moorland-Spingarn Research Center	1497	Museum of the National Center of	
Morehouse College	527	Afro-American Artists	1404
Morehouse School of Medicine	528	Museums of the University of	
Morgan State University	544	Mississippi	1413
Morris Brown College	529	Muslim Journal	1782
Morris College	589	Mutual Federal Savings & Loan	
Morris Ltd., E.	12	Association	82
Most Worshipful National Grand		Mutual Savings & Loan Association	112
Lodge Free and Accepted Ancient			
York Masons	445	NAACP Henry Lee Moon Library &	
Mother A.M.E. Zion Church	2114	National Civil Rights Archives	1539
Mother Bethel African Methodist		NAACP Historical & Cultural Project	732
Episcopal Church	2116	NAACP Historical & Cultural Project	1569
Motown Museum	1654	NAACP Legal Defense and Education	
Mount Tabor Baptist Church	2123	Fund Inc.	485
Mount Zion United Methodist Church	2112	NAACP Legal Defense and Education	
Multicultural Publishing and Education		Fund Inc.	1315
Council, The	2060	NAACP Legal Defense and Education	
Murphy Productions Inc., Eddie &		Fund Inc.	2056
Eddie Murphy Television		Naismith Memorial Basketball Hall	
Enterprises Inc.	1031	of Fame	138

❋ OTHER OWL BOOKS OF INTEREST ❋

If you would like to suggest corrections and/or new entries to be listed in future editions of *The African-American Yellow Pages*, please write to:

Editor, The African-American Yellow Pages
Henry Holt and Co., Inc.
115 West 18th St.
New York, NY 10011